BUYING AND BELIEVING

BUYING AND BELIEVING

Sri Lankan Advertising
and Consumers
in a Transnational World

Steven Kemper

The University of Chicago Press
Chicago and London

Steven Kemper is professor of anthropology at Bates College and the author of *The Presence of the Past: Chronicles, Politics, and Culture in Sinhala Life.*

The University of Chicago Press, Chicago 60637
The University of Chicago Press, Ltd., London
© 2001 by The University of Chicago
All rights reserved. Published 2001
Printed in the United States of America
10 09 08 07 06 05 04 03 02 01   5 4 3 2 1

ISBN (cloth): 0-226-43040-5
ISBN (paper): 0-226-43041-3

Library of Congress Cataloging-in-Publication Data

Kemper, Steven, date
    Buying and believing : Sri Lankan advertising and consumers in a transnational world / Steven Kemper.
            p.   cm.
    Includes bibliographical references and index.
    ISBN 0-226-43040-5 (cloth)—ISBN 0-226-43041-3 (pbk.)
    1. Advertising—Sri Lanka.   2. Marketing—Sri Lanka.   3.Consumption (Economics)—Sri Lanka.   I. Title.
    HF5813.S72 K46   2001
    659.1'095493—dc21   00-012205

CONTENTS

PREFACE

I started this project in the late 1980s just before I finished *The Presence of the Past*. That book considered the relationship between contemporary Sri Lanka and its past; this one considers the relationship between Sri Lanka—as a society, an economy, and a locality—and the rest of the world. Moving from a concern with temporality to one with spatiality is also a transition from exchanges framed in a primarily religious idiom to talk that is largely commercial. Even in retrospect I am not entirely sure how I moved from the temple to the bazaar. One day I was walking to monasteries, hoping to meet the village monk; the next I was telephoning multinational firms, scheduling appointments with executives.

It is hard to imagine two localities less similar, and moving from monasteries to advertising agencies forced a change in my intellectual identity. Talking with monks requires Sinhala, lots of waiting, and deference (easy enough for a beginner with sketchy language skills and great respect for Buddhism). Talking with advertising executives requires English, watching the clock, and bursts of sociability (is this an ethnographic project or my life?). I started across the bridge between these two venues as I tried to make sense of the *Mahavamsa, Nutana Yugaya,* the most recent updating of a tradition of historical writing that began in the sixth century. That chronicle recounts the relationship between Buddhism and the Sri Lankan state. Its most recent installment celebrated the inauguration of an elected government committed to free-market capitalism. It was overseen by a committee and modeled on the *Cambridge History of India.* As the project languished I discovered that carrying on the tradition was more important than producing the text, celebrating the government's virtue on television more important than anything that the history might say. I began to think about advertising, media, and a society adapting itself to new circumstances.

This book is the result. It approaches Sri Lankan society as part of a global system of culture and commerce, working not so much across expanses of time, but synchronically across the world. Advertising functions as a second-order business, serving the interests of firms that produce goods and services. Unlike legal services and accountancy, advertising plays a public and highly political role in linking together far-flung parts of the planet—connecting Western sources of production with consumers around the world, converting commodities into libidinal images of themselves, and reimagining products and services for local consumption. To this extent advertising produces culture (which is what makes it anthropologically interesting). Unlike other businesses that also depend on print and electronic media—the book, magazine, movie, and music industries are obvious examples—advertising is parasitic on something else, the daily ration of commodities that enter human lives. To this extent, advertising has an everydayness and a materiality that makes advertising culture even more consequential.

What follows is a transnational ethnography. It begins by approaching advertising as a modern practice, tied to Western centers of material and symbolic production, dependent on media, and implicated in the interests of nation-states, multinational corporations, and nongovernmental organizations. When the J. R. Jayewardene government came to power in 1977, I expected an explosion of capitalist activity, advertising, and consumption. And there have been signs of all three. But Sri Lankans have become ever more skillful savers, and I have concentrated on banking as a conduit that links Sri Lanka to the larger world, a source of legitimacy and economic support for the state, and a critical link between global forces and ordinary people living lives dependent on values and long-term strategies that often work at cross-purposes with the interests of capitalist institutions. By focusing on two families, I have tried to bring the global system to ground, for it is by scrutinizing lives of local design that the transnational becomes the ethnographic. My hope is that the transnational character of the project—its focus on how forces that originate far away bear on people living in Sri Lanka—provides a better sense of just how they are "us" while remaining distinctively themselves.

In pursuing this project, I have accumulated a set of debts to the institutions that helped me along the way. Several sources of support allowed me to carry out five periods of fieldwork in Sri Lanka and Malaysia. Early on in the project, the Social Science Research Council supported two periods of fieldwork in 1987 and 1991; the National Endowment for the Humanities made possible two longer periods of fieldwork in 1990 and 1995. The American Institute for Sri Lankan Studies underwrote summer fieldwork in 1997. Bates College has been consistently generous in supporting my research. I thank them all and acknowledge Sylvia Hawks who skillfully oversaw the manuscript.

Many practitioners took time from their hectic days to talk to an outsider whose questions ranged from the irrelevant to the vexatious. Guy Halpe in particular gave more of himself than I had any right to ask. To a person who stopped to talk to me rather than return home to be with his family, there is little I can say but to make public my debt. Over the last decade, a large number of people in the advertising, television, and newsprint industries have shared their knowledge with me. In particular I want to thank Kenneth Abeywickrama, Sanjiva Ahangama, Mel Assauw, Angelo Assauw, Reggie Candappa, Stanley Carvalho, Shaan Corea, D. S. Dayaratne, Anandatissa de Alwis, Tissa de Alwis, Felicia Dean, Nishamani de Mel, Nihal de Silva, Ranil de Silva, Ruwan de Silva, Stephen de Silva, Lilamani Dias, Victor Gunewardena, Upali Herath, Laddie Hettiaratchy, Suresh Jayawickrama, Podma Pathirane, Cyril Perera, M. J. Perera, Chandini Rajaratnam, Sandya Salgado, Ajit Samaranayaka, Jayantha Sittampalam, Caryll de Silva Tozzer, Ananda Wedaarachchy, and Irwin Weerackody. In Thailand and Malaysia I owe thanks to Chris Baker, K. C. Lee, S. P. Lee, Tony Lee, J. Matthews, Richard McDonough, Harmandar Singh, and Roziah Osman.

A number of people not directly involved in the advertising and media business have also helped me with the project in Sri Lanka. They include Kumar Abayanaike, Nate Bowditch, Chandra, Indira, and Dinusha Corea, C. R. de Silva, Ven. Ampitiya Dhammakitti, H. D. C. Dissanayake, Tissa Jayatilaka, Stanley Jayawardena, Talbot Penner, I. G. Sumanasena, and Abhaya Weerakoon.

At home I have received intellectual reinforcement from Arjun Appadurai, Carol Breckenridge, Loring Danforth, Val Daniel, Nick Dirks, Ulf Hannerz, David Kolb, and Dennis McGilvray. My wife, Anne, soldiered on while I was away in Asia. I appreciate her many gifts—love, character adjustment, and publicity, but especially love—and thank her and my daughters, Jordan, Shannon, and Jessica, for being who they are. When I was in the seventh grade, I had an English teacher who I did not fully appreciate. I doubt that anyone ever thanked Helen Wingfield. I remember her laughing over a critic's review of Katharine Hepburn's first stage performance—"her emotions ran the gamut from A to B"—which went past most of us students. But she also asked us to think about advertising as an imaginative literature. It all makes sense to me now, and I happily acknowledge her distant influence. Miss Wingfield will not read this note, but some of the people who never get recognized will.

Domesticating the Imagination

Superficially, the world has become small and known. . . . Yet the
more we know, superficially, the less we penetrate. . . . We, bowl-
ing along in a rickshaw in Ceylon, say to ourselves: "It's very much
what you'd expect." We really know it all. We are mistaken.

D. H. Lawrence, *Phoenix*

This book concerns the economic and cultural connections that
tie the world together. It is also a book about consumption, advertising,
the production of a public culture in a postcolonial nation-state, and the
way people make use of modern institutions. These issues—which, to cut
to the heart of the matter, are organized by the practices and passions of
buying and believing—confront all societies. They are especially conten
tious in postcolonial places. Here the distinction between that which is
local and that which is foreign weighs on issues that at first seem remote.
What one consumes becomes a matter of national identity, or modernity,
or decency. How commodities are advertised poses a political dilemma,
forcing the state to protect local values and interests while also encouraging
development and other connections to transnational forces. Between the
allure of the foreign and sentiments that derive from more proximate
forms of community, postcolonial societies find their way.

The nation-state is the venue for the interaction of these competing forces, but in most cases not itself an object of powerful feeling. When
people defend the local, they speak less for the nation-state than for other

forms of association (an ethnic group, religion, caste, or linguistic community), which are clearly more compelling. At the same time, the people who defend the local may favor foreign goods over their local equivalents, linking them to forms of community that transcend the nation. Participation in virtual communities of consumption depends on advertising, electronic media, and patterns of living that link individuals to the deterritorialized world of commodities. In these circumstances, advertising threatens not only the postcolonial state but also local tradition, morality, and the relationship between young people and old.

All that said, we are mistaken if we think that a global culture will soon dominate the planet or that advertising will soon destroy local traditions. Advertising has its effects, and they are real and deep, if not always what the advertiser intended. But those effects need to be accounted for along with other forces—from media in general to local credit arrangements—that confront people in postcolonial societies. The very fact that consumption is so widely seen as bearing on local tradition or morality suggests that consumers do not consume passively or read advertisements without resistance. A globalized economy and culture are not overwhelming the societies of the world, but distant forces are causing the people of Africa, Asia, and Latin America to act on new sources of desire, fear, and possibility.

Where capitalism goes, advertising goes. That affinity means that advertising is as much a part of commercial life in Colombo and Port Moresby as New York and Tokyo. In transferring commodities and ideas between places all across the planet, the advertising business functions alongside a number of other transnational institutions. Like media companies, public relations firms, wire services, the music, movie, and telecommunications industries, nongovernmental organizations, accountancy and legal firms, multinational corporations, press and broadcast services, and development agencies, it links persons in far-flung parts of the globe in a way increasingly less constrained by distance. Advertising's role as a site of cultural production in a network that links every place with every other place makes it the transnational profession par excellence, a site where the relationship between things and their meanings is always under construction, always responding to imagination and economic interest.

Advertising people—account managers, copywriters, and graphic artists as well as executives—are part of a global class of people concerned with symbol work. In this sense, the advertising business is bound to those other transnational businesses in a second way. They all produce, manipulate, interpret, and traffic in forms of signification. As a site of cultural production, advertising is a primary channel through which the blandishments of the modern enter Sri Lankan life, but it is even more a cutoff point where the modern is domesticated by being translated into a vocabulary that makes sense to local consumers. To that extent, advertising influences Sri Lankan understandings of what is modern and what is traditional, constantly readjusting local definitions of each. This process is interesting in itself, the more so for an anthropologist because of its resonance. The disciplinary language of the advertising profession parallels and sometimes converges with the disciplinary language of anthropology.

ADVERTISING KNOWLEDGE AND ETHNOGRAPHIC KNOWLEDGE

My interest in the advertising business grew initially from the idea that I could learn something new about Sri Lankan society by asking people who have a professional interest in understanding that society just what they know about it. To the extent that advertising copywriting and artwork requires and produces knowledge of local life, advertising executives are ethnographers.[1] Anthropologists interested in Sri Lanka fix their professional gaze on matters as various as ritual behavior, kinship, caste, and land tenure. More recently, they have turned to new expressions of Buddhism, ethnic violence, and the historical memory. These research interests produce a view of Sri Lanka that is not so much narrow as distinctive. Advertising people are interested in the same society. They simply picture it in different terms. For them, Sri Lanka is a society of consumers. It fans out from Colombo and divides neatly into two groups—the middle class, typically English-speaking and living in Colombo, and a provincial city and village Sri Lanka.

Ethnographic interest in the island's peoples began with the Seligmanns' 1911 account of Sri Lanka's only aboriginal people, the Veddas,[2] and that focus on the primitive, the traditional, and the unspoiled is instructive. By the 1950s and 1960s ethnographic interest had settled on village life. Only recently—and then haltingly—have anthropologists looked to urban settings, modernity, and transnational processes in the island. The focus of advertising practice, by contrast, fell first on a small, Westernized elite living mainly in Colombo and spread to the majority of Sri Lanka's people living in villages and towns only in the 1960s and 1970s. For the first two-thirds of the last century, advertisements were framed in English, ignoring the great majority of the island's peoples. Where the direction of ethnographic interest spread from village to town and city, advertising moved in the opposite direction.

Ask anyone to reflect on his or her own society, and they will produce a folk ethnography. But advertising executives are folk ethnographers with a critical difference, for they are professional observers who make a living by convincing clients that they understand how the natives think. Agencies compete with one another by claiming better knowledge of how that thinking will affect a particular product or service. Having a stake in knowing what Sri Lankan society is like does not guarantee the reliability of that knowledge, but it surely increases the knower's self-awareness and interest. As the demographics evolve, as businesses seek to know what is going on right now, advertising executives try to keep pace with a society changing rapidly. They should have ethnographic knowledge, perhaps more than professional ethnographers, that is not only sophisticated but less prone to essentialism and ahistoricism.

When advertising executives use the word *segment,* they employ it not as a noun but as a verb. To segment a market is to create a market segment, not merely respond to an existing one.[3] As in the expression *young urban professionals,* segmenting a market begins with an act of demographic phrase-making, but it does not end there. Advertising cannot create that segment without inventing tropes of gender, ethnicity, class, and locality that cause consumers to identify with the people and places depicted in advertisements. Independent of whether advertising executives are well informed about what their public is like, they create new and often startling images of the people who read advertisements and watch commercials. They are hardly the only source of images of Sri Lankan society, and they are themselves reinterpreted by consumers.[4] But once in the public domain, advertising representations of Sri Lankan society become one way in which the people of that society acquire a sense of locality and thus of themselves. Whether it sells commodities or not, advertising creates culture, and that second function has great importance apart from the role advertising plays in the economy.[5]

Whatever part the representations of garment factory workers and paddy farmers play in the production of culture, ordinary people lack the mechanical power and distributional range of electronic and print media. Academic interpretations of Sri Lankan society have their own disadvantages. Occasionally an academic will write something that riles up popular feelings—Romila Thapar's work on ancient India and S. J. Tambiah's *Buddhism Betrayed* accomplished that much—but most academic work, even when the focus falls on issues of great importance, never receives public discussion. Academic hopes for critique and social renewal duly noted, it is hard to imagine any book—this one included—producing culture. Creative directors, graphic artists, copywriters, and television production people produce a relentless, ever-growing flow of it.

When I started this project in the late 1980s, I expected that the street smarts—from an intuitive sense of what makes people laugh or cry to the ability to exploit popular culture in inventive ways—that characterize the American advertising profession would have a Sri Lankan equivalent. This book is the product of my testing those assumptions. Some distinctions that advertising executives and marketing people impose on Sri Lankan life do not come to much. What to make of the fact that scent companies in Sri Lanka sell their strong fragrances in village markets and their subtle ones in more urban ones? The truth of the assertion aside, I do not learn anything substantive about either village or town by having discovered the distinction. By contrast, knowing that Sri Lankans spend large percentages of their income (relative to places such as the Philippines and Indonesia) on products associated with children and health forces me to think about domestic life and kinship in unfamiliar ways.

Approaching Sri Lankan society from an advertising executive's point of view has allowed me to think about Sri Lankan society itself as a distinctive kind of theoretical object. On the one hand, I have been led to think of that society as a single entity. Sri Lanka, so conceived, is something different from Sri Lanka understood as local ethnographers do—as the longest reach to which their assertions apply, the national entity that is the nominal context of their work (even when the focus falls on a single village). It is instead a market for commodities and advertising.[6] And Sri Lankans under this description are a community of people known for what and how they consume. On the other hand, when I have thought about Sri Lankan society in terms of its internal differences, thinking about Sri Lankans as a community of consumption leaves the ubiquitous distinction between Sinhala and Tamil behind. The distinction that counts more in this context falls between middle-class people and the generality of Sri Lankans. And once I begin to approach Sri Lankans as people who own cell phones and VCRs, people with whom I communicate by e-mail, it becomes difficult to imagine their living in a historical moment different from my own.[7]

In some ways advertising executives are not the ethnographers I had anticipated. Advertising accounts move between one agency and another for all manner of reasons, but the explicit rationale that agencies employ to pitch some other agency's client is often some version of this argument: "We can sell your products because we can think in the same terms as most of Sri Lanka's people." I have heard some advertising people make quite a lot of the "local idiom" notion and others dismiss it out of hand. Its natural venue is local advertising agencies, which seek to compete against multinational agencies by claiming to share more in common with the average Sri Lankan consumer. When executives claim the ability to understand Sri Lanka's peoples, their knowledge of how the natives think is anecdotal, unsystematic, and motivated by rhetorical figures. The same words, of course, have been used to critique ethnographic knowledge.

Whether they claim to have mastered the "local idiom" or to be able to exploit strategic thinking from the home office in New York for the sake of selling things in Sri Lanka, advertising executives work with real disadvantages. As part of an urban-dwelling middle class, they have negligible contact with people who live in villages. Executives invariably speak English as their first language and transact business in English. Most Sri Lankans do neither. Disproportionate numbers of advertising executives come from minority communities. Some are Burghers, that is, European and Eurasian descendants of Dutch colonists, and others are Sinhala or Tamil Christians. And whatever their ethnic origins, advertising executives are cosmopolitan people, putting them at a remove from most Sri Lankans. The social distance that separates the people of the advertising profession from their public is probably no greater than the situation in many postcolonial countries, but that distance reinscribes in their own lives the distinction between foreign and local, the modern and the traditional that figures prominently in advertising copy.

The people who work in the Sri Lankan advertising industry are heirs to a class of colonial middlemen, the "brown Englishmen" found all across South Asia. I will use their interstitial position as a vehicle for thinking about how they link ordinary Sri Lankans to commodity exchange, their government, and the world beyond. The island's position in the larger scheme of things is suggested by the fact that this linkage works in only one direction. The Sri Lankan advertising business plays no part in representing exports—tea, rubber, coconut, and clothing—to the larger world. Its usual function is to represent local and imported commodities to the Sri Lankan people. Doing so puts advertising people in the position of ventriloquists—in order to speak to the people of Sri Lanka they have to speak for them. To repeat a point I made previously: advertising executives are not only middlemen to the national imagination, they are sources of it, producing new images, to name the categories most relevant here, of what it is to be a woman, a man, a parent, a responsible person, a Sri Lankan, and, naturally, a consumer.

However much advertising people claim to speak the local idiom or to understand conditions at the point of sale, their fundamental dilemma is selling things to a society where many people get by on very little. When I first lived in Sri Lanka, I spent an afternoon with my friend Razik in his *kade* (shop) in a town in Sabaragamuva province. A small boy ran in and bought half of a bar of soap. Razik told me that sometimes people buy a quarter of a bar. Then as now, over half of the shelf space—itself a notion alien to stores built of rough-hewn wood and lighted by petromax lamps—in village shops was taken up with dried milk powder—Nestlé, Lakspray, and Anchor milk—and Unilever products, which are largely food items (soap and toothpaste are the leading exceptions). Sri Lankans spend some 60 percent of their income on food. For many people in one of the world's twenty poorest nations, the high proportion of income spent on food means that deciding how to spend one's money is typically a matter of splurging on a bar of Lux soap or a choice between buying the local milk powder or the foreign equivalent, which people think is more nutritious.

Marketing people trying to introduce consumers to toothpaste and shampoo put their products in small packets known as sachets. They know that the price of the ordinary-sized container is beyond the reach of many Sri Lankans. At the same time, some village families that would otherwise face these conditions have a daughter, son, wife, or husband working in the Middle East who sends home money in amounts sufficient to put up a new house or purchase a television. Other young women work in a growing number of free-trade zones, and, living with their parents, they often have discretionary income. Business people in Colombo move about in expensive cars and talk to one another on cellular telephones. When human circumstances range from subsistence to serious wealth, when some people in the neighborhood are suddenly doing very well and others are not, when new consumer items appear in shops that earlier offered far less dazzling fare, talk centers on who is getting what.

A second problem with characterizing advertising people as ethnographers comes from their being professionals trained in a Western practice. Advertising the world over is produced by a profession that has its own disciplinary practices and vocabulary. This is a language practitioners speak with one another and their clients, and they spend much more time interacting with each other than thinking about consumption or Sri Lankan life. In the late 1980s I heard an advertising executive address the Sri Lanka marketing institute on what advertisers had to keep in mind during a time of civil war and ethnic crisis. My assumption was that her remarks would reveal what she knew about how consumers were coping with years of terrorist bombings and growing estrangement between Sinhalas and Tamils. Here I thought I would hear an ethnographic account organized in terms of the language of a kindred profession.

She talked instead about maintaining brand identity, working cooperatively with clients, resisting the temptation to cut prices. All matters important to marketing people during an economic downturn—they are

just nothing that speaks to the troubles that confront Sri Lankan consumers themselves. Her audience thought her remarks were pertinent, and
that is a point worth emphasizing. Advertising is a profession. Having an
agreed-on set of assumptions, a disciplinary language, and everyday practices makes the advertising business a community as well as a profession.
That community is worldwide and in many ways stronger than the ties
that join the advertising profession to its public. But the extent to which
advertising people can communicate with local society is an open question.
When it succeeds, the advertising business becomes an interactive site that
links people of all types—executives who are chauffeured about as they
talk on cell phones and the little boy whose family sends him to the *kade*
to buy half a bar of soap—to the world beyond.

LONG-DISTANCE FORCES AND LOCAL SOCIETIES

The circulation of things around the globe itself is hardly new. Eric Wolf's
account of the world in 1400 shows the complex interconnection of faraway places long before European trading companies appeared in Asia.[8]
A millennium earlier there were Arab traders doing business in China. At
a time when Europeans were counting wealth in terms of cattle, Arab traders could write a check on a bank in Baghdad and have it honored in
Canton. With time the "subtle play of indigenous trajectories of desire and
fear with global flows of people and things" grows in intensity and magnitude.[9] Nowadays a list of leading transnational forces includes electronic
media, development projects, labor migration, and tourism. Advertising
is a phenomenon centrally implicated in all of these other transnational
forces, but I begin from the assumption that the new in this case emerges
from something old: long-distance trade and the allure of the foreign.

As Marshall Sahlins puts it, the Western rush of the last two decades to sell things to the Chinese is today's installment "of a dream that
has been playing in Europe for three centuries now—all those hundreds
of millions of customers just waiting for British woolens, then cotton textiles, steel cutlery, guns, and ships, and latterly jeeps, perfume, and TV
sets."[10] The long-distance character of the trade has not changed, yet the
appeal of foreign things depends in altogether unprecedented ways on
advertising. Until the recent collapse of Asian currencies, 40 percent of
French luxury production in watches, liquor, and scent was sold in Asia.
The premium prices attached to such goods makes advertising, marketing,
and packaging possible. They also make those exercises of the imagination
necessary.

When European societies began to enjoy high levels of consumption in the eighteenth century, commodities flowed to Europe from many directions. And these commodities—not local ones, however expensive— were fundamental to the transformation of European societies; they were "conspicuous components" in the construction of a particular kind of society, a society of consumers.[11] It was the appeal of sugar, tea, coffee, porcelain, and Indian and Chinese textiles that led to the emergence of this new social order. Speaking of the growing English fondness for sugar after the sixteenth century, Sidney Mintz writes that a change in taste brought with it "profound alterations in people's images of themselves, their notions of the contrasting notions of tradition and change, the fabric of their daily social life."[12]

To this extent, the rise of a European consumer society depended on the presence of commodities that were foreign and carried irresistible symbolic loads. The growth of consumer societies in Asia involves similarly high stakes, but the imaginative forces working on consumption nowadays are many times more powerful. "Subtle play" has become heavy traffic. This time around, Europe and the United States (and Japan) supply the commodities, while newly prosperous Asians provide the discretionary income that drives trade. And now foreign commodities carry symbolic loads skillfully constructed and widely advertised.

The speed with which things circulate, the volume of foreign things in the hands of ordinary people, the variety of things that show up in odd places—all define a new world order. The conventional wisdom is that the source of cultural production is the West, and it is true that entertainment is the United States's second largest export. In the late 1980s, a Chinese student from Shanghai, Zhou Zou-Ren, won a trip to the Grand Ole Opry for his essay "What Country Music Means to Me."[13] I think I know what *native land* or *family* means to people who speak in those terms; I have no idea what country music could mean to a Chinese student, but it obviously means something. As commentators have said in a variety of ways, the West is everywhere.

But the transnational phenomenon is more interesting because it is more complicated. Japanese musicians play Cuban music so convincingly that a Japanese *salsa* band, *Orquesta de la Luz,* has acquired a following in New York, Puerto Rico, Panama, Venezuela, and Madrid. Americans now consume more *salsa*—to move from the musical to the culinary—than ketchup. Parisians go out to eat in some thirty Tex-Mex restaurants, although neither Texans nor Mexicans would recognize the cuisine. It is not so much that the West is everywhere; everywhere is everywhere.

Asia has become a large consumer of Western music, and sales of music are still growing despite the economic downturn of 1997. Western performers—from Elton John to Michael Jackson—perform regularly before large crowds in Asian venues. But the Western things that appear in non-Western places are not necessarily what they seem—Asia has created its own transnational system of production and distribution for Western music. English is the language of pop music in Asia, and Asians want Western music to be sung by Westerners. But they disdain the "in-your-face" quality of some Western music in favor of romance and soft melodies. Some British and Danish pop singers—Alex E, Aqua, and Michael Learns to Rock, for example—produce music exclusively for the Asian market.[14] They perform in Asia, and their music companies promote them only there. This is Western music sung by Westerners not intended to be heard in the West.

Amidst the rising tide of everything being everywhere, Western music created by Asian taste recalls Marshall Sahlins's insistence on agency in the interaction of local societies and the world beyond. Societies shape their encounter with the larger world, at the level of both national governments and individual taste. As local trajectories of desire and fear meet new commodities, they oscillate between the adoption of Western ways (which happens when desire is realized or fear forestalled) or resistance (which follows desire rejected or fear enacted). What makes it harder to detect local agency is the frequent asymmetry between a powerful outside world and overmatched local societies, and economic and political advantage have their effects, to be sure. But we can surely do better than reduce the intercultural encounter to materiality on one side and an "unrelieved chronicle of cultural corruption" on the other, a kind of physics supplied by the West and a teleology that determines the course of local people.[15]

Sahlins's point is less a humanistic claim than an epistemological one. The force of the Western intrusion into non-Western places and the blandishments of foreign things—clothes, liquor, guns—is undeniable. But to leave matters there is to underestimate both sides of the encounter. Along with markets and commodities, capitalism brings with it a set of values—individualism and material gusto are two—as well as a set of material interests, and local societies enter the intercultural encounter with their own economic and political interests (as well as a distinctive way of life). What follows is a history of juncture in which change is balanced by continuity, and foreign forces by local ones. When Certeau argues that the future enters the present in the mode of alterities, he emphasizes the reciprocal strangeness that initiates the encounter between the local and the foreign.[16] But difference is a historical moment, soon gone.

As most accounts of nineteenth-century Fiji have it, the establishment of trade in sandalwood and European muskets led to warfare and eventually state formation. But where those accounts say that muskets made Fijian chiefs powerful, Sahlins insists it was the other way around. The importance of Fijian chiefs—whose existence, as Sahlins puts it in Kantian language, "was the condition of the possibility of [their] people's social existence" and whose death by musket fire could give the opposition a military victory with a single shot—owed to the local scheme of things, the way cultural order was constructed long before Europeans and their goods got to Fiji.[17] The local scheme of things, not any objective quality that muskets might have had, made muskets important.

As wave after wave of foreign goods and ideas wash over faraway societies, it is important to remember the durability and cunning of local realities.[18] It is all the more important to remember such things in the face of multinational corporations and their products, electronic media, and advertising. All of these institutions serve to rechannel those waves and reconstruct the content of those venerable categories—the local and the foreign. Let me make that argument by turning to a society that insists on that distinction. Many Japanese writers evaluate their country's role in the world by beginning from the assertion of Japan's uniqueness, and that claim—the discourse of *Nihonjinron*—is itself a force in maintaining that distinction between the local and the foreign.

Japan is a market where products are understood as either traditionally Japanese or foreign. Department stores separate the two categories, present each differently, and steer foreign customers away from areas offering traditionally Japanese products.[19] It would be hard to find another society that marks consumption practices so starkly. But consider in this light a newspaper account of the process by which a very American institution, Disneyland, has been made Japanese: "On a recent spring day Mieko Sano paid a visit [to the Tokyo Disneyland] with her daughter, who was about to move to the United States with her husband and children. 'It's a special occasion,' she said. 'Maybe It's the best way for them to remember the real Japan.'"[20] Disneyland, the "real Japan"?

But who is to deny that the Japanese have made the Tokyo Disneyland distinctively theirs:

> For though it was based, down to the last detail, upon its American counterpart, its effect was to serve as a shrine to Japan's validating beliefs. . . . In the Meet the World pavilion—a ride not to be found in American Disneylands—a sagacious crane guides a little boy and his kind sister around what is not only a history of Japan but also a defense of the Japanese way. The bird points out a group of cavemen seated around a campfire. "They have

learned," pronounces the Feathered One, "the importance of banding together to survive." Then it goes on to introduce the children to a samurai. "At least," boasts the warrior, "we never became a colony." [21]

The Japanese have transformed Disneyland in ways more penetrating than simply adding something, in this case, pavilions to dramatize Japanese values. They have taken Disneyland's efficiency, cleanliness, and the idealization of nature and pushed them even further. By being more American than the paradigmatic American institution, the Japanese have made it Japanese. On leaving home, the Japanese call by Disneyland to remember Japan, even though they are headed to the country that created the institution and, in the minds of other Disneyized countries (such as France), remains irremediably tied to it. As Sahlins says, "the very ways societies change have their own authenticity, so that global modernity is often reproduced as local diversity." [22]

VENUES OF INTERACTION

The interaction between Europeans, muskets, and Fijian society that Sahlins describes occurred—to use Greg Dening's language, "on the beach"— and the place shaped how the encounter developed. The beach or the estate or the colonial port city became more than an arena for interaction between Western capitalist interests and non-Western peoples. Speaking of the zone where the people of the Marquesas Islands met the outside world, Dening characterizes the beach as an area of generative power:

> Whatever [the middlemen, traders, beachcombers] did on the beach, they had to carve out a new world for themselves. This new world could not be the one they left: it lacked all the essential ingredients. It could not be the world on which they had just intruded: none could be born again so radically. So on the beach they experimented. They made wives, children, relations, property in new ways. The beach that was the boundary between the old world and the new ran down the very centre of their lives.
>
> On the beach, [they] were ordinary men to [Marquesans]. Perhaps they were strange, indecent or improper, but their needs and functions were recognizable. They merely solved familiar problems in unfamiliar ways. . . . But they were not bound by the rules of their new world. By breaking its rules and not suffering for it, they weakened its sanctions, made absolutes relative to their

> condition. They enlarged the experience of the island by translat-
> ing islanders' roles into their own familiar ones. . . . They knew
> the moods and motivations of both sides and made intercourse
> possible.[23]

The beach is betwixt and between and a place with its own practices and powers. What started out as a beach or a harbor became a port city and later still a colonial capital, always a place out of place, seductive, and dangerous.

But what happens when the encounter takes place on neither the beach, the port city, or the colonial capital but in bureaucracies and transnational corporations, some local and others half a world away? What happens to the encounter of cultures when governmental agencies and advertising agencies turn their attention to matters of consumption? What, for instance, would have been the Fijian response to European muskets if advertising practice and government policy had been focused on them? If muskets had not reached Fiji until today, would television commercials construct them as the latest condition for the possibility of social existence? Or would the government of Fiji ban their import as dangerous to the local way of life?

Then again, what happens when the interstitial zone between things local and foreign moves to the newspaper, movie screen, television, cassette tape, and CD-ROM, when mechanically produced images bring that contrast into the workaday world of paddy farmers, schoolteachers, and merchants who would have never gone close to the beach or colonial port city? The pervasiveness of these intrusive forces, their accessibility to the eye (always present and always changing) balanced by their unavailability to the purse (what ordinary consumers could afford these things, and where would they be able to buy them if they could?). The capacity for startling figures of desire and fear has implications, Arjun Appadurai argues, for the very way the imagination operates in the modern world:

> No longer mere fantasy (opium for the masses whose real work is
> elsewhere), no longer simple escape (from a world defined princi-
> pally by more concrete purposes and structures), no longer elite
> pastime (thus not relevant to the lives of ordinary people) and no
> longer mere contemplation (irrelevant for new forms of desire and
> subjectivity), the imagination has become an organized field of so-
> cial practices, a form of work (both in the sense of labor and of
> cultural organized practice) and a form of negotiation between
> sites of agency ('individuals') and globally defined fields of possibil-

ity. It is this unleashing of the imagination which links the play of pastiche (in some settings) to the terror and coercion of states and their competitors. The imagination is now central to all forms of agency, is itself a social fact, and is the key component of the new global order.[24]

Although Appadurai lays out the consequences—fields of possibility, pastiche, terror and coercion—that follow the liberation of the imagination from place, he says less of how modern institutions reterritorialize that imagination, and that second element is as important as the first. Advertising agencies in Sri Lanka—not to say, Bombay, Madras, and Karachi—engage high-flying South Asian imaginations, freed up from place by television, music, films, the World Wide Web, tourist travel, and other forms of the modern by constructing advertisements in ways that return those imaginations to their place of residence. Advertising practice in postcolonial markets gets pulled in two directions. On the one hand, there are economies of scale that follow transnational campaigns, the homogenization of taste, and the deterritorialization of the imagination. On the other, advertising "in the local idiom," caters to, not to say creates, local preferences.

As much as the people who mediated on the beach, advertising executives have real skill in understanding the moods and motivations of their superiors, colleagues, clients who live outside of Sri Lanka, and the public they address inside. But people who work in the advertising business nowadays have lithography, photography, mechanical reproduction, and electronic resources that their forebears on the beach lacked.[25] They can reimagine the local and the foreign in ways that ignore circumstances. They can remake the foreign for local consumption (just as they regularly remake the local). They can experiment. Sometimes they domesticate the foreign by shooting advertisements with local faces, retaining both the same script used in other markets and a "zone of display"—an unbelievably blue lagoon, a sailboat in high seas—just as beguiling as such scenes are for a Western audience.[26] On other occasions, they relocate an alien commodity amidst faces, places, conversational patterns, and practices that are locally familiar, speaking to their audience in terms of the "local idiom."

What makes foreign commodities engaging is often something independent of the commodity itself. Often it is seeing that commodity in a "zone of display" that is also foreign—a luxurious locale, a situation where men and women are brought into close contact, the surface, color, and form of the human body, most often the female body. Those "zones of display" may work perfectly well with some commodities and in some markets. Sometimes the advertisement can rely on an unearned advantage. Potential consumers may have previously viewed, let's say, a pair of blue denims in a Western film or music video. When it comes to advertising denim trousers for the local market, the qualities that made them attractive in other contexts—their youthfulness, sensuality, unisexuality—offends local standards of decency. In such cases, the deterritorialized imagination gets brought to ground by recasting alien pants in a "zone of display" that is as reassuring and unthreatening as a family setting, reterritorializing the imagination in the process. The allure of the foreign does not disappear, it is simply left to work its effects beyond the advertisement itself.

Several forces shape the way the imagination gets domesticated, but the postcolonial state is fundamental. Where colonialism shifts the focus—and the chief source of symbolic production—in traditional societies from the cosmo-magical relationship of human beings and gods to the relationship of European officials and the local elite, postcolonial circumstances shift it again to the relationship of the national government and the most ordinary of people, citizens. Although it is ordinary people who matter, once the nation-state enters the scene, it becomes important to determine who is an insider and who an outsider, what is domestic and what is foreign. Maintaining those distinctions derives from a fiduciary responsibility to the people that postcolonial governments proclaim far more insistently than their colonial predecessors. After the Second World War, that responsibility led the leaders of African and Asian nations to conceive of their task as tied to development and modernization.

Fifty years later, those citizens are linked to the world beyond the nation-state by television, movies, print journalism, and travel itself, and they are increasingly aware of global changes in fashion, everyday practices, and consumption itself. Under these circumstances, national governments still exert a trusteeship over their people, only nowadays that responsibility often entails attempts to protect local culture and standards of decency. That responsibility often puts national governments at cross-purposes with advertising practice. Sometimes that means that certain commodities are made unwelcome altogether; more often it causes creative directors to find a "zone of display" acceptable to local critics of Western values, modernity, and materialism. Meantime, creative directors cannot afford to forget the allure of the foreign.

In what follows I practice a variant on the "follow the thing" anthropology that characterizes studies of transnationalism.[27] Sidney Mintz's account of the worldwide dispersal of sugar—first as a luxury spice, preservative, and ingredient in decorative confections and medicines, later as a workaday commodity—traces the transformation of a single commodity.[28] Instead of following a single commodity, I scrutinize a single profession that promotes, constrains, and configures the flow of many things, global and local. In the Sri Lankan case, advertising is a transnational profession that gazes in two directions—outward toward the world economy of commodities and culture and inward toward a small society. Whether the profession succeeds in domesticating the imagination depends on householders and their interests. To that end, I eventually move from advertising as profession and process to two families saving, consuming, and taking risks. The focus falls between the executives who are chauffeured about Colombo while they talk on their cell phones and the little boy who buys half a bar of soap. For all of its complexity and power, the world system exerts its claims only to the extent that it touches people living lives of local design.

NOTES

1. Keith Basso premises his study of Apache joking behavior (*Portraits of "the Whiteman"* [Cambridge: Cambridge University Press], 1979) on the argument that ethnographers are not the only people who do ethnography, although most Apaches would not recognize their jokes as the "microsociological analysis" that Basso asserts them to be (17). Advertising executives are folk ethnographers in a more systematic and self-conscious way—they speak in terms comparable to "microsociological analysis," and their livelihood depends on convincing others of their ethnographic skill.

2. C. G. Seligmann and Brenda Seligmann, *The Veddas* (Cambridge: Cambridge University Press, 1911).

3. Richard S. Tedlow, *New and Improved: The Story of Mass Marketing in America* (New York: Basic Books, 1990).

4. Michel de Certeau, *The Practices of Everyday Life,* trans. Steven Rendall (Berkeley: University of California Press, 1984).

5. Michael Schudson's study of American advertising dismisses advertising's role in influencing consumption decisions, but it ignores advertising as a source of cultural production (*Advertising, The Uneasy Persuasion: Its Dubious Impact on American Society* [New York: Basic Books, 1984]).

6. Where the nation-state is often the nominal background for ethnographic work—an article may be called "Kinship in Sri Lanka," for instance, although it really focuses on a small part of Sri Lanka—so it is with the discourse of advertising people. Executives speak of selling things to Sri Lankans, even while their efforts are aimed at Colombo or the western province.

7. See Johannes Fabian, *Time and the Other: How Anthropology Makes Its Object* (New York: Columbia University Press, 1983).

8. Eric Wolf, *Europe and the People without History* (Berkeley: University of California Press, 1982), 24–72.

9. Arjun Appadurai, "Disjuncture and Difference in the Global Cultural Economy," *Public Culture* 2, no. 2 (Spring 1990): 3.

10. Marshall Sahlins, "Goodbye to Tristes Tropes: Ethnography in the Context of Modern World History," *Journal of Modern History* 65 (1993): 2.

11. John E. Wills, Jr., "European Consumption and Asian Production in the Seventeenth and Eighteenth Centuries," in *Consumption and the World of Goods,* ed. John Brewer and Roy Porter (London: Routledge, 1993), 133

12. Sidney Mintz, *Sweetness and Power: The Place of Sugar in Modern History* (New York: Viking Books, 1985), 13.

13. *Voice* (Voice of America), no. 28 (August–September 1988): 24.

14. Alexandra A. Seno, "Manufactured for Export," *Asiaweek,* 8 May 1998.

15. Marshall Sahlins, "Cosmologies of Capitalism: The Trans-Pacific Sector of 'The World System,'" *Proceedings of the British Academy* 74 (1988): 4.

16. Michel de Certeau, *Culture in the Plural* (Minneapolis: University of Minnesota Press, 1997), 131.

17. Sahlins, "Goodbye to Tristes Tropes," 22.

18. For a useful treatment of the role of commodities in drawing the line between that which is local and foreign in Latin America, see Benjamin Orlove, ed., *The Allure of the Foreign: Imported Goods in Postcolonial Latin America* (Ann Arbor: University of Michigan Press, 1997).

19. Millie Creighton, "Maintaining Cultural Boundaries in Retailing: How Japanese Department Stores Domesticate 'Things Foreign,'" *Modern Asian Studies* 25, no. 4 (1991): 675–709. See also, Joseph Tobin, ed., *Remade in Japan: Everyday Life and Consumer Taste in a Changing Society* (New Haven, Conn.: Yale University Press, 1992).

20. Laurie King, "Tokyo Disneyland as Cute as Ever, but Slowing Down," *Lewiston (Maine) Daily Sun,* 7 April 1993.

21. Pico Iyer, *Video Night in Kathmandu* (New York: Knopf, 1988), 351.

22. Sahlins, "Goodbye to Tristes Tropes," 2.

23. Greg Dening, *Islands and Beaches: Discourse on a Silent Land, Marquesas 1774–1880* (Honolulu: University of Hawaii Press, 1980), 129–30.

24. Appadurai, "Disjuncture and Difference," 5.

25. In the age of mechanical reproduction, advertising avoids issues of authenticity that characterize the mass reproduction of art. Instead, by rechanneling and extending the social transmission of culture, it calls into question the very definition of art. See Walter Benjamin. "The Work of Art in the Age of Mechanical Reproduction," in *Illuminations* (New York. Harcourt, Brace and World, 1968), 222 23.

26. I have taken the expression "zone of display" from Stephen J. Greenblatt, *Learning to Curse* (New York: Routledge, 1990), 161–63.

27. George Marcus, "Ethnography in/of the World System: The Emergence of Multi-Site Ethnography," in *Ethnography through Thick and Thin* (Princeton, N.J.: Princeton University Press, 1998), 91.

28. Mintz, *Sweetness and Power,* 74–150.

CHAPTER ONE

Advertising as a Global Business

If advertising is defined as a system of proclamation and announcement, it predates the modern world of consumer capitalism. "Advertising is consistent with most types of human society," a study of communication begins, "and in fact was not unknown in ancient Greece and Rome."[1] I take such statements as reflecting not life in classical times but the desire to find venerable origins for the profession. By my definition, advertising of the modern kind, which depends on persuasion by a variety of rhetorical effects for the sake of selling commodities, arose in the late nineteenth century along with the department store, mass-produced, standardized, and branded products, the growth of the newspaper business, unprecedented material prosperity, and the transformation of fashion into a popular phenomenon.[2] To locate its origins in space as well as time, advertising began as a Western practice, and more narrowly an American one. In its origins it had no connection to colonialism or Western domination. But wherever advertising has spread—and in the early twenty-first century, few places on the planet lie beyond its reach—it has carried with it values, assumptions, and economic interests that are also Western.

Over the past one hundred years, the "official art of capitalism," to use Raymond Williams's expression, has itself become a multibillion dollar business.[3] In 1993 New York advertising agencies had billings of US $26.5 billion, which Tokyo agencies virtually equaled at US $25.4 billion. To the extent that advertising celebrates desire, the pleasure of calculation and choice, not to say the very possibility of paying mind to an unlimited array of things, advertising represents capitalism's love song to itself; to the extent that advertising is a profession composed of firms that meet payrolls, compete against one another, take over rival organizations, and hire and fire employees, advertising is simply one profit-seeking enterprise among many.

This duality defines advertising as a profession—on the one hand, a business among businesses; on the other hand, a business about business, a metabusiness. Marx's characterization of advertising—a parasite feeding on the rotting corpse of capitalism—inadvertently makes something of advertising's second-order position in the social organization of capitalism. As advertising agencies—headquartered in Western capitals—have established offices in faraway places, they have often done so by following a major corporate client into a market where the corporation wanted to do business. In recent years the modular character of economic development has allowed a second-order business to be installed in an economy before those first-order businesses are firmly established. In the early 1990s China became the world's fastest growing economy, and advertising was its fastest growing business.[4] Part of that growth owed to agencies' willingness to set up shop many years before they can attract clients in sufficient numbers to be profitable.

Especially in postcolonial settings, advertising is tied to the state in revealing ways. In some places, it celebrates the nation-state itself.[5] In Sri Lanka, a few agencies survive by depending on government accounts— for lotteries, development projects, and government corporations—or by representing various nongovernmental organizations. In the 1980s representing the state in its several forms constituted some 50 percent of all advertising revenues. Most of these advertisements, including the lotteries, are tied to development: "Your lottery ticket supports government's development projects; if you win, you win twiceover." The Chinese State Administration for Industry and Commerce acted in 1994 to control advertising rates in hopes of restraining unacceptable levels of inflation.[6] By treating advertising rates on a par with interest rates, the Chinese state assumed that what corporations pay to advertise governs economic expansion at least to an extent that warrants controlling them.

Advertising, by my definition, depends on mass media, first in the form of newspapers, and later radio and television broadcasting. Its association with print journalism means that advertising participates in the construction of "imagined" communities, not simply national ones, but also communities of consumption. Newspapers, novels, and periodicals bring contradictory forces to bear on the way human beings are organized in groups—their quotidian, demotic, and encyclopedic character creating a "national" world by leveling difference across regions, while their peculiar editorial orientations create new patterns of desire and fear appropriate to various social classes, age groups, genders, and cognitive interests.[7]

Television pushes the democratizing, intrusive, and vulgarizing aspects of advertising to new limits. Because television advertisements move, they are engaging in quite new ways—fully exploiting the rhetorical turn that print advertisements had taken much earlier. Television advertisements speak to particular kinds of people just as much as newspapers and periodicals, but television broadcasting brings with it an endless flow. Once switched on, television addresses anyone who enters the room—not just the viewers whom advertisers had envisioned. Its omnipresent, always at-the-ready quality creates a "national" world in ways much more thorough-going than print journalism. A nation that wakes up to a morning news program, watches a *telenovella,* or tunes in a lottery drawing is brought into an unprecedented kind of community, marked by a simultaneity and intensity that a newspaper cannot produce.

As an institution, advertising mediates an extraordinary variety of social forms—the nation and what lies beyond the nation (the global system of capitalism and politics, transnational flows of people, ideas, and things, the community of nations) as well as a variety of other relationships—between culture and commerce, producers and consumers, city and countryside, and government and its citizens. Because advertising produces not only profits but also culture, the advertising business not only links these social forms, it reimagines the relationship between them. What is powerful and frightening about this transformative process is that advertising—at least in its exemplary forms—works by indirection and metaphorical association. Rather than focusing on the commodity itself, it puts the commodity in contexts marked by signs of class, gender, nation, and personhood. The commodity is more accessible; the context more engaging. In that interaction, the commodity acquires meanings otherwise unearned.

There is nothing strikingly new about exploiting the imagination to sell things, but making a living by exploiting one's imagination as part of a job description and doing so for the benefit of other businesses has few precedents. The variety of people who work in an advertising agency—account managers, copywriters, art directors, graphic artists, and creative directors—come at the manipulation, articulation, and celebration of symbols from distinct directions. Once a creative director envisions a campaign, copywriters do a literary kind of interpretation, while graphic artists and film directors do the visual equivalent. Together they represent "a form of negotiation between sites of agency and globally defined fields of possibility" because the advertising imagination can be liberated from time and place.[8]

By the nature of their work, symbol analysts relate to other human beings, and thus to space and time, in distinctive ways.[9] Workers who provide in-person services such as waiters and waitresses, real-estate brokers, physical therapists, and child-care providers provide those services in a face-to-face way. Their services cannot be sold worldwide, which ties these workers to a particular place. What advertising people—as well as development specialists, corporate headhunters, systems analysts, architects, cinematographers, publishers, writers and editors, journalists, musicians, and university professors—trade in is the manipulation and analysis of symbols. No practical problem prevents their services from being traded and put to work far from where they were conceived. By that logic the transnational advertising firm and the global campaign are the logical extension of the very nature of the advertising business.

To the extent that advertising practice depends on electronic and print media to unleash the imagination, it is a relatively new form of work. To the extent that advertising agencies are organized as bureaucracies, it represents an older innovation in business practice. The trick is knowing how to join individual creativity to bureaucratic efficiency: some agencies are worldwide corporations that operate like corporations, others allow creative people to run with their imaginations.[10] Agencies such as Ogilvy and Mather and J. Walter Thompson fall on the first side, disciplining the imagination by way of demographic research and focus groups, while smaller agencies such as Weiden and Kennedy tend toward the affective side.

Two impulses have dominated the business in America.[11] One has been an advertising style driven by riotous, carnivalesque values; the other, by rationalization and scientism. The latter, centered on the theories of Frederick Winslow Taylor, shaped advertising text and graphics through the 1950s, squeezing out the carnivalesque. An aesthetic of play and defiance came to the fore in the 1960s, paralleling the ascendancy of one part of the agency—art directors and copywriters—in some firms. Art directors and copywriters had never been comfortable with the emphasis on "unique selling propositions" and hierarchical forms of business practice. Now they would run the business. In other words, the conflict between styles of advertising practice—the carnivalesque and the rationalistic—is reflected in the bureaucratic history of the profession.[12]

Advertising practitioners typically bring a high sense of their own life conditions to their work. Part of that self-consciousness owes to their being symbol analysts who make a living from acts that require skill and confidence. Another part owes to their making a living in a profession often looked down on and sometimes despised by the larger society. Any profession that depends on "manipulation" (of symbols or anything else) is likely to face resistance and critique. Under these circumstances, practitioners learn to defend their profession and their participation in it. Much of that self-reflection is apologetic and defensive, but it nonetheless produces the profession's vernacular theory. In contexts that range from professional meetings to regulatory hearings, advertising executives insist that advertising has social benefits.[13] The arguments are familiar: the consumer is sovereign, advertising simply responds to human nature, it informs and plays a role in fostering rational choice on the part of individuals, and, by increasing sales, it reduces the cost of products. In developing economies, advertising finds additional rationales—it creates economic development and turns peasants into consumers and citizens.

When advertising executives reflect on their own practice, when they are not apologizing for the profession but trying to collect their thoughts after a career of meeting deadlines, launching new products, and "knowing where the brand is today," they have more interesting things to say. They talk about the rise and fall of agencies and the extremely competitive nature of the business. Anyone who has worked in the business has seen accounts lost for no discernible reason (a client met an executive of another agency at a social occasion and was swayed by a convincing pitch), employees move on to new jobs at delicate times (after the agency had spent thousands of dollars on training), and national governments fall (threatening local business, not to say advertising). Advertising executives do their share of theorizing about what kinds of advertising succeed and how the imagination serves these ends, remembering great campaigns and talented copywriters. Most of the time, talk gravitates toward how much the business depends on managing employees, keeping clients happy, and using people properly.

Advertising around the Globe

Advertising executives constitute a small part of a cosmopolitan managerial and entrepreneurial class that runs the world economy.[14] As a modern kind of work centered on the construction and manipulation of symbols, the profession's defining characteristics link it to the movie, television, music, newspaper, magazine, and public relations industries. But advertising practice depends not only on a transnational class of managers. It has increasingly come to link local agencies into global networks, outstripping even a newspaper industry moving in the same direction. The advertising profession has well-known firms with global reach—J. Walter Thompson and Saatchi and Saatchi are the best known—but it also has a network structure that creates great flexibility. Local advertising firms attach themselves to transnational agencies with home offices located in New York or London, and just as quickly drop that affiliation to make another.

At the individual level, there is just as much movement. An agency in Sri Lanka gets an important account from Unilever to "refresh" the market for the most venerable consumer product in Asia, Sunlight soap. Unilever has money to spend, and the agency brings in a film director from Singapore to produce a new television commercial. Suddenly Sri Lankan television viewers are watching a local rendering of an advertisement that began in Southeast Asia as a regional campaign. Transnational firms such as Lintas, J. Walter Thompson, and Bates stage regional workshops that draw junior employees from various parts of the region. Over a two- or three-day period, they receive instruction from more experienced people, raising their level of professionalism. They also meet their peers who manage the Sunlight account in, let's say, India, Pakistan, Malaysia, and Thailand. Together they discuss what advertising seems to work and what does not, what attributes this product brings to the market, and how best to differentiate the product from its competition.

Most often senior people move into the managerial part of the business, handling accounts, keeping clients content, and making final decisions. Younger people pursue expressive tasks, writing copy, conceiving and producing television commercials. In an inchoate but growing market, an agency has to cope with a number of employees who leave their jobs each year for more attractive positions and better salaries. An agency can lose a copywriter without his or her taking accounts along. What it cannot afford to lose is a creative director (who manages all of the agency's creative work), putting such people in positions of great power. J. Walter Thompson has an expatriate holding this position, using its large scale and high profitability to ensure that their creative director in Colombo is fully competent and unlikely to leave his job at JWT to take another local job. Having an Australian in that job in Colombo gives global clients more confidence in the quality of the local office's work. It also insults local employees.

Graphic artists in Third World settings are usually more tied to place than their bosses. In my experience, they tend to be less well-educated, less often fluent in English or any world language, and more local in taste and sensibility. In Sri Lanka they derive from different social classes—executives are comfortably middle class in their origins, often coming from Colombo. Graphic artists, by contrast, come from all over the island, having found a place in the business because of an ability to draw that they developed in school.[15] Copywriters and graphic artists operate at a remove from the executives who manage the business. But even more social distance separates copywriters from artists. On the glass partition behind which graphic artists work at one Colombo agency is taped a sign, "English only to be spoken here." Doing so is a tall order for people who speak only Sinhala.

Just as advertising goes where capitalism goes, where transnational corporations go, transnational advertising firms—along with accountancy firms, management consultants, and legal services—follow. These are the service industries that have taken most successfully to supporting other global businesses. The synergy that advertising agencies create with transnational corporations depends on economies of scale, which in turn gives the advantage to the biggest agencies and forces smaller ones to get bigger. Through the 1980s, nearly 90 percent of all advertising revenue was produced by the economies of North America, Europe, and Japan. This economic concentration favors agencies headquartered in such places. But the effect of economic concentration does not end there. Some two to three hundred advertisers produced over 70 percent of advertising revenue worldwide.[16] Holding onto these accounts determines whether agencies survive or not.

What prevents the unlimited growth of economic concentration in transnational agencies is the desire of transnational corporations for unique representation for their products. Thus, the existence of some twenty transnational food companies ensured the existence of twenty transnational advertising firms.[17] One of those companies may also have food products that they want represented by a different advertising firm, and that preference creates space for a twenty-first advertising agency that can represent a single food product the world around.[18] But that agency may not have an office in a particular market, which allows still more advertising firms to acquire a piece of that food product's global business.

The center of gravity of these global networks rests in the world's most economically developed nations. Of the ten largest advertising organizations in 1993, five were based in the United States, three in Europe, and two in Japan. The Western origin of most of these global firms reflects the hegemony of Western—and more narrowly, American—forces in the global production of culture, just as the presence of Japanese transnational agencies reflects Japan's more recent economic power.[19] The centers of sophisticated symbolic production, in other words, operate alongside the centers of sophisticated material production and, to that extent, increase the hegemony of the world cities where they are based. When the New

York firm Revlon decided to mass market cosmetics with a global image in recent years, it had only to look down the street, giving its $70 million media-buying account to the sixth largest advertising organization in the world, Young and Rubicam.[20]

Corporations that operate around the world—Coca-Cola, Kodak, Sony, Mercedes-Benz, Pepsi-Cola, Nestlé, Gillette, Colgate, Adidas, Volkswagen—get several benefits from their transnational advertising firms. Besides economies of scale, worldwide representation gives them assurance of consistent and high-quality advertising, and unified advertising promises that world brands will be clearly differentiated from their competition in the way that Coca-Cola and Pepsi-Cola—independent of their negligible difference in taste—are clearly differentiated products. McCann-Erickson Worldwide represents Coca-Cola in eighty-seven national markets, Lintas does so in thirty-three, D'Arcy Masius Benton and Bowles in seven, the Low Group in seven, while Coke is sold but not represented in Bulgaria, Rumania, Jordan, and Tunisia. BBDO Worldwide handles Pepsi-Cola's advertising business in forty-nine markets, but Ogilvy and Mather Worldwide (eleven markets), Saatchi and Saatchi (twelve markets), J. Walter Thompson (twelve markets), DDB Needham Worldwide (seven markets), and Wunderman Cato Johnson (five markets) also have portions of Pepsi's advertising.[21]

Over the past decade, accounts have increasingly gravitated toward a single worldwide advertising agency. Neither Coke nor Pepsi has unitary representation across the globe, although Coke has consolidated more of its business.[22] All the virtues of worldwide representation duly noted, a practical constraint makes it difficult to achieve. No global agency is global enough to have offices in every national market. Moreover, there is local resistance. Several nation-states have resisted foreign advertising firms' plans to set up shop. In this regard, a handful of substantial economies—France, Sweden, Brazil, Japan, and South Korea—stand apart from the world system of commodities and commercial culture.[23] By closing their advertising markets to transnational agencies, they protect local culture, not to say local advertising firms.

Transnational agencies—British ones such as Lintas and hybrid British-American ones such as Ogilvy and Mather—spread with the growth of global manufacturing and marketing companies in the period between the two world wars.[24] The first American agency in Asia was established in 1955 when J. Walter Thompson and Company opened an office in Manila. American firms expanded rapidly in the decade that followed, often taking control of some of the European agencies. A few American firms linked up with Japanese ones in joint international ventures (as the American firm McCann did in 1961 when it joined forces with the Japanese firm Hakuhodo). But, then and now, the more common form of alignment occurs when a global agency, headquartered in Europe or North America, establishes an alliance with a local agency in a market where the transnational agency wants to do business.

These arrangements have always been unstable. The transnational agency has a falling out with its local affiliate and looks for a new partner in that market or it wins a new global account, which requires a new local affiliate because the present one handles a competing brand. In other words, an increasingly globalized economy works sometimes to complicate, not simplify, the relationship between advertising firms and clients. Anheuser-Busch employed D'Arcy Masius Benton and Bowles for seventy-nine years to advertise Budweiser until 1994 when D'Arcy Masius's Televest unit in New York accepted a media buying assignment from Miller Brewing. That account came to Televest because of its standing relationship with Miller's sister company, Kraft General Foods. Televest, however, neglected to tell either the agency's St. Louis office or Anheuser-Busch; and that act of disloyalty so angered Anheuser-Busch that it gave its $110 million account to DDB Needham Worldwide. It also took its international advertising business away from D'Arcy Masius, only to find that it could not give it to DDB Needham because its London office was already handling several competing accounts.[25]

American agencies developed networks in distinctive ways. Because they were more driven by profit-seeking, they preferred to find locally owned agencies and enter into working agreements rather than establish fully owned branch offices. Where European firms moved key managers to their branch offices, invested in training, and tried to develop regional and global integration, American firms took the cheaper course.[26] Often these joint ventures amounted to little more than an agreement to cooperate and new names added to the local firm's nameplate, although the enormous expansion of Asian economies in the 1980s led American firms with global aspirations to invest more resources in their local affiliates. At the same time, European and American firms in Asia have grown increasingly more autonomous. Only one firm, Ogilvy and Mather, has tried to establish a training scheme to be used around the world.

One process is general: when they are able, advertising agencies hire local staff. In Colombo almost all key executives are Sri Lankans. Transnational agencies, however, often have foreign "hires" in junior positions—an Indian, Malaysian, Australian—working on a short-term contract, before moving into a better position in the firm's other offices. In Kuala Lumpur, Europeans, Americans, and Australians—as well as Malaysians—run global (and local) agencies because the much larger Malaysian economy makes agency profits higher and hiring foreign executives possible. But the general pattern is clear all across Asia. Europeans who ten years ago held key positions have been replaced by local employees. Those same Europeans may now be working in Prague or Nairobi.

As the people working in transnational agencies in Asia have come to look more like the societies they inhabit, these agencies have tried to make brand identities, advertising campaigns, and sales strategies more centralized. In other words, as advertising offices have become more localized, the cultural forms—the advertising techniques, the media that carry advertising they produce—have begun to move in the opposite direction, becoming more centralized and more cosmopolitan. The move toward centralization began in the 1980s when the London firm Saatchi and Saatchi began to speak of "global advertising," arguing that by creating a single identity for a commodity the world over it could sell products the same way in Uruguay as the United Kingdom.

Global advertising took its cue from a *Harvard Business Review* article that announced in 1983 that the globalization of markets was at hand. The article argued that "different cultural preferences, national tastes and standards, and business institutions are vestiges of the past," and its oracular tone convinced substantial numbers of businesspeople that history had taken a real turn.[27] The future lay with globally standardized products. The article made a distinction—"multinational companies that concentrated on idiosyncratic consumer preferences have become befuddled and unable to take in the forest because of the trees . . . [and] the modern global corporation. . . . Instead of adapting to superficial and even entrenched differences within and between nations, it will seek sensibly to force suitably standardized products and practices on the entire globe" (91, 102).

For all of its bluster, the article was wrong about the short-term and the long-term alike. But it had a noticeable effect on both corporations and advertising agencies. Transnational agencies began to present themselves as uniquely qualified to service multinational business by calling on their size, well-defined organizational structure, and global reach. If a corporation was going to be able to sell a standardized product with a single identity the world over, common sense suggested the advantages of a single transnational advertising firm to handle that product's advertising. "We're seeing," argues the vice president for worldwide client services for Backer Spielvogel Bates Worldwide, "that increasingly clients are operating on a global basis and the agency of the future will run its multinational business through a global, not a local or regional structure."[28] In principle a global agency could use its organizational strength to coordinate activities all over the world, while reconceiving multinational campaigns in ways that accommodated local sensibilities. But maximum advantage—because of economies of scale and scope as well as increased market power—would require world-standardized products represented by a global agency using a global advertising campaign.

Seen in historical perspective, global advertising is today's installment of the capitalist dreamlife. Today those dreams have drawn closer to reality. Manufacturing, research, and packaging and design have all grown more centralized. There are signs of the creation of communities of consumption that transcend small localities. Judging simply from the worldwide spread of fast-food franchises such as McDonald's, television programming and Hollywood movies, brand names such as Levi Strauss and Coke, and commodities such as cigarettes and liquor, it might be possible to speak of the unification of taste across the world.[29] And it might be possible to imagine a global campaign that celebrated the universality of these tastes or their Western connections in a way that could reach people living in wildly different settings.

Global advertising has another advantage. For managers, it offers convenience: "you work for Saatchi and I'm at British Airways and I only have to deal with you and can ask you if the advertising in Zimbabwe is doing all right and you assure me that it is."[30] When IBM began to reorganize its floundering computer business in early 1993, it also reorganized its advertising business, taking accounts from nearly eighty advertising agencies worldwide and giving the works to Ogilvy and Mather.[31] This level of economic concentration and the ability to make worldwide media purchases—across different media as well as markets—means that tomorrow's installment of the capitalist dream will include capital flows directed by alignments of global corporations (such as IBM), global advertising agencies (such as Ogilvy and Mather), and global media companies (such as Rupert Murdoch's News Corporation). Ogilvy and Mather's campaign for IBM, "Small Planet," stressed the world-shrinking character of the computer, but the premise applied equally well to the agency's own strategic plans.

As it has turned out, selling standardized products worldwide has not been so easy. Some products cross national borders more easily than others. Even in Europe, where the emergence of an integrated market in the early 1990s and the relative similarity of life in modern, industrialized states made the possibility of pan-European advertising campaigns look realistic, there were problems. The financial unification of Europe aside,

Europeans live largely in a world of national meanings and practices. Consider one advertising executive's assessment of how liquor settles into various localities:

> "In Northern Europe—in Germany and the U.K., especially—
> Scotch has an aging profile. . . . Gin is young and trendy and excit-
> ing, except in the U.K., where it's a stuffy old drink that majors
> and bishops and retired members of the Tory Party drink. Vodka is
> the party drink of Europe. Bourbon is sexy and imported—the
> whiskey of the new generation. Tequila is "Let's get pissed." And
> rum—well, Bacardi is the product of advertising. Bacardi is es-
> cape." What about Scotch? "In Greece and Italy, it's a hip drink."
> And everywhere else? "It's 'my father's drink.'"[32]

On the possibility of regional advertising for liquor, the executive comes down on both sides. Some liquors cannot escape their localities, others can.

GLOBAL ADVERTISING RECONSIDERED

For every economy of scale there is a problem of scale. And however confident the assurances that the Zimbabwe advertising is doing all right, the fact of the matter can often be different. Notable failures of global campaigns—the House of Chanel's problems selling its products globally is an example—have caused advertising executives nowadays to invoke some version of the "think globally, execute locally" theme. Or else they speak of global advertising with reduced expectations, as in the words of an executive who runs Coca-Cola's advertising around the world—"centrally designed and centrally executed advertising will solve the problems of most people [will work in most markets] and establish quality standards for the remainder."[33] But even this more modest vision may not withstand close scrutiny. The founder of an American agency suggests his doubts about the success of global advertising:

> Interviewer: So you don't believe in the concept of global adver-
>   tising?
> Jay Chiat: No. And I've looked at Coca-Cola advertising from
>   around the world. Now, Coca-Cola is probably one of the
>   most simplistic products you could advertise for, right? With
>   the exception of possibly China and Russia—where Pepsi has
>   the franchise—Coke is pretty much all over. This is a com-
>   pany that's trying to be global, and they have an international

> task force that works on adaptations of Coke's ads. The reality
> is that the ads probably don't work in half the places.
>
> Interviewer: What do you mean by adaptations?
>
> Chiat: They change the ethnicity of the cast, the language, and
> reshoot the ad using the same premise. But it's like translating
> a joke from one language to another—it's not funny in trans-
> lation. . . . I've never seen a locally adapted campaign of an
> American or British advertising campaign adapted successfully
> enough that it was applauded or won anything at interna-
> tional advertising festivals. The advertisements that always
> win are those that were generated locally, in a particular
> community.[34]

Sometimes a local adaptation entails only reshooting an advertisement with local actors, reanimating a global campaign with recognizable faces. Other times local execution entails a form of cultural translation. East Asians drink beer in distinctive contexts—in mixed company, with family members of all ages. For this audience, the unremitting youthfulness of American beer commercials—as well as their sexuality—is off the mark, if not offensive.[35] Those advertisements need to be completely replotted. Multinational advertising aspires to universality of a kind, aiming for a similar response—let's say, "drinking Heineken makes the occasion special"—from consumers.[36] Who it is who come together to enjoy that special occasion may differ—young men in North America, family groups in East Asia—but the advertising means to celebrate something universal by manipulating local symbols.[37]

A transnational advertising firm has an office in Caracas. That lo-cal office acquires the Venezuelan accounts of a corporation that has ne-gotiated a worldwide contract with the advertising firm's head office in New York or London. Those connections do not prevent the local office of the global agency from competing with local firms for purely Venezue-lan accounts. Under these circumstances, the logic of contention usually takes this form. For accounts that they represent in many different places, transnational firms promise sophisticated advertisements, executed consis-tently across all of those markets. For local accounts, they promise to bring their clearly delineated marketing structure, market research, and a repu-tation for high quality to bear on a local campaign.

Local agencies compete by claiming better knowledge of the local market, while trading on social proximity to local clients, and lower, some-times much lower, cost. Dealing with local clients, those virtues go a long way. I know of smaller advertising firms in Sri Lanka that survive on the business provided by three or four accounts, and they maintain those accounts by way of family ties or long-standing social relationships with their clients. A few local firms can compete with the transnationals for important local clients. Some survive by offering extraordinary service. Even though his product is cheaper than the competition, let's say that a businessman finds that he just cannot sell cash registers. His advertising man does impromptu market research to keep him happy, driving round town and asking shopkeepers along the way why they are not interested in an efficient machine at a reasonable price. The advertising executive returns to his client and tells him that the last thing shopkeepers want is any kind of cash register (which produce register tapes in a political system where a trail of paper subjects a merchant to having to pay taxes). The rest make a living by finding various market niches that no multinational would consider. At the lower end of the market, advertising firms specialize in art-work—exhibition stalls, nameboards, tee-shirt printing, and conference materials.

Against local competition, the transnational firms have major advantages—larger organizations and better resources—from in-house production teams to professional training for staff. Doing business with Grant, McCann-Erickson, J. Walter Thompson, or Lintas offers local clients the prestige that goes with being served by the same agency that handles global clients. Prestige counts in the advertising business: when a creative director I know in Colombo established his own agency, he created a fictional nameplate for it—thus, a man named Rajapakse established an agency named Williams, Fletcher, and Stoltz—on the logic that local clients would believe the agency was less local than it really was and direct their business to an agency with Western founders. For their part, transnational agencies claim to be more local than they might appear by making a localizing promise: we can "think globally, execute locally" by exploiting our organizational advantage, while recognizing the need to approach local markets with the same sensitivity that local agencies claim for themselves. In their view, they replace the product-oriented thinking of local agencies—"here is a product, now let's see who will buy it"—with market research that can locate needs and preferences waiting to be addressed.[38]

If global advertising has become less global than promised, there are forces that push advertising in directions that transcend markets centered on individual countries. The fundamental one is competition. The advertising business in Asia is dominated by transnational agencies, and as competition among these agencies increases, so does the drive to economize by putting on campaigns that are global or at least regional in scale. Although the Japanese alter their products to sell in different markets much more so than Western corporations do, they also market those products in much the same way everywhere—"same brandnames, same packaging, same slogans, and same ad strategies."[39]

A second globalizing force is the evolution of communications technology. When satellite transmission began to bounce television signals from space, reception areas began to leave national boundaries behind, in turn forcing corporations to name, package, and manage their products in a unified way. In this case the technology itself created transnational communities of consumption. Because StarTV—the first pan-Asian network, based in Hong Kong but now owned by Rupert Murdoch—reaches an extraordinary viewing area, from the Mediterranean to Japan, television itself creates economies of scale and scope that favor both standardized products and standardized advertising. How else to speak to 2.8 billion people living in thirty-eight countries? Bouncing different broadcast signals off satellite transponders makes it possible to adjust programming and advertising to local audiences, but concern for profitability makes it unattractive to do so.

The simple way to lay out the social topography of advertising as a global phenomenon is to locate a postmodern sensibility in advertising viewed by people who live in industrialized countries and the earnest sales pitch in advertising regimes characteristic of developing economies. According to this argument, Chinese consumers watch advertisements high in informational content, and Japanese viewers watch television commercials that have little to do with selling and quite a lot to do with the character of life in a postmodern society.

> Any American who has gone to Japan and watched TV has been struck by the commercials—their blinding pace, their fragmentation, their high-tech construction, their wild and seemingly meaningless juxtaposition of language and images. To add to the perplexity of the newcomer, Japanese commercials often do not even refer to the product being sold; it is often difficult to ascertain either the sponsor or the product. For devotees, the commercials themselves often become highly valued aesthetic artifacts, and their creators respected and famous artists.[40]

Although it is true that the Chinese watch a lot of deadpan advertising and the Japanese see many commercials of the kind Marilyn Ivy describes, the broad distinction between sensibilities fails to do justice to the complexity of the situation. In my view, transnational corporations and the agencies that represent them expose people in most parts of the world to random parts of that postmodern sensibility—playfulness, depthlessness, pastiche. By the same token, Western consumers receive a large share of very unpostmodern advertising for foodstuffs, toiletries, and local services. Taken in the aggregate, the most one can say, I think, is that the effect of advertising derives from a variety of production values and sensibilities, and television pushes this variety to an extreme.

Consider advertising in the larger media context. When the Singer corporation sells sewing machines, refrigerators, and televisions in developing countries, it pays no attention to emotion or ambience. It simply proclaims the product's virtues. For almost a decade, Singer also sponsored *Dynasty* around the globe, projecting the highly imagined doings of the American rich into a world of unlikely places. It might be plausible to treat the joining of melodrama with earnest commercials as postmodern pastiche, now available in village and countryside. But why approach television by desegregating it even at the level of an hour-long production and its attendant commercials? As Raymond Williams says, the unprecedented quality of television is its flow, that is, the coursing of images across the screen that begins when the television is turned on and continues until it is turned off.[41] To that extent advertising is part of a communicative regime that has postmodern qualities intrinsic to this medium. How Singer advertises its products is only a small part of the flow.

Advertising in Asia

In Asia global advertising confronts a variety of powerful local forces. Two are especially important—rapidly rising standards of living and a strong sense of Asia's distinctive identity. Even with the economic downturn in Southeast and East Asia in late 1997, the expansion of these economies over the last thirty or forty years is extraordinary. Many Asians have discretionary income to an extent unknown to their parents. In China wages are doubling each year. By some definitions, half of the people of South Korea, Taiwan, Hong Kong, and Singapore are now middle class. The middle-class figure for Thailand, Indonesia, and Malaysia now approaches 20 percent. For some Asians prosperity entails food and shelter; for others it makes possible consuming goods and services associated with status and sophistication. In 1993 some 40 percent of the exports of French luxury goods went to East Asia; at the same point the Swiss watchmaker Piaget regarded Asia as its main market.[42] Looked at in comparison to the rise of a consumer society in eighteenth- and nineteenth-century Europe, prospering Asian societies are acquiring a fashion system similarly fixed on foreign luxury goods.

Chinese advertising expenditures have grown at a staggering rate since the economy was opened up in 1979. They still amount to a small fraction of their potential—some $91 million in 1992—compared with annual billings in Japan at that time of some $25 billion. While advertising budgets typically grow at an annual rate of single-digit proportions, annual billings in the most dynamic economies in Southeast Asia—Taiwan, South Korea, and mainland China, for example—have grown 25 to 50 percent each year since the 1980s.[43] Indian advertising expenditures grew at a 12 percent rate through the late 1980s, causing new advertising agencies to proliferate. Where there were 93 advertising agencies in Bombay in 1960, there were 425 by 1988.[44] By paying handsome salaries, firms have attracted talented and energetic people. In the late 1980s a copywriter in Bombay could earn 15,000 rupees (US $1,200) a month, one-third more than India's president. When middle-class South Asians question me about my research, conversation has often drifted toward their own aspirations for their children's finding a job in the advertising business. A generation ago, these same people would have been thinking about a position in the civil service.

Asia still represents the most important investment market for all global advertising agencies. With 200 million middle-class consumers, the Indian advertising market has become the fourth largest in the world. The Chinese national savings rate is some 36 percent, wages are doubling each year, and the number of Chinese with rising expectations can be calculated in the hundreds of millions.[45] Long-term prospects have made advertising agencies doing business in China write off short-term losses. In China, according to J. Walter Thompson's regional director in Southeast Asia, "our revenues doubled last year, but we still lost money because of salary and expansion costs and general operating expenses. . . . we are looking at 140 percent revenue growth and projecting a $500,000 loss."[46]

Despite the fact that setting up business in the developed markets of Asia is expensive and the short-term prospects for profits in markets such as China are negligible, transnational agencies, wanting to do business in one part of Asia, often choose to establish agencies all across the region. By making a bet on being able to do business regionally in the future, advertising agencies make themselves a transnational force. By wanting to be on the ground when transnational corporations enter a market, a second-order business sometimes precedes first-order businesses. The same is true of the exploding number of commercial television networks in Asia.[47] The cost of communication satellites is such that hardly any of the television networks broadcasting across Asia are making money. But they will be in the air when business arrives.

There is increasing talk across Asia of the cultural distinctiveness of the region as a whole—Asians are family and group oriented, they respect tradition, and they value work and thrift—and each of these values has implications for consumerist practices, advertising, and material life in general. To that extent, a ready-made account of Asian identity has been transnationalized as much as the advertising business. The invocation of Asian values has produced a new discourse, treating Asia as a single place governed by values that always seem to do their work independent of either political or economic forces or other local realities.[48] All of the usual anthropological critiques—essentialism, reductionism, and ventriloquism—duly noted, the pertinent issue when Asian values are invoked is whether any particular Asian society in fact endorses these values or whether they encode the interests of Asian leaders, governments, and advertising agencies.[49]

Although the values most often celebrated in distinguishing Asian societies have Confucianist origins, similar arguments have been made about the cultural distinctiveness of South Asia. The importance of the family and religion looms large in most of these arguments, and advertising is often seen as threatening both. Gandhi wanted to run his journals without advertising, but the attitude of the generality of Indians toward advertising is another thing altogether.[50] A tribal society in Andhra Pradesh, the Muria Gond, values self-restraint, the importance of the commonweal, and thrift to an extent that would please Gandhi.[51] A populist movement in Sri Lanka has recently decried Coca-Cola and Western practices such as dancing, and a former Janata Dal minister, George Fernandes, persistently campaigns against Pepsi-Cola in India.[52] But the generality of South Asians have opinions about consumption and advertising that are as various as their reactions to Gandhi himself have been.

In 1990 a talk show aired on Sri Lankan television interviewing people on the streets of Colombo about advertising.[53] An older woman said advertising was good, equating advertising with programming in general, which she said was also good. A man followed who argued that, without advertising, consumers would not know anything about products, a sentiment echoed by another man seen later. He was followed by a man who said that advertisements influence people. A third man remarked on the catchy slogans and added that manufacturers have a responsibility to make products as good as their advertising. A male executive said that advertisements must be impressive. Two younger people argued that television advertising was not up to foreign standards and that Sri Lankan commercials are very slow. There were only two negative voices, one saying that advertisements appeal to foolish people and the other characterizing advertising as a science designed to attack people's weaknesses. No one made any comments about materialism as such, and no one said anything about advertising as a threat to Sri Lankan values.

But there is considerably more resistance from the nation-state itself. When Singapore's former Prime Minister Lee Kuan Yew used to argue that Confucianist values were the foundation for the public culture of Singapore, he seemed to be making a claim about values that resided in the minds of Singaporeans, not only in his own or his ministers' and bureaucrats'. But the government's position has great force in itself, whatever ordinary people believe and do. Even if the people are indifferent to those values, legitimating and projecting those values, according to Confucian tradition, is an obligation of leadership. "The grass will bend with the wind"—the people will be influenced by what the leader does. If they do not understand, they will follow. And of course there are political imperatives at work in all pronouncements about culture. When the government of Vietnam denounces the effects of "toxic cultural imports" by publicly burning videocassettes with violent and sexual content, calendars, books, posters, and playing cards, and by tearing down Pepsi signs because they were written in a foreign language, such actions reflect the government's sense of how well Vietnamese society is being served by its contact with the outside world. But they also reflect power struggles within the ruling party.

On occasion South and Southeast Asian societies respond to television advertisements in ways that suggest—appropriate disclaimers noted—that the relationship between parents and children is a sensitive issue all across the region, no matter how different these societies may be in other ways. In Sri Lanka children can appear in advertisements, but they cannot recommend a product—on the premise that a child's testimony has too much effect on other children. What a child does say can violate local expectations of proper behavior between children and parents. A recent example comes from the Singapore government and, more specifically, Goh Chok Tong, Lee Kuan Yew's successor as Prime Minister. He objected to a print advertisement for a nutritional supplement featuring a boy with clenched fists saying to his father, "Come on Dad. If you can play golf five times a week, I can have Sustagen once a day." [54]

A recent Sri Lankan advertisement that parallels the Singapore example was even less confrontational. By Western standards, it was gentle enough to be quaint. A little girl appeared in a television advertisement, drinking milk with great enthusiasm. She speaks to the camera, saying that her mother thinks she drinks the milk because she understands how nutritious it is. Actually she drinks it because she likes the taste. "Don't tell Mommy!" The *Ammata kiyanne epā* ("Don't tell Mommy!") commercial was withdrawn just as quickly as the Sustagen advertisement in Singapore. If one wants to find difference here, it is clear that the Sri Lankan advertisement would not have met any objections in Singapore, and the Singaporean advertisement would not have drawn comment from a Western audience. But in the way advertising practice handles the relationship of children and parents, Singapore and Sri Lanka have more in common than their sharing a media policy inherited from the British.

There is a global system of advertising that ties Asia to centers of industrial production in a variety of places beyond Asia. But that global system—where transactions across national borders increase in importance relative to those within nation-states and where national boundaries cease to be a significant obstacle to the movement of goods and services— is scarcely seamless.[55] It is flexible in organization and global in reach. Consider the case of Sustagen, whose advertising provoked government feelings in Singapore. It is manufactured by Mead Johnson, a U.S.-based corporation, which was acquired by another U.S.-based corporation, Bristol-Myers, which subsequently merged with Squibb in 1989.

Sustagen is just one nutritional product that Bristol-Myers Squibb sells worldwide, along with infant formulas, medical nutritionals, and other consumer nutritional products. This division of Bristol-Myers Squibb employs 5,200 people worldwide. Since April 1997 the president of Mead Johnson has been a Scotsman, Ian Stuart, who received his education at the Glasgow College of Technology and Newcastle-upon-Tyne Polytechnic in the United Kingdom. Prior to joining Bristol-Myers Squibb, he held management positions with Gillette, Cheeseborough-Ponds, and Unilever in Europe, Japan, and Africa.[56] He now lives in Evansville, Indiana, where he directs Mead Johnson's efforts to increase sales for Sustagen and other nutritional products.

Although Mead Johnson is headquartered in Indiana, Bristol-Myers Squibb does not market Sustagen in the United States. It has been sold from Brazil to Thailand for almost thirty years. Stuart inherits a problem from his predecessors—selling a milk product in parts of the world where milk is not consumed regularly or at all. In Indonesia, Sustagen's advertising agency has tried to increase its market by targeting adults with a new product, Sustagen HP, and to segment the adult market with a skimmed milk product aimed at young urban professionals. The same emphasis on fitness and energy appears in the product's Singapore advertising. In the controversial advertisement Sustagen's advertising agency tried to address the adolescent children of young urban professionals—"Come on Dad. If you can play golf five times a week, I can have Sustagen once a day."—and their parents at the same time.

There are many obstacles to the globalization of trade, but putting commodities in idiomatic "zones of display" is not the least of them. In the Singapore case, even a local agency did not recognize the limits beyond which a son's cajoling his father cannot go. Sometimes the commodities are foreign and need to have their dangerous qualities domesticated without losing their allure, but just as often the commodities are produced locally and advertised in "zones of display" that differentiate them from the competition or convert local culture into a sign of itself in a way that benefits the commodity. When it occurred on the beach—a few foreigners selling commodities and locals buying—the translation process was straightforward but considerably less interesting.

N O T E S

1. Gillian Dyer, *Advertising as Communication* (London: Methuen, 1982), 5.

2. For a different conception of the origins of advertising, see Brian Moeran, *A Japanese Advertising Agency: An Anthropology of Media and Markets* (Honolulu: University of Hawaii Press, 1996). On Moeran's definition, Japanese advertising began almost 1,300 years ago when market stall operators were allowed to use their name and their products' names on signboards. By the Edo period (1603–1868) department stores were doing advertising in the form of mass communications (6–7).

3. Williams elsewhere characterized advertising as "a highly organized and professional system of magical inducements and satisfactions functionally very similar to magical systems in simpler societies but rather strangely coexistent with highly developed scientific technology" (Raymond Williams, *Problems in Materialism and Culture* [London: Verso, 1980], 185).

4. Jinhao Hong, "The Resurrection of Advertising in China," *Asian Survey,* 34, no. 4 (April 1994): 328.

5. See, for instance, Robert J. Foster, "Print Advertisements and Nation Making in Metropolitan Papua, New Guinea," in *Nation Making: Emergent Identities in Postcolonial Melanesia,* ed. Robert J. Foster (Ann Arbor: University of Michigan Press, 1995), 151–81; and Steven Kemper, "The Nation Consumed: Buying and Believing in Sri Lanka," *Public Culture* 5, no. 3 (Spring 1993): 377–93.

6. Sheila Tefft, "Ad Boom Unsettles China," *Advertising Age,* 19 September 1994, 13.

7. The paradigm source is Benedict Anderson, *Imagined Communities* (London: Verso,1983). For an account of how consumption figured in the rise of English nationalism, especially through the distinction between English and French dress, see Gerald Newman, *The Rise of English Nationalism: A Cultural History, 1740–1830* (New York: St. Martin's, 1987).

8. Arjun Appadurai, "Disjuncture and Difference in the Global Cultural Economy," *Public Culture* 2, no. 2 (Spring 1990): 5.

9. I take the expression "symbol analyst" from Robert B. Reich, *The Work of Nations: Preparing Ourselves for 21st Century Capitalism* (New York: Basic Books, 1991). He has it "symbolic analyst."

10. See Thomas McLaughlin, *Street Smarts and Critical Theory: Listening to the Vernacular* (Madison: University of Wisconsin Press, 1996), 121.

11. T. J. Jackson Lears, *Fables of Abundance* (New York: Basic Books, 1994), 138, 162, 197, 216–17. Also see Thomas Frank, *The Conquest of Cool: Business Culture, Counterculture, and the Rise of Hip Consumerism* (Chicago: University of Chicago Press, 1997).

12. Moeran says that there are no Japanese agencies where creative people actually run the business (*Japanese Advertising Agency,* 97 n. 8).

13. McLaughlin, chapter 5 in *Street Smarts and Critical Theory.*

14. Useful accounts of this transnational class include Robert Redfield and Milton Singer, "The Cultural Role of Cities," *Economic Development and Cultural Change* 3 (1954): 53–73; Ulf Hannerz, "The Cultural Role of World Cities," in *Humanizing the City?* ed. Anthony Cohen and Katsuyoshi Fukui (Edinburgh: Edinburgh University Press, 1993), 67–84; and David Harvey, *Consciousness and the Urban Experience: Studies in the Theory of Capitalist Urbanization* (Baltimore: Johns Hopkins University Press, 1985).

15. Because qualified creative directors are hard to find locally, creative directors frequently are Indian nationals who come to Sri Lanka with a degree in graphic arts and English, becoming creative directors straightaway.

16. Thierry J. Noyelle and Anna B. Dutka, *International Trade in Business Services* (Cambridge, Mass.: Ballinger Publishing, 1988), 40.

17. Noyelle and Dutka, *International Trade in Business Services,* 101. In the mid-1980s the biggest agencies, such as Saatchi and Saatchi, attempted to run a network of several agencies under one roof, in this case, Saatchi and Saatchi, Compton and Ted Bates. Success at doing so requires serving different corporate clients with similar products under that same roof.

18. Moeran provides a useful account of the split account system (*Japanese Advertising Agency,* 46–48).

19. Dentsu and Hakuhodo are among the largest advertising agencies in the world, but Japanese firms are situated in the global system of culture in a distinctive way because they largely represent Japanese firms. Dentsu has offices in 18 countries, and its chief clients are Canon, Japan Airlines, Kao, Nestlé, Nissan, Panasonic, Sony, and Toyota; Hakuhodo has offices in 13 countries and represents ANA, Ajinomoto, Canon, Honda, Isetan, Kao, Konica, Matsushita, and NEC ("'AAI' Picks Next Major Marketers," *Advertising Age,* 18 September 1995, 143).

20. To quote the President of Revlon International: "The basic strategy of Revlon is to use the North American, U.S.-based positioning worldwide, so that the excellent Cindy Crawford/Claudia Schiffer-type core ad vehicle is present throughout all markets in which Revlon advertises" ("Revlon Eyes Global Image, Picks Young and Rubicam," *Advertising Age,* 11 January 1993, 1).

21. Laurel Wentz, "Upstart Brands Steal Spotlight from Perennials," *Advertising Age,* 19 September 1994, 113–114. Coca-Cola often has several agencies represent it in one market, different agencies handing different media; Pepsi tends to have a single agency representing it in any national market, handling all media.

22. McCann-Erickson Worldwide handled most of Coca-Cola's business worldwide for forty years. In 1991 Coca-Cola began working with a new agency, Edge Creative, which had Coke as its sole client. That relationship produced the "Always Coca-Cola" theme

and polar bear imagery. That relationship broke up in 2000, and Coke went back to Madison Avenue for representation ("Coke to Disband In-House Agency That Handles Its Flagship Brand," *New York Times,* 4 April 2000.

23. Noyelle and Dutka, *International Trade in Business Services,* 101. If one tallies the national origins of the fifty or so top multinational advertising firms in any recent year, five or so will be French and five Japanese. The remainder are American, with a handful of British and German agencies. But even the paltry representation of French and Japanese firms is no indication of their global competitiveness or their being a source of global cultural production independent of the United States. French and Japanese firms rank as high as they do not because of international accounts but by doing enormous amounts of business in their own economies, where government policy protects them from foreign competition.

24. Chris Baker, "Who Are the Space Invaders Now?" (paper presented at the Social Science Research Council Conference, "Advertising, Consumption, and the New Middle Class in India," Monterey, Calif., April 1991), 11.

25. Ira Teinowitz, "Why A-B Bounced Bud," *Advertising Age,* 21 November 1994, 1–2.

26. Baker, "Who Are the Space Invaders Now?" 10.

27. Theodore Levitt, "The Globalization of Markets," *Harvard Business Review* 3 (May–June 1983): 96. Levitt attributes the "convergence" idea to Daniel Boorstin's *The Americans* (3 vols. [New York: Random House, 1958–1973]), which itself has a genealogical relationship to the "modernization" theory of the time. Benjamin Barber's *Jihad vs. McWorld* (New York: Times Books, 1995) extends Levitt's argument, balancing it against the gathering force of Muslim resistance to the encroachment of Western institutions.

28. "BSB Sharpens Its 'Global Focus,'" *Advertising Age,* 7 June 1993, 12. Its early celebration of local values and dispersed responsibility notwithstanding, Apple Computer recently decided it needs global advertising ("Apple Wants Unified Worldwide Image," *Advertising Age,* 12 April 1993, 3).

29. Most of the contributions to a recent account of the Asianization of McDonald's suggest the opposite conclusion. See James Watson, *Golden Arches East: McDonald's in East Asia* (Stanford: Stanford University Press, 1997).

30. Carol Squiers, "Big Brother Goes Bicoastal: An Interview with Jay Chiat," in *Global Television,* ed. Cynthia Schneider and Brian Wallis (New York: Wedge Press; Cambridge, Mass.: MIT Press, 1988), 176.

31. Bradley Johnson, "IBM Hammers out Worldwide Media Deals," *Advertising Age,* 8 January 1996, 4. Ogilvy and Mather has only sixty-one offices worldwide, so Grey Advertising represents IBM in markets such as Russia, Slovenia, and Israel where Ogilvy has no office.

32. John Heilemann, "All Europeans Are Not Alike," *New Yorker,* 28 April and 5 May 1997, 175.

33. William O'Barr and Mauricio Moreira, "The Airbrushing of Culture: An Insider Looks at Global Advertising," *Public Culture* 2, no. 1 (Fall 1989): 7.

34. Squiers, "Big Brother Goes Bicoastal," 176.

35. "Targeting Asians," *Far Eastern Economic Review,* 21 January 1993, 40.

36. To clarify matters, I follow the practice of describing instances of centrally designed advertisements reshot with local actors as an example of global advertising, but treat ones involving changes in context and plot as multinational advertising. This distinction derives from "Global Campaigns Don't Work; Multinationals Do," *Advertising Age,*

18 April 1994, 23. While distinguishing two types of advertising campaigns, I have relied on another term to refer to advertising agencies that do business around the world regardless of whether they emphasize global or multinational campaigns. I will call them "transnational firms." All I want to establish here is a distinction between different kinds of campaigns—global and multinational—carried out by transnational advertising firms—firms that do business around the world.

37.   Whether one can make sense of the idea of universal meaning as distinct from the local expression of meaning is a question that interests anthropologists more than advertising executives. See Rodney Needham, "Inner States as Universals: Skeptical Reflections on Human Nature," in *Indigenous Psychologies: The Anthropology of the Self*, ed. Paul Heelas and Andrew Lock (London: Academic Press, 1981), 65–78.

38.   "The Selling of Asia," *Far Eastern Economic Review*, 29 June 1989, 61.

39.   Baker, "Who Are the Space Invaders Now?" 3.

40.   Marilyn Ivy, "Critical Texts, Mass Artifacts: The Consumption of Knowledge in Postmodern Japan," *South Atlantic Quarterly* 87, no. 3 (Summer 1988): 434.

41.   Raymond Williams, *Television: Technology and Cultural Form* (Hanover, N.H.: University Press of New England, 1974), 72–112.

42.   Peer Meinert, "Culture of Consumption Sweeps Newly-Wealthy Asia," Deutsche Presse-Agentur, 7 October 1994 (available from Lexis-Nexis).

43.   "The Selling of Asia," 60.

44.   John Battenfeld, "Diversity Makes Indian Advertising Boom," Reuters News Service–India, 9 March 1988 (available from Lexis-Nexis).

45.   What makes that unimaginable savings rate possible is the small percentage, 5 percent, of household income that Chinese families spend on housing, health care, education, and transportation, giving consumers equally unbelievable amounts of spendable income (Hong, "Resurrection of Advertising in China," 333.)

46.   Gail Kemp, "How to Set Up Shop in Asia," Reuters Textline, 27 January 1995 (available from Lexis-Nexis).

47.   Tim Healey and Law Siu Lan, "New Bird in an Overcast Sky," *Asiaweek*, 8 December 1995, 55.

48.   The most recent example is Mahathir Mohamad and Shintaro Ishihara, *The Voice of Asia: Two Leaders Discuss the Coming Century* (Tokyo: Kodansha International, 1995).

49.   These notions have a clear effect on advertising firms in Asia, which regularly call for advertising that respects Asian values. "Asian Advertising Conference," *Daily Yomiuri*, 8 November 1993, 5.

50.   Judith M. Brown, *Gandhi: Prisoner of Hope* (New Haven, Conn.: Yale University Press, 1989), 135.

51.   For both an example of a tribal society whose consumption values are tied to group identity and a contrast with the individualizing and extravagant consumption practices of Sri Lankan fishermen, see Alfred Gell, "Newcomers to the World of Goods: Consumption among the Muria Gonds," in *The Social Life of Things*, ed. Arjun Appadurai (Cambridge: Cambridge University Press, 1986), 110–38.

52.   Fernandes's anxiety about advertising is itself instructive: "I used to think that Western television and advertising would create in people an anger and revulsion and that . . . would help the radical movement . . . by showing people the life that was denied them. Now I just feel that people treat the ads as just another form of entertainment" (*Guardian*, 8 April 1994).

53. "Feedback," Sri Lanka Broadcasting Corporation, May 1990. The balance of the program consisted of a discussion with three advertising executives.

54. Sumika Tan, "Sustagen Ad PM Objected to Will Be Withdrawn," *Straits Times*, 23 August 1994, 3.

55. I take this characterization of globalization from Wyn Grant, "Perspectives on Globalization and Economic Coordination," in *Contemporary Capitalism: The Embeddedness of Institutions,* ed. J. Rogers Hollingsworth and Robert Boyer (Cambridge: Cambridge University Press, 1997), 320.

56. "Ian Stuart Named President, Mead Johnson Nutritionals," (www.pslgroup.com/dg/24336.htm), August 1997.

CHAPTER TWO

Facing the Nation

Feelings about the nation-state—patriotism, chauvinism, civic-mindedness—are no more natural than the nation-state itself. The nation has to be forged, in both senses of the word, as part of a self-conscious attempt to create a kind of community that transcends local forms of belonging.[1] In postcolonial states such as Sri Lanka and Malaysia, the nation as an object of loyalty has been overwhelmed by older affiliations—ethnic group, religion, region, race, language, and culture. But in a less-noticed way, the birth of national feeling has been undone by forces even more workaday and unassuming than these sources of identity. People have simply been more interested in other things.

Anthony Burgess's fictionalization of the last years of British colonialism in Malaysia goes to the heart of the matter. A British teacher— newly arrived and hopeful for a Malaysian nation—encourages a Chinese student with a flair for composing music.

> Crabbe got up from the arm-chair and walked the sitting-room. He entered a belt of sun from the window, gazed out for an instant on palms and Government houses, wondered dizzily for a moment what he was doing here anyway, and poured himself gin and water.
>
> "So," said Crabbe to the boy's back—thin nape, plastered hair, white shirt soiled from travel—"you just write for yourself, is that it? You don't think other people might want to hear it? And you've no particular love for your country?"
>
> "My country?" the boy looked around, puzzled.

"Some day Malaya might be proud to have a major composer."

"Oh, I see." He giggled. "I don't think that will happen."

"Music can be a big thing to a country finding itself. Music presents a sort of image of unity."

"I don't see that."

"No, I suppose not. Your job, as I say, is just to compose. But even a composer has to have some sense of responsibility. The best composers have been patriotic."

"Elgar is not one of the best composers," said Robert Loo, with a boy's smug dogmatism. "His music makes me feel sick."

"But look what Sibelius has done for Finland," said Crabbe. "And de Falla for Spain. And Bartok and Kodaly. . . ."

"The people of Malaya only want American jazz and ronggeng music. I am not composing for Malaya. I am composing because I want to compose. Have to compose," he amended, and then looked embarrassed, because he had admitted to a daemon, an obsession. He had very nearly been seen without his clothes.[2]

At Independence the ordinary run of Malaysians may not have had commitments as forceful as the boy's need to compose, but they had other things to look after—fishing, farming, and tending to their gardens, running small businesses, raising families, listening to jazz and ronggeng music. Relative to the routines of life, the nation has simply not been able to make a claim on most people.

The prospects of a patriotic music for Malaysia also confronted ethnic difference. The Chinese were not citizens of British Malaya and, unbeknownst to Crabbe, not offered citizenship until 1955. But had he known more about the anomalous position of the Chinese in Malaysia, Crabbe would not have been deterred. For him, music has spirit, and that spirit has irresistible force. It constitutes the nation, virtually independent of local people, their feelings, and their different interests. He tries to enlist a Malay teacher in Loo's cause.

"You see," said Crabbe, "apart from its aesthetic value—and I'm not really capable of judging that—it's just come at the right time from the political point of view."

"Music? Politics?"

"Yes. You know, of course, that they made Paderewski Prime Minister of Poland. Paderewski was a great pianist."

"A bit before my time."

"This symphony could be played as a big gesture of independence. 'We in Malaya have thrown off the shackles of an alien culture. We have gotten past the nose flute and the two-stringed fiddle. We are adult. We have a national music of our own.' Imagine a full orchestra playing this symphony in the capital, imagine it on the radio—'the first real music out of Malaya,' imagine the pride of the average Malayan. You *must* do something about it."

"Look here . . . the average Malayan won't care a damn. You know that as well as I do."

"Yes, but that's not the point. It's culture, and you've got to have culture in a civilized country, whether the people want it or not. That's one of the stock clichés—'our national culture.' Well, here's the first bit of national culture you've ever had—not Indian, not Chinese, not Malay—Malayan—just that."

"What sort of a thing is it?" asked Nik Hassan suspiciously. "Is it modern—you know, Gershwin stuff? Has it a good tune? Do you really think it's any good?"

"I'm pretty sure it's good. I've not heard it, but I've read it. Whether it's good or not is not really the point, anyway. It's a work of art, it's extremely competent, it's probably highly original. But don't expect sound-track slush. It's not got a good tune anywhere in it, but it's terrifically organized, tremendously concentrated. That boy's a genius."

"Chinese, isn't he. Pity about that." Nik Hassan made a sour gangster's face. "Pity he's not a Malay. Though, of course, he could use a what-you-call . . ."

"Pseudonym?"

"That's right, a Malay pseudonym. It might carry a bit more weight. After all, everybody knows the Chinese are clever. We're a bit sick of hearing it. We're just dying for a Malay genius to turn up."

"Well, here's a Malayan genius for you." (372–73)

Forget the matter of who would be the first Malayan composer. Or the first Malayan genius. The issue was who would be a Malayan, early or late, composer or paddy farmer? Who would identify themselves with the nation-state? The Chinese were "clever," but Malay opinion did not accept local Chinese as legitimate participants in the polity. They were newly arrived (most had come in the nineteenth century to work tin mines, grow pepper and gambier, and trade), culturally alien, and joined to the economy in ways that made their national-feeling suspect. The Chinese guerrillas who began fighting the invading Japanese ended up in the 1950s fighting against British and Malay troops. At one point they proclaimed the annexation of Malaysia to China, putting the loyalty of all local Chinese at issue. The Malays were people of the place but had little more reason to conceive of themselves as Malayans than the Chinese. They were Malay, and that was enough.

With a few exceptions, nation-states have always had to be constructed from congeries of ethnicities. Against this standard, Sri Lanka and Malaysia had no special burden. They both confronted historical forces—the rise of a world system of political and capitalist institutions, the proliferation of electronic media (which created alternatives to both "national" music and nose flutes), and an unprecedented onrush of commodities—besetting all nations that came into being after World War II. Economic development was expected to proceed in step with the political development of the nation, forward movements drawing people into newer forms of belonging. And advertising was increasingly to play a part in both projects.

Both Malaysia and Sri Lanka were British colonies, constructed as import-export economies in a larger colonial system. They have roughly the same population (in 1992 Sri Lanka had 17.7 million citizens; Malaysia, 18.8 million). Post-Independence politics in both places has been organized around developing the economy in ways that have linked the nation to the larger world of economic interests, foreign lenders, development experts, multinational advertising agencies, and free-trade zones. They have a comparable ethnic mix. Sri Lanka has a Sinhala majority (of some 70 percent) and Tamil and Muslim minorities. Malaysia has a Malay majority (of 55 percent) with Chinese and Indian minorities.

At Independence Sri Lanka looked to have much greater potential for avoiding ethnic conflict and just as much potential for developing economically. Neither prospect has been borne out. Although the country's annual growth rate of some 5 to 7 percent looks anemic compared to Malaysia's, it has grown at a respectable rate, the more so considering that it has grown amidst a civil war that has dragged on since 1983. Sri Lanka also escaped the currency collapse and economic downturn of late 1997. Both countries have established a network of free-trade zones, become increasingly dependent on foreign aid, investment, and commodities, and been challenged by electronic media and advertising. But the economic prospects of the generality of people in each place are considerably different. The Malaysian per capita GDP has reached US $2,500 per year. Sri Lanka's hovers at US $500.[3]

In the production of the nation, one element seems unproblematic—the representation of what Malaysians and Sri Lankans look like. As long as a foreign master was around, that local face was established by what it was not: it was not European.[4] Once free, that local identity became problematic. As Benedict Anderson puts it, a "remarkable confidence of community in anonymity . . . is the hallmark of modern nations."[5] Nineteenth-century newsprint journalism could nurture the national imagination while ignoring its improbabilities. And even through the first half of the twentieth century, sticking Robert Loo with a pseudonym might have worked for a while. After all, how many Malaysians would have known him personally? But visual media traffic in particularity, not anonymity, and persons with ethnic characteristics are not the "people," abstractly understood. Some readers and viewers see like kinds of people represented in electronic and print form. Others do not.

Picturing people is the most forceful and straightforward way to represent either commodities or nations, the ultimate and simultaneously most proximate "zone of display" for products to be purchased and nations to be celebrated. But that embodiment means that choosing one ethnic type excludes another. Any choice undermines the unity in anonymity that enables the nation-state. The national physiognomy ceases to be a generic Sri Lankan or Malaysian and becomes an entirely particular one. Organizing an advertisement around a model uses that person in two contradictory ways—as a unique human being and as a collection of signs that reference that person's race, religion, gender, ethnicity, and national identity. The national face carries significance that is as much political as commercial. When "we Malaysians" or "we Sri Lankans" see ourselves consuming in advertising contexts, who exactly is the "we"?

Developing the Nation

Ever since World War II, the new states of Asia have undertaken two simultaneous tasks: growing the economy and creating stable political institutions. These two tasks have been imagined in ways that join citizenship to economic life. As we grow the economy, we leave behind our past as a colony and create the nation-state. But this campaign to join the political task to the economic one has developed in league with a set of exclusions because some local people are more fully Sri Lankan than others and some are more Malaysian. These exclusions fly in the face of the secular and democratic values of the nation-state, and they may not even be much discussed. But they weigh on who feels the call of citizenship.

The need to feed, shelter, and employ people has been only part of the state's motivation to make the economy grow. For the state has also needed development to create itself, fostering a sense of national identity and civic feeling sufficient to balance ethnic identities. The first generation of postcolonial leaders in Africa and Asia—Nkrumah, Nasser, Sukarno, and Nehru are the usual examples, although Kim Il Sung and U Nu suggest the full range—tried to create civil sentiments by founding the state as an ideological project. Grandiloquent and often unrealistic, these ideologies have given way to a project that almost everyone can agree on, development. What the emphasis on development means for the advertising business is that consumption can be tied to, and justified by, its role in supporting high national purposes—we are developing the nation so that we can consume more; we must consume more now or we must buy local products in order to jump-start the development process.

Ethnic conflict has made development even more urgent, leading each nation to pursue policies that discriminate in favor of the majority community. Malaysia experienced anti-Chinese riots in 1969, bringing to the surface the estrangement of Malaysia's Malay majority from the more prosperous, better educated, and more urbanized Chinese minority. By 1971 the Malaysian government had established a New Economic Plan, designed to enhance Malay participation in the economy by setting aside educational opportunities and development contracts for *bumiputras* (sons of the soil). It is not hard to imagine Chinese reaction to the government's goal of creating 30 percent Malay ownership of the corporate sector by 1990.[6] But the Malaysian economy grew handsomely over the last three decades, the Chinese have adapted, and the potential for civil strife has been contained.

The contrast between Malaysia's having been able to contain ethnic strife since 1969 and the ethnic disturbances—first in 1958, but again in 1977, 1981, and 1983—that have overtaken the Sri Lankan state is still more to the point. By 1983 relations between the state and some parts of the Tamil minority had deteriorated to the point of a guerrilla war that has now taken some sixty thousand lives. Although there has been occasional talk of following the Malaysian example by discriminating in favor of *bumiputras* (in this case, Sinhalas), the government has not imposed measures that would challenge the mercantile position of the Tamil minority.[7] Instead, it limited Tamil access to higher education by imposing in the 1970s a "standardized" and then a regional formula in determining who gained places in the universities. Educational discrimination in turn became a central grievance for young Tamils who took up arms against the national government.[8]

In almost any context, the expression "sons of the soil" carries a full measure of irony. It envisions the people least likely to have benefited from previous political regimes (including indigenous polities as well as colonial and postcolonial ones) as the primary beneficiaries of future development. Putting aside the question of who has been helped in Malaysia and Sri Lanka by postcolonial economic policies, the notion that the last will be first is part of the national imaginary, that vision of both the nation and the people who are its historical subjects that allows power to hide itself while producing "the effect of unity by virtue of which the people will appear, in everyone's eyes, 'as a people,' that is, as the basis and origin of political power." [9]

The nation-state's most unlikely formula for helping individuals forget their class and ethnic differences and see themselves as citizens is to privilege the culture of some part of the society and use it as a metonym with which the entire society can identify. Or the nation can celebrate its variousness, as Singapore and Indonesia have done, drawing on either ethnic stereotypes or cultural practices in ensemble as a way to represent unity in diversity. It can hark back to a noble past, as India tried just after Independence, letting the achievements and artifacts of an estimable Buddhist emperor serve as a symbol of unity for a nation of Hindus and Muslims. In the Sri Lankan case, making Sinhala culture and Sinhala persons stand for the nation at large derives from many sources. Sometimes it has been policy recklessly asserted; other times, an almost unwitting assumption. In practical ways, giving advantage to Sinhalas is the natural outcome of majoritarian politics. But doing so is also motivated by a less attractive desire to get even for Tamil advantages in the past.

The Malaysian government has also assumed a special obligation to its majority and favored Malays in ways unimagined in Sri Lanka. That policy has been explicit and transparent, as well as balanced by equally explicit and growing concern about foreign influence on all Malaysians. Part of that anxiety was generated by the extraordinary burst of television broadcasting, material consumption, and Western influence that marked Malaysian life over the last two or three decades. Part derives from a growing sense of Muslim identity, and another part is the product of Mahathir bin Mohamad's campaign both to accomplish big things in Malaysia and counteract what he sees as the arrogance of the West. [10]

In both cases—in Sri Lanka, where cultural policy has been shaped by shifting assumptions about Sinhala predominance, and in Malaysia, where the minority Chinese have entered into a compact with the Malay majority—advertising practice and government policy move together. [11] The Malaysian state has intervened—regularly if erratically—in deciding what kinds of Malaysians will be seen taking up those objects of desire (from soft drinks to automobiles) and wisely shunning provocations of fear (from drugs to childhood diseases). For its part, the Sri Lankan state has high expectations about propriety, especially in the representation of women and children in television advertising, and the reigning political parties have depended on Sinhala predominance for winning elections and, once in power, staying there. In ways both economic and cultural, the nation-state stands between the global system and the people of both places.

MALAYSIAN FACES

In the days when newsprint was the chief vehicle of public communication, advertising copy was written and line drawings were made in London, airmailed out to Colombo, and run in local newspapers. Singapore and Penang may have been larger markets, but advertisements here too spoke to a small local elite—part local, but mostly European—of products that were manufactured elsewhere. Their foreignness was one of their attractions, because the goods and services advertisements urged consumers to purchase were well beyond the means (and often contrary to the inclinations) of almost everyone but an elite that consumed European automobiles, household appliances, and foodstuffs.

From the early nineteenth century, newspapers in Singapore, Malacca, and Penang were dominated by print advertisements placed by traders from around the world, indicating the availability of recently arrived products.[12] During the First World War, an English firm placed a newspaper advertisement that suggests the identity of local consumers: "Messers. Crosse and Blackwell much regret that for the first time for a hundred years war conditions prevent many of their products being shipped to Singapore. They much appreciate the letters they are receiving, and in reply would state that it is fully recognized here that under the circumstances of life in Singapore the absence of English delicacies and food is a very real hardship."[13] In such cases, the imagination did not have to be brought down to ground. It had never left England.

Nowadays the growth of the Malaysian economy has attracted an unusually large number of transnational advertising firms, and the goods and services they represent are consumed by a burgeoning middle class. Some twenty-two transnational advertising firms do business in Malaysia, centered in Kuala Lumpur.[14] By the late 1980s, their gross incomes came to US $626 million, a figure large enough to suggest that as the Malaysian economy has grown in the last three decades, advertising has become a major beneficiary of the emergence of a consumer culture.[15] The contrast with Sri Lanka is striking. Sri Lanka's development trajectory trails Malaysia by some ten to fifteen years.[16] Colombo has six transnational advertising firms, and a gross income of US $22 million.[17]

Transnational advertising firms established offices in Kuala Lumpur and Colombo in the same years as the national governments were beginning to take threats to the local way of life very seriously (a paradox I would address by saying that change and preservation in postcolonial states have come in a single package, the development package). Until the mid-1970s, the models who appeared in Malaysian television commercials were Europeans, but from that point onward the Ministry of Information proposed various ways to protect local identity.[18] In the 1980s it began to require agencies to air advertisements that met certain expectations regarding "local content."[19] Those regulations required that advertisements be filmed in Malaysia with Malaysian models, allowing no more than 20 percent of advertising footage to be filmed outside the country. The motivation was not to limit the influence of transnational firms themselves, and it was not entirely a scheme to set aside part of the market for local agencies. The policy was driven by Prime Minister Mahathir's anxiety over the rising tide of Western influence on the television screen, coupled with his perception of British arrogance.[20]

Before a commercial could be aired on television or radio, all advertising agencies had to obtain a "Made in Malaysia" certificate from a government board. Restricting the amount of foreign footage to 20 percent of the total ensured that the great majority of scenes and shots would be done in Malaysia. If a corporation required a snow-covered mountain peak, shooting in the Himalayas was acceptable because there was no local equivalent, and tourism to other ASEAN countries could be advertised without Malaysian content. Yet even in these cases, the processing of advertisements had to be done in Malaysia. The general rule was that the content of advertisements as well as the production staff that made them had to be Malaysian. Especially in television advertisements, the foreign could never be promoted in a way that put the local at a disadvantage. As the advertising code had it, "Strong emphasis on the specialty of the country of origin of an imported product is not allowed. Any reference made should only state the name of the foreign country. Words should not be used to suggest superior quality or promise a greater benefit."[21]

When an agency representing Washington State apples advertised them by emphasizing their crispness and intense flavor, the creative director portrayed a Malaysian consumer biting lustily into a whole apple, juices flying in all directions. Where the agency saw exuberance, the Ministry saw the celebration of Westernness and the implication that eating fruit whole was a superior practice. The Ministry wanted the commercial reshot in a way more consistent with Malaysian values. Malaysian television view-ers saw a group of Malaysians offered apple sections on a plate. The creative director insisted that apples should be represented in a way that captured their intrinsic character. They are crunchy; they just are. Eating apples, he added, was not a local tradition, so there was no reason to expect a local way of serving and eating them.[22] The Ministry responded that Malaysians should eat apples in the same polite way they eat other things.

Although they groused about it, advertising agencies complied, knowing that business would keep coming their way. In the matter of mod-els, the advertising code required that commercials reflect the multiracial nature of Malaysia. Racial groups could not be identified with a trade or vocation. Caucasians, the regulations said, could not be shown advanta-geously (or disadvantageously) vis-à-vis other groups by such variables as lifestyle, vocation, mode of transportation, dress, environment, or housing. Instead, advertising agencies were asked to project a balanced proportion of Malaysia's main ethnic groups. The advertising code's summarizing statement allowed no pretense: "models, narrators and singers must be Malaysians projecting the Malaysian identity."[23]

Always troubled by the bureaucratic complexities of getting the content of advertisements approved by the Ministry of Information, the advertising business regarded these new regulations as another obstacle to be gotten over. And creative directors had an ace in the hole—a way to comply with the regulations without the complications of presenting a Chinese, Malay, and Indian in every scene. They began to use more and more so-called "pan-Asian" talents, actors of complicated origins whose appearance could stand for "Malaysian identity" as such by appearing to be Southeast Asian in an unmarked way (see fig. 1).[24] The Ministry would be happy; and the agencies, economical. Instead of having to find three models to maintain ethnic balance, agencies could hire one or two models whose diffuse origins could stand for all Malaysians. Voila! The nation in all its variety compiled as a person.[25]

The pan-Asian phenomenon pulls together forces that are as much demographic as semiotic—the reproduction of new human types as a product of the colonial and postcolonial encounter of different kinds of people, the uncanny way such faces have of evoking Westernness and Western ideals of physical beauty while also looking Southeast Asian, not to say their ability to occlude difference, standing as a figure of bleached-out Malaysianness. Here was a face that was Malaysian, but no particular type of Malaysian. Here was an exemplary figure, capable of representing the nation because of what pan-Asians lacked—a clear connection to any one ethnic group presently living in Malaysia. Pan-Asian faces had other practical virtues. They could be dropped into any "zone of display" and shown performing any occupation. "The industry made a conscious move to a 'neutral race'," according to the manager of Lintas Kuala Lumpur, Khairudin Rahim, "in answer to the government's call not to typecast the various races." [26] Instead of having to film a Malay family at dinner, then a Chinese one, and finally an Indian one, the scene could be shot with a pan-Asian family standing for all of them.

The idea of banning pan-Asians was mooted from the late 1980s onward, but a compromise held until March 1993, when the Minister of

FIGURE 1.   Malaysian models, one Chinese (left), two pan-Asian ("Gold & Dreams," Benson and Hedges advertising supplement, September/October 1999).

Information, Datuk Mohammed Rahmat, tightened up policy, prohibiting advertisements featuring generic, pan-Asian, or Eurasian models (as well as advertisements "suggesting Western superiority") as of July of that year.[27] Government anxiety about Western superiority derived from advertisements featuring either Western commodities or local faces with any Western appearance, regardless of whether the commodity those actors promoted was Western or local. Pan-Asian models felt blindsided: "'I was born this way, so why am I being singled out from other Malaysians?' complained Stephen Sta Maria, a mix of English, Portuguese, and several Asian ethnic groups. 'I sing the national anthem, respect all races, and have no police record.'"[28]

Practices might in principle escape categorization as either local or foreign, but Malaysian models with no clear ethnic identity are not as neutral as Khairudin Rahim made out. Pan-Asians can be the product of a Eurasian marriage or a local one, and the Ministry became especially concerned with Eurasian models. A spokesperson from the Information Ministry made the distinction explicit: "This ruling does not refer to pan-Asians who look like Asians. What's not allowed is the Caucasian look."[29] The straw that broke the camel's back was the appearance of a pan-Asian model with blond hair. If advertisements relied on models no more local in appearance than that, why exclude Caucasians? Models with features that would have cost them dearly during the colonial period had come to profit from their eclectic appearance. Now they were going to lose that advantage.

Many pan-Asians are considered beautiful—they are "the yardstick of beauty," according to the pan-Asian head of a Kuala Lumpur casting agency, "because they [do not] have a definite ethnic look."[30] Local models with that Caucasian look have an even greater advantage. In addition to their ability to represent generic Malaysianness, their partially European origins give them stronger noses and sharper jaw lines than most Southeast Asians. Why would Malaysians find such features attractive? "The faces we see on television and in the movies, Sylvester Stallone, Tom Cruise, Cindy Crawford, whoever, have strong features," according to one executive. "They play heroes, so they look heroic." So what is the attraction of Eurasians? "They look like heroes and they look like us." In this case, advertising placed Eurasians in the same liminal position that their birth placed them, the advertising business wanting to exploit their association with Western standards of physical beauty (not to say their practical virtues), the government acting against Eurasians with egregious attributes of Westernness such as blond hair.

When Malaysian viewers look at pan-Asian actors, they do not see pan-Asians as such. They see handsome people. But that is just why the Ministry found reason for action. Television viewers were watching unrealistic portrayals of local people, as well as ones that carried Western associations. The 1993 decision of the Minister of Information prohibiting the use of pan-Asians insisted that viewers watch advertisements that featured models who were clearly Malay, Chinese, or Indian, and that policy met criticism for encouraging racism. He proposed another compromise, allowing the use of pan-Asians if they appeared in the company of Malays, Chinese, and Indians. Including pan-Asians in the mix suggests an inclusionary policy approaching its logical extreme, although no minister suggested the use of *orang asli* (Malaysia's aboriginal people). By implication, it treats pan-Asian as an identity on a par with the major ethnic identities, transforming a null category into a new ethnicity.

The portrayal of "Malaysianness" as opposed to "Malayness"—of citizenship in the nation-state as against birth in the state's dominant ethnic group—in advertising practice has been shaped not only by the government's changing policies but also by its presenting one face to the larger world and another in local contexts. "Visit Malaysia Year" in 1994 showed Malaysia for foreign visitors as a multicultural society; governmental attempts to represent the nation to the people of Malaysia invested more in Malay faces and places.[31] On the domestic side of the contrast, the Chinese are cropped out of the national photograph. The motivations for that disparity are not far to seek, for the state's attempt to create a national identity has been confounded by the emergence of satellite broadcasting, Malaysia's new economic power, and long-distance tourism and its interests.

What complicated the representation issue was advertising agencies' search for economies of scale by creating campaigns that could be aired in several parts of Southeast Asia and beyond. Hong Kong's Star TV reaches almost three billion people living in places from the Mediterranean through South and Southeast Asia and on to eastern Siberia. With satellite transponders stationed all over the region, Malaysian "local content" regulations begin to lose all meaning. But the government insisted that if an agency wanted to do business at all in Malaysia, it had to produce advertisements locally. Advertising agencies in turn pursued a strategy shaped by far more interests than Sahlins's example of the Fijian appropriation of Western muskets. In this case, the issue was not so much finding a way to make the foreign acceptable to the local scheme but discovering how to comply with the government's frequently changing conception of what constitutes the "local" in order to preserve the right to sell to markets both local and foreign. Advertisements filmed in Malaysia, using "pan-Asian" actors could be shown all over the region on the logic that a generic Malaysian makes a pretty good generic Sri Lankan, Nepalese, or Southeast Asian.[32]

Advertising produces culture shaped by both government concerns about national identity and market forces that care nothing about it. The economic policy that came to the fore in the 1980s intended to stimulate the growth of businesses related to advertising, such as film production. It also fostered the growth of a few *bumiputra* advertising firms, such as PTM Thompson and Idris Associates.[33] But the inadvertent effects of "Made in Malaysia" regulations were more substantial. Faced with the choice of producing two television commercials—one filmed in Thailand and another in Malaysia—or one commercial filmed in Malaysia that could also be shown in Thailand, advertisers took the obvious decision.[34] For them, filming in Malaysia offered economies of scale; for Malaysian advertising firms, it created a lot of business.

Regional advertising remains a small part of media spending in Asia, but the products advertised regionally are directed at affluent consumers, giving regional advertising disproportionate importance. As Southeast Asia has begun to produce a middle class with substantial discretionary incomes and as satellite transmission has made reaching these consumers increasingly economical, the region's bourgeoisie has been joined to the world's circulatory system of culture and commodities. When a government acts to shape the representation of desire, it limits not only the consumption of foreign goods but also images of well-to-do consumers consuming. Television viewers continue to see pan-Asians as a "zone of display" for particular products, such as cigarettes and fashions. It is in such contexts that pan-Asian and Caucasian models find their place, their appearance implicitly serving as signs not only of physical beauty but also of success.[35]

The managing director of a Kuala Lumpur advertising agency suggests ways that faces reference class as well as ethnicity. He had a model he wanted to use for a facial cleanser, and he tried to convince his clients to choose his favorite by showing them a selection of eight choices on a videocassette. When everyone was seated, he asked, "Are you looking for a face that could appear on the cover of *Cosmopolitan* or *Vogue?*" The clients nodded in agreement. "Then look at these faces. I won't tell you who they are. All you have to do is tick off your favorite on the sheet with the numbers I've given you." He showed the videocassette, and one woman came out on top. When the Sikh executive showed his clients her personal data, they discovered she was Indian. "Is she a Sikh? Your sister?"

He explained that she was Kashmiri but a third-generation Malaysian, pleading her case by saying that she was as Malaysian as they were. In any case Indian women had recently won the Miss World and Miss Universe contests. His clients remained unpersuaded, settling on a face that he describes as "cute" and "local." According to the executive, his clients wanted a face everybody would be comfortable with, not one that would "seduce" the viewer. He went on to analyze for his clients the Malaysians who live in the Klang Valley, where some 50 percent of affluent Malaysians now reside. He asked whether they knew that one of the most affluent communities in Petaling Jaya (a commercial city just outside of Kuala Lumpur) was Indian? Had they ever visited Bangsar (an Indian neighborhood)? In the end, he interpreted their unwillingness to identify their brand with an Indian face as lack of imagination. A Malaysian Indian face, he thought, has a quality that resembles the pan-Asian advantage. It is local on the one hand, yet fair and shaped like a Caucasian face on the other.

The sophistication of his response notwithstanding, there is something to be said for the way his clients reasoned. They have a good sense of the demography of class in Malaysia. Certain faces—the fair and angular ones—have the cachet of Westernization (even when the West is Kashmir) and success. They have the power to beguile. But if a firm wants to sell a facial cleanser to the generality of Malaysians, it may be wiser to emphasize local class aspirations and settle on someone who looks like most Malaysians. Over the past thirty years, Malaysia has become hugely urban. In 1970 only 28.7 percent of Malaysians lived in cities of more than ten thousand people. By 1990 that figure reached 75 percent. Even after the economic troubles of 1997, they have discretionary income quite unlike their parents. For some products—cigarettes, liquor, fashion, luxury automobiles—Eurasian, pan-Asian, and Indian faces have become appropriate "zones of display." For commodities that are less expensive, there is a lot to be said for "zones of display" centered on a model who resembles the majority of Malaysians.

SRI LANKAN FACES

Malaysia is a newly industrialized economy surrounded by other newly industrialized economies. Singapore is its chief trading partner, and the two strong economies create all manner of commercial flows between them: Malaysia even sends untreated water by pipeline to Singapore, where it is purified and piped back to Malaysia to be consumed. Sri Lanka, by contrast, exchanges relatively little with South India, except for smuggled goods.[36] It does most of its foreign trade with the United States, Germany, and the United Kingdom. Political difficulties with India suggest that the growth of a regional economy on a par with Southeast Asia lies far in the future. And while there has been real economic expansion in both South India and Sri Lanka over the last two decades, there are few prospects for regional development linking Sri Lanka and the subcontinent. Occasionally one hears talk about regional ties to Southeast Asia, but India, north or south, is seldom talked about. Tamil Nadu's entanglement in Sri Lanka's civil war and the movement of refugees between Sri Lanka and India make it is easier to speak of regional conflict than regional development.

But even if forging closer economic ties to South India were possible, there is an overriding force that is simultaneously cultural, political, and economic—Sri Lanka's long engagement with the West, set off against a set of regional ties considerably weaker than Malaysia's. Just as during colonial days, when the island was administered separately from India, there are few cross-cutting ties to India. Sri Lanka's involvement with the West has its ambivalences, but for many Sri Lankans—especially middle-class people—the ties that link it to the West override any regional connection. And for Sri Lankan advertising agencies, the issue is not balancing local ethnic types, but speaking to Sri Lankans by way of actors who are either Sri Lankan in a generic way or recognizably Sinhala.

Although Malays and Chinese continue to have their problems, the striking characteristic of Sri Lankan life is the near invisibility of Tamils in Sri Lankan public culture. The occasional advertisement aims at a Tamil audience, but the general assumption that Sri Lankan culture is Sinhala culture is replicated in Sri Lankan advertising practice. I once asked a senior executive at a Colombo agency whether there were any contexts where one would use a recognizably Tamil model to sell things to Sinhalas.[37] He laughed out loud. How about showing a woman with a *pottu* (the red dot Tamil women wear in the middle of their foreheads after marriage)? The kiss of death. How about showing scenes comprising people of different ethnic types? Not realistic and not done. How about using Tamils to assume advertising roles that appear to be Sinhala? Yes, that happens, even though a huge number of Tamil "talents" have migrated to Canada.

Of the roughly one hundred advertising agencies in Colombo, only one specializes in Tamil advertising. Tamils purchase products they see advertised in either English-language or Sinhala advertisements. Indeed, having to negotiate a public order in one's second language is what it means more generally to be a Sri Lankan Tamil. Under these conditions, the axis of difference runs in an East-West direction: advertisements that invoke local practices do so by drawing on either Sinhala culture (because it stands for the nation) or they employ actors whose ethnic characteristics are hard to pin down. Advertisements for goods linked to modernity, luxury, or simply their Western origins occasionally employ European actors. Western faces predominate in advertisements for milk products, chocolate, and soft drinks. But, all in all, one sees relatively few Western faces, although there is no governmental policy prohibiting the practice.

When one does see those faces, they are not Western in a diffuse way, and they do not stand for success or anything aspirational. If the model is European, the advertisement is selling, let's say, a dairy product, and the model appears as Swiss in a marked way, wearing Swiss peasant dress. Or a foreign chocolate is represented by a model of the same ethnic identity as the product. The low visibility of Western models derives in part from the minimal number of Western consumer products—relative to Malaysia—in the Sri Lankan market. But it derives just as much from what the majority of people want to see represented in television and news-print advertisements—themselves. The problem is that that self, that face, is Sinhala, or at least it is taken to be Sinhala. A consumer who watches a television advertisement sees actors whose identity is interchangeably Sri Lankan or Sinhala. When actors appear marked as Tamils, the advertising motivation is perfectly clear—the client wants to speak to Tamil consumers and ignore Sinhala ones.

Were the Sri Lankan focus on one ethnic type transferred to a Malaysian public setting, the faces that one would observe in television and newsprint advertisements would all be Malay. The faces one sees in Sri Lankan newsprint and television contexts are automatically taken to be Sinhala. They could be argued to be Sri Lankan as well because of the metonymic connection by which Sinhala culture represents Sri Lankan culture. In this case Sinhala identity stands for the national identity. So where the Malaysian state has invested twenty years trying to enhance the life-chances of *bumiputras*, it has also pursued a media policy that disaggregates the national identity into the three dominant ethnic groups. The Sri Lankan government has no comparable policy, but the tacit assumption in advertising is that the national identity has a Sinhala physiognomy.

For an outsider, Sinhalas are hard to distinguish from Tamils as physical beings, but Sinhalas are quite sensitive to cultural differences—language, dress, and self-presentation—between themselves and Tamils. I once saw an Indian television production of R. K. Narayan's *Malgudi Days,* dubbed in Sinhala and broadcast on Sri Lankan television. I was impressed by the unusually high quality of the production; what struck my Sinhala friends was how implausible it was to hear Tamil actresses speaking Sinhala. For them the whole production was not to be credited. Watching dramatic action in dubbed form requires a turn of mind that is routine only for certain kinds of moviegoers—it presumes that the viewer can suspend the disbelief that characterizes giving credence to actors who speak a language that is alien to the time and place being represented. In this case it requires the viewer to take seriously the performance of Tamil actors and actresses, appearing in distinctly Tamil dress and cosmetics, even while hearing them carry on in Sinhala.

The ads that strike viewers as troubling are not ones that mix up these categories or try to manipulate them. Neither, in fact, occurs very often. To this extent Sri Lankan advertising practice is straightforward—at first glance, everything is what it is and not another thing. The advertisements that trouble local consumers are ones that put local faces in alien "zones of display." The affluent Sri Lankan drinking a tumbler of scotch is a good example. The scotch appears in a "zone of display" that aspires to be local but glamorous—often the drinker appears at a beach resort or tea estate; the sun is usually setting in the background. At the same time, the Western liquor in his hand and the bottle from which he is served puts him in another zone, and that zone is foreign. As Mary Douglas said of another context, confusion is danger. A woman appearing in a sophisticated advertisement for a local gold shop is not troubling. She can be put in a relatively sexualized posture and costume without offending people's sensibilities, because gold—for Sinhalas, Tamils, and Muslims alike—is itself a local decency, and a part of a calculative strategy that is commonly shared.

Just below the surface there are subtleties in the representation of Sri Lankan identity. Appropriate disclaimers duly noted—Sinhala is an Indo-European language and Tamil a Dravidian one, Sinhalas often say that their complexions are fair and Tamils are dark—the pertinent fact is that Sinhalas and Tamils are South Asians. The other human beings with whom they share the most in common culturally are likely to be the people with whom they share the most in common genetically. In some cases dress, adornment, and speech reveal different identities, but their faces do not. When actors appear in advertisements representing middle-class Sri Lankans—women dressed in sarees or dresses, men in trousers—their facial appearance bespeaks an identity that few Sri Lankans find compelling. They appear to be Sri Lankan without any marked ethnic reference.

In this regard Sri Lankan advertising agencies begin with an advantage—the actors they work with are unaccommodated human material, their bodies unmarked for any of the local ethnicities. The same human material can be pushed in several directions. By altering dress and context, those bodies can be constructed to emphasize difference—as in those cases where an advertisement speaks directly to Tamil consumers. By choosing ethnically neutral clothing and contexts, those same bodies serve as tokens of local types: "a housewife," "a trousered gentleman," or a "high-achieving

Sri Lankan." Compare the Malaysian case, where the same middle-class tokens—unless the actors were pan-Asians—would be either Malay, Chinese, or Indian housewives, gentlemen, or high-achievers. But what masking ethnic difference cannot produce is a representation of "Sri Lankanness." In advertising contexts, unmarked identity settles out by default as Sinhala identity.

A second subtlety hides below the first. The actors who represent Sinhala culture in print and electronic advertisements, the faces that stand for the nation itself, are often not Sinhala, but Burgher.[38] For their part, the public is none the wiser. Just as Burghers are overrepresented in other parts of the advertising business—as account managers and executives—they are even more overrepresented in the ranks of models who appear in advertisements. I know of one client who insists that his advertising agency always employ Burgher models to represent his product. Several informants suggested that upward of 50 percent of advertising models are Burgher by origin.[39] A few male Burgher models, such as Peter Almeida, are known by name. His name identifies his ethnic origins as Burgher, but it is known because of his work as an actor, not as a model.[40] Most Burgher models are simply assumed to be Sinhala, and their names never enter the picture.

In the 1970s the election of the SLFP government and the loosening of immigration policy in Australia drew a substantial proportion of Sri Lankan Burghers to Australia and other places where their ethnic identity was less problematic. Back at home, the expansion of advertising expenditures also drew some Burghers into the modeling business. Some Sinhalas and Tamils also found employment as models, but Sinhalas and Tamils were put off by the business's reputation for defying local expectations for decent behavior. Appearing in advertisements is not as stigmatized as appearing in films, but it suffers from the same association with promiscuity (conditioned by perceptions of modeling as a profession similar to acting, well-paid and alien) and impropriety (deriving in part from the simple act of endorsing a product). If they were asked, an advertising executive told me, most Sri Lankans would be reluctant to say in a public context that they prefer this over that. Burghers do not share those reservations.

Other characteristics recommend Burghers. The first is that the Burghers who appear in print or electronic advertisements look like Sinhalas (and Tamils for that matter) because they have intermarried with local people since the days when they were an expatriate European community (see fig. 2). Indeed, a European line of descent has been a critical

The sign of rich good taste

JOHN PLAYER

GOLD
LEAF

Price : Rs. 30.80 for 12 Rs. 51.00 for 20

GOVERNMENT WARNING:
SMOKING CAN BE HARMFUL TO HEALTH.

FIGURE 2.   Who are these people? Sinhalas? Tamils? Burghers who can be Sinhalas
or generic Sri Lankans but never themselves? (*Island* [Colombo], 16 February 1992).

issue for membership in the Dutch Burgher Union, creating a distinction between Sri Lankans who claim Burgher identity by virtue of their ancestors marrying exclusively within the community and those who carry Burgher names but who make no such claims. Not all Burghers are regarded as attractive, and Sri Lankans would find some Burgher physical features—blue eyes, brown hair, and freckles—quite off-putting. Sometimes fair Burgher actors can be used to represent Europeans in advertising contexts, and Burghers who look European are not reviled. But Burghers who have black hair, brown eyes, and fair skin have features that most people regard as ideal. These are the Burghers who model on television and in newsprint, where they are seen as Sinhala and attractive.

Most Burghers tend to be fair by Sri Lankan standards. When television viewers see them, they see them as "sophisticated Sinhala," not Burgher. The importance of a light skin goes well beyond advertisements. Read a page of classified advertisements for marriage proposals in a Sri Lankan newspaper, and one will quickly see that a fair complexion shows up as a virtue in many advertisements. Looking at an old Sunday newspaper I had in my files confirmed my sense that the virtue of fair skin, not to say physical appearance in general, is more important for brides than for grooms.[41] Of the marriage proposals that appeared that day, there were sixty-five classifieds placed for brides, and thirteen mentioned that the bride was fair. Of the forty-two grooms listed that day, only two were described as fair, although three prospective grooms had classifieds indicating that they were looking for a fair bride.

There are at least two products on the market in Sri Lanka that promise to lighten one's skin. The first is Morison's Calamine Lotion, which has been on sale in Sri Lanka for many decades. The advertisement promises that the "goodness of pure Calamine and Witch Hazel in every drop of Morison's Calamine Lotion makes your skin look soft, fairer, and more radiant. . . . a powder base . . . pampers your complexion, making it lighter, smoother, and vividly clear . . . bringing a blush of spring to your skin."[42] A recently arrived Indian product, "Fair and Lovely," makes stronger claims:

> You were born with a certain colour. But, today, you're many
> shades darker. You blame it on the sun. After all, you know how
> quickly the rays of the sun can darken you. But this is not the only
> reason. Besides external factors such as the ultraviolet rays of the
> sun which penetrate your skin, there are other factors that influ-
> ence the colour of your skin. Within your skin there is a dark pig-
> ment called melanin. This "spreads" in some individuals more
> than in others. The more it spreads, the darker you appear.[43]

"Fair and Lovely" claims to reverse these effects. It promises to control the darkening process without using bleach or other harsh ingredients, although the advertisement concedes that at first "you may notice a slight tingling sensation." It acts in two ways, by being absorbed by the skin to check the darkening process and by acting as a sunscreen. "In 6 to 8 weeks, the new skin layers that emerge are naturally lighter in colour." The advertisement features a drawing of a woman who appears in duplicate. On the left, a vignette shows an attractive young woman with a light brown complexion. Her double just to the right radiates whiteness.

The sources of Sri Lankan (and for that matter, South Asian) conceptions of beauty and preference for fair complexions are unclear, but it seems unlikely that the preference for fairness has origins that predate colonialism.[44] When I have asked people in the advertising business, they have typically attributed the idealization of fair skin to colonialism, the dominance of the West, and American movies, but some people have told me that fair complexions simply film better. According to this logic, the attraction of fair skin is purely technical. In any case, the preference for fair complexions stops short of white skin, which Sri Lankans see as pasty and prone to freckles, blemishes, and redness. Sri Lankans want to see not Westerners but people who look like them, and Burghers fill the bill.

European models, according to several executives, have their uses, but they come across as too sophisticated for most products. Their appearing in the advertisement suggests the product is expensive, and to that extent, they drive people away. They are too remote and not "us." With the exception of high-end banking products and luxury cosmetics, advertisements made elsewhere with Western models are irrelevant to the Sri Lankan market. Burghers, by contrast, have the quality of looking Sinhala in a way that can be both beautiful and familiar. They have a facial structure, people say, that is also more Western than the generality of Sri Lankan faces. In that regard Burghers function like pan-Asians in Malaysia. They split the difference. They look sophisticated and heroic, but they also resemble the people who view Sri Lankan television and read local newspapers.

Burghers have a second virtue as models, a virtue especially important for women. The modeling part of the advertising business is quite small, and the number of women who work as models—body models, teenage girls, and young women—comes to about forty people. Of those forty models, some twenty are Burghers. When an advertising firm needs a female talent, it chooses one from that short list. "We always use these forty," a creative director told me. "Who wants to recruit and train new people only to discover that they cannot act?" Advertisers sometimes want a new face, but finding one usually means looking further down the list and using a talent who has not been seen much recently. Burghers have a body language, an exuberance, that allows them to act. They can project themselves in a way that many Sinhala and Tamil women cannot. He described that exuberance as Western, which of course is exactly why Burghers would be seen as having this quality. Like the "cheerful Goan" in India, Burghers are renowned in Sri Lanka for drinking, dancing, and expressing their feelings publicly.

Of the remaining twenty women who are not Burghers, the majority are Sinhala. There is obviously no biological reason why Sinhalas and Tamils cannot project themselves before a camera as well as Burghers. But young women in Sinhala families are brought up to be demure and modest, qualities that advertising uses on occasion but which have to be available to be turned on and off on short notice. Burgher women often are brought up under less scrutiny and constraint, a failing in Sinhala eyes that justifies the reputation that Burghers carry for looseness and promiscuity. In the modeling business, that liability becomes an asset. What the majority community interprets as looseness is the quality that allows a woman to be exuberant when the camera is fixed on her. Minutes later the same woman can affect modesty.

Cost factors also constrain who appears in advertisements. J. Walter Thompson maintains a bio-data file of all kinds of models—attractive young people, children, older people, and character actors. When a creative director who works at a smaller agency needs a particular kind of actor, he calls his friend at J. Walter Thompson and she sends over a collection of photographs. He hires the model directly, knowing that these people have a track record.[45] He knows that the photo shoot will get done the first time around. Established models know how to take makeup, work with lights, and pose. And another Burgher quality makes them cost-effective. When a Sinhala, Tamil, or Muslim model marries, she gives up her career. Modeling was strictly something to occupy her interests between school and marriage. Not so for Burghers, who continue to work after marriage. Because they continue in the business for ten to fifteen years, relying on Burgher models reduces the need to train new talent. A reliable name on file remains on file.

Burgher men are less dominant in their end of the modeling business, but there are other connections between advertising and ethnicity. Sinhala men play a larger role in the male modeling business, although Sinhalas have historically been reluctant to do modeling, on the grounds that the work was too girlish. Their reluctance meant that Tamil men—quite unlike Tamil women—were overrepresented. Many of them had been first involved in theater in Colombo, moving on to modeling as a way to cash in on their theatrical skills, a necessity because acting in Sri Lanka often pays no salary. Almost twenty years of civil war has sent many Tamils to Canada and Europe, and those effects have even been felt in the modeling business. Sinhalas have taken their places. When I reminded one executive of his having told me earlier that Sinhalas were reluctant to model because of its connection with woman's work, he said it was not hard to find Sinhala men nowadays who were sufficiently uninhibited. Money is the great lubricant.

Over the last few years, there have been new Indian forces at work in the modeling business. The most fashionable model of the day is a Muslim woman, Sooraya Hussein, and several Bohra (a Shi'a Muslim community from Bombay, famous for their business success) men have also started to appear in Sri Lankan advertisements. These models are sophisticated, well-to-do, and urban. Their families move between Colombo and Bombay. They know the Bombay film industry in a direct way and are interested in the modeling business because they see it in that light. However Sinhala men view modeling, Muslims see it as Bollywood South. To cap off the irony, when Sri Lankan consumers look at newsprint and television, they see these models—whether they are Muslim, Tamil, Burgher, or Sinhala—as "sophisticated Sinhala."

The growing availability of Hindi films on Sri Lankan television has similar results. The process began when a Sri Lankan network began to steal Star TV signals from India and broadcast them on local television. There are now three channels that beam Hindi songs and dance at Sri Lankan homes, giving viewers daily exposure to North Indian glamour. Hindi film actresses have a growing reputation as beautiful and fair. When I asked one executive why people found Indians beautiful, he said he could not say exactly, but it was "in our genes. It is part of our mythology. The *Mahabharata* and the *Bhagavad Gita*. We are all Aryans, no?" Tamils, by contrast, simply do not exist. Nor does Tamil dress appear in contexts aimed at the general public. Sinhalas think of Tamils in a variety of unattractive ways—as bucket lifters and conservancy workers, estate laborers, and domestic servants.[46]

In Sinhala eyes, Sri Lanka is a land of beauty. India is a land of poverty. Sinhalas consider the movement of Tamil estate laborers and domestic servants into Sri Lanka as evidence of that poverty. These associations make Tamil faces unlikely candidates for the operations of the imagination. That Tamils have been historically overrepresented in the professions and civil service functions in another way as a source of Sinhala resentment, while resting—the contradiction unrecognized—beside the notion that Tamils occupy the bottom of Sri Lankan society.

North India figures in Sri Lankan advertising production in another way. If an agency is putting together a campaign for a global client, they may choose to have the film production done in Bombay because of its reputation for high quality production and skillful directing. Sometimes an Indian film crew comes from Bombay and films in Sri Lanka; other times the Sri Lankan creative team goes to Bombay. But in all cases it is essential that the advertisement have an entirely Sri Lankan look. That is easily achieved on a stage set, although it can also be achieved when shooting outside in India. The agency brings along several people whose job it is to monitor the cameras, making sure that no foreign elements intrude. As the chief executive of an agency in Colombo put it, "We want Sri Lankan grass and Sri Lankan trees, and we get them in Bombay."

Shooting a television commercial in Bombay requires avoiding signboards painted in Devanagari script and any telltale sign of the Bombay skyline. A creative director once described for me a commercial he had shot on the beach in Bombay with a horse. He pulled off the deception by keeping the focus tight and the action moving quickly. Whether an agency brings an Indian woman down from Bombay to appear in a television commercial or films in Bombay, the agency can ensure that she will appear to be Sinhala. Her Hindi is dubbed in Sinhala, and her saree has to be cut in Sri Lankan style. That style itself has Indian origins, but what must be avoided are recent innovations in Indian fashion. The sleeves of the saree blouse must not go below the elbow or end at the shoulder. The neckline must not move about, and the model cannot be seen wearing fancy necklaces or dangling earrings. All the positive qualities of fair complexion and Indian facial structure are lost if some part of the model's appearance reveals that her face is not Sinhala but North Indian.

Sometimes North Indian men appear in Sri Lankan advertisements for razors and toiletries, and an Indian model was recently used for a Black Knight cologne advertisement filmed in Sri Lanka. All things considered, idealized men seem to be more able than female models to slip out of their ethnic character and still satisfy creative directors' notions of what the public wants to see.

The ethnicity of children follows a complicated trajectory. It is irrelevant for infants, and a cute baby of any ethnic identity would be suitable for a baby lotion commercial. But ethnicity becomes critical for schoolchildren. Consider the deception involved in a Nespray commercial organized around five hundred Indian children filmed in Bombay. The creative director checked each one of them to make sure that they looked Sri Lankan. "You cannot distinguish a Sri Lankan face from an Indian one," he told me, "but I can." Neither can the Sri Lankan public, at least not those Indian faces chosen to stand for Sri Lankan ones.

Both Malaysia and Sri Lanka share a practice by which imaginations freed up by newsprint and electronic media are domesticated. Consumers look at advertisements for commodities that appear in "zones of display" featuring local faces. They see themselves in idealized form wearing those new fashions, smoking cigarettes, admiring the fresh shine of a polished floor. There are some exceptions—for upmarket products, Malaysians sometimes see Western faces, and Sri Lankans see European faces and costumes in advertisements that celebrate commodities (such as Swiss chocolate) directly linked to a national identity. The contrasts are more instructive. In Malaysia the national physiognomy is government policy; in Sri Lanka the state takes no position on what kinds of faces people see in advertisements, tacitly assuming along with the advertising profession that Sri Lankans look and dress like Sinhalas. But the general point is clear. The notion that the West is everywhere has its limits.

Pan-Asians in Malaysia and Burghers in Sri Lanka have physical features that reveal the wondrous effects of the intercultural encounter, the play of different types of people meeting and mating. Over the long term, colonial port cities have produced physical types that have come to represent local ideals of postcolonial beauty. The irony of their position becomes even greater when they are used to evoke Sinhala culture, for portraying tradition and the local way of life requires actors who have little contact with either, but whose social origins make them willing to take up a profession that insiders regard as contrary to those traditions. No matter how subject to external threat Sri Lankan identity may be, no matter how unique and long-lived Sinhalas see themselves as a community, they are often represented in advertisements by people whose ancestors came from Europe and whose status is still betwixt and between.

NOTES

1. Gananath Obeyesekere makes the pun on the title of Linda Colley's book (*Britons: Forging the Nation, 1707–1837* [New Haven, Conn.: Yale University Press, 1992]), which uses the word to suggest simply the "creating" or "bringing together" of the nation. See his "On Buddhist Identity in Sri Lanka," in *Ethnic Identity: Creation, Conflict, and Accommodation,* ed. Lola Romanucci-Ross and George A. DeVos (Walnut Creek, Calif.: AltaMira Press, 1995), 226.

2. Anthony Burgess, *The Long Day Wanes: A Malayan Trilogy* (New York: Norton, 1992), 354–55.

3. United Nations Development Programme, *Human Development Report 1994* (Oxford: Oxford University Press, 1994), 16.

4. Clifford Geertz's formulation is to the point: "Most Tamils, Karens, Brahmins, Malays, Sikhs, Ibos, Muslims, Chinese, Nilotes, Bengalis, or Ashantis found it a good deal easier to grasp the idea that they were not Englishmen than that they were Indians, Burmese, Malayans, Ghanaians, Pakistanis, Nigerians, or Sudanese" ("After the Revolution: The Fate of Nationalism in the New States," in *The Interpretation of Cultures* [New York: Basic Books, 1973], 239).

5. Benedict Anderson, *Imagined Communities* (London: Verso,1983), 40.

6. By 1990 some 20 percent of corporate equity was held by Malays, although some in

the form of Malay holding companies. *Financial Times Survey* (London), 28 August 1992, 6.

7. In the 1980s some Sinhala legislators looked directly to Malaysian *bumiputra* legislation as a model for discriminating in favor of the Sinhala majority. The most notorious example was Cyril Mathew.

8. See C. R. de Silva, "The Politics of University Admissions: A Review of Some Aspects of the Admissions Policy in Sri Lanka, 1971–1978," *Sri Lanka Journal of Social Sciences* 1, no. 2 (December 1978): 85–123; and K. M. de Silva, "Discrimination in Sri Lanka," in *Case Studies on Human Rights and Fundamental Freedoms: A World Survey,* vol. 3, ed. W. A. Veenhoven (The Hague: Martinus Nijhoff, 1976), 73–119.

9. Etienne Balibar, "The Nation Form," *Review* 13, no. 3 (Summer 1990): 346.

10. One initiative was Mahathir's encouraging the governor of the Central Bank of Malaysia to aggressively trade in foreign currencies. That ultimately ruinous policy had origins that were as much cultural as economic. In the same spirit, his Ministry of Education has acted to create a sense of Malaysian identity that can stand up to the onslaught of foreign culture and commerce. See Mahathir bin Mohamad, *The Challenge* (Petaling Jaya, Malaysia: Pelanduk Publications, 1986); and Boo Teik Khoo, *Paradoxes of Mahathirism: An Intellectual Biography of Mahathir Mohamad* (Kuala Lumpur: Oxford University Press, 1995).

11. Malaysia has the advantage of more heterogeneous parliamentary constituencies than Sri Lanka, making coalition politics at the local level essential to win a single-member constituency. Donald Horowitz argues that "the Malaysians took no chances with ethnic conflict in the 1950s, and the structures they established could later be modified to take account of changed conditions. The Sri Lankans took no precautions" ("Incentives and Behavior in the Ethnic Politics of Sri Lanka and Malaysia," *Working Papers in Asian/Pacific Studies,* Duke University, 1989, 21).

12. Adnan Hashim, *Advertising in Malaysia* (Petaling Jaya, Malaysia: Pelanduk Publications, 1994), 5–6.

13. "A Review of Advertising in Singapore and Malaysia during Early Times," (Kuala Lumpur: Federal Publishers, 1971), 19.

14. These figures, and the ones that follow, derive from the "53rd Annual Agency Report," *Advertising Age,* supplement, 21 April 1997, S41–S42.

15. That figure makes Malaysia the thirty-seventh largest advertising market in the world in 1994; see *World Advertising Trends, 1996* (Oxfordshire: NTC Publications, 1996), 106.

16. The contrast between the largest sources of advertising revenues makes the point most forcefully. In Sri Lanka, the largest amounts of advertising derive from the banks and insurance companies, food products companies, and government agencies (these are my rankings based on what various executives have told me, and the rank order may be arguable). In Malaysia, the ten top product categories in 1996 were (1) classifieds and appointments (a category I did not consider in the Sri Lankan case), (2) telephones, pagers, and phone dealers, (3) entertainment and franchise advertisements, (4) corporation, government agencies, and utilities, (5) real estate, (6) banks and credit cards, (7) communication, publishing, media, and exhibition, (8) department stores and emporiums, (9) entertainment, lounge, cinema, and leisure activity, and (10) education and bookstores. The source of my data is an in-house publication, "Media Scene, Peninsular Malaysia, 1996," made available to me by the Director of Batey Ads (Malaysia).

17. *World Advertising Trends, 1996,* 144. In 1994 Sri Lanka was the fifty-eighth largest advertising market in the world.

18. I hesitate to use expressions such as *race* and *Caucasian* because of their ideological power. But I will do so because the alternatives are cumbersome, and these expressions are the terms Malaysians themselves use.

19. "Medium and Message," *Far Eastern Economic Review,* 25 February 1993, 52.

20. A recent account of Mahathir's confrontation with Britain can be found in Yao Souchou, *Mahathir's Rage: Mass Media and the West as Transcendental Evil* (Canberra: National Library of Australia, 1994).

21. Kementerian Penerangan Malaysia, "Advertising Code for Television and Radio" (1989, typescript), 6. These regulations went into effect 1 January 1990.

22. Before Malaysia got rich in the 1970s and 1980s, Malaysians ate very few apples.

23. "Advertising Code," 7. The code prohibited "advertisements that employed any professional, public figure or anyone who by their position is deemed by the Ministry of Information to have authority in convincing public opinion such as School Teachers, College Professors, University Lecturers, Doctors, Dental Practitioners, Surgeons, Pharmaceutical Chemists, Veterinary Surgeons, Members of Nursing Profession [sic], Judges, Religious Teachers including 'Alim Ulama', Senators, Members of Parliament and Public Figures." At the same time, it allowed the use of celebrities: "singing artistes, actors, actresses, sportsmen, sportswomen and entertainers" (10). The use of the phrase "deemed . . . to have authority in convincing public opinion" implies that celebrities are acceptable for an unlikely reason—because they cannot influence public opinion.

24. As it is used in Malaysian English, "pan-Asian" includes the offspring of both various Asian ethnic groups—Malays, Chinese, and Indians—and Asians and Europeans. I will try to retain the local usage, but in some circumstances it makes sense to speak of advertising models who derive from a marriage of a European and Asian as "Eurasians."

25. Richard Handler's account of the way the nation appears in nationalist thought as a collective individual as well as a speciated being suggests the other side of the linking together of the nation-state and the individuals it comprises. See *Nationalism and the Politics of Culture in Quebec* (Madison: University of Wisconsin Press, 1988), 30–51, esp. 39–47.

26. "Seeking the Right Look," *Asiaweek,* 21 April 1989, 39.

27. "The Selling of Asia," 61.

28. Lai Kuruk Kim, "Malaysian Television Ban on 'Pan-Asian' Models under Fire," Reuters Library report, 14 April 1989.

29. "Seeking the Right Look," 39.

30. "Seeking the Right Look," 39.

31. This policy too has been applied inconsistently. See David Camroux, "State Responses to Islamic Resurgence in Malaysia," *Asian Survey* 36, no. 9 (September 1996): 855.

32. Even the newer formula that Malaysian advertisements must use recognizably Malaysian ethnic types—Malays, Chinese, Indians—gave advertisers a familiar identity for places beyond Malaysia where those same kinds of people live, namely, Thailand and Singapore.

33. "From a Toe Print to a Giant Foothold for Bumi Ad Agency," *Star* (Kuala Lumpur), 6 March 1993.

34. Alain Fairnington, "Kuala Lumpur—The Imminent Ad Capital of Asia," *Malaysian Advertising Association Bulletin* 8, no. 1 (February 1980): 12.

35. "Ads: Truth Should Be Stressed," *Business Times,* 22 March 1989.

36. The same pattern is true of South Asian trade in general—only 3 percent of all trade flows between countries in the subcontinent.

37. There are at least two contexts where Malaysian Tamils serve to sell commodities to other kinds of Malaysians, Milo, a nutritional supplement, and Guinness Stout. Tamils are known for their physical prowess—an association embodied in the success of a track star of Tamil origin—and serve as appropriate zones of display for drinks associated with strength.

38. Sri Lankan categories for the interstitial social types—pan-Asians and Eurasians— which I discussed in the Malaysian case, break out rather differently. No one speaks of "pan-Asians" in the Sri Lankan case, and Sri Lankans encode people who could be called Eurasian in distinctive ways. The hegemonic category is Dutch Burgher in the strict sense, namely, Sri Lankans who have strictly European ancestors despite long-time residence in the island and genealogical evidence on record at the Dutch Burgher Union in Colombo. But there are also Burghers in an extended sense of the word—descendants of marriages between a European (let's say a certified Dutch Burgher of the nineteenth century) and a local person. People in the latter category gravitate over time toward either a Sinhala or Tamil identity. There is another Eurasian category—Portuguese "mechanics" who are few in number but retain a distinct identity as children of a Portuguese and a local person. See Dennis McGilvray, "Dutch Burghers and Portuguese Mechanics: Eurasian Ethnicity in Sri Lanka," *Comparative Studies in Society and History* 24, no. 2 (April 1982): 235–63; and Michael Roberts, Ismeth Raheem, and Percy Colin-Thome, *People Inbetween: The Burghers and the Middle Class in the Transformations within Sri Lanka, 1790s–1960s* (Ratmalana: Sarvodaya Book Publishing, 1989). For other treatments of the calculus of Eurasianness, see Kenneth Ballhatchet, *Race, Sex, and Class under the Raj: Imperial Attitudes and Policies and Their Critics, 1793–1905* (New York: St. Martin's, 1980); Ann Laura Stoler, "Rethinking Colonial Categories: European Communities and the Boundaries of Rule." *Comparative Studies in Society and History* 13, no. 1 (1989): 134–61; and Ann Laura Stoler, "Making Empire Respectable: The Politics of Race and Sexual Morality in 20th-Century Colonial Cultures." *American Ethnologist* 16, no. 4 (1989): 634–60.

39. That estimate is more accurate, I suspect, of female models than male ones, where Burghers are less common. Nowadays modeling is a profession that attracts aspiring models from all kinds of Sri Lankans.

40. That a person with a Portuguese surname is categorized as a member of an ethnic group identified with the Dutch suggests the fluidity of these categories.

41. *Sunday Observer* (Colombo), 26 October 1990, 22. For a fuller account of marital classifieds, see Steven Kemper, "Sinhalese Astrology, South Asian Caste Systems, and the Notion of Individuality" *Journal of Asian Studies* 38 (May 1979): 477–97.

42. *Daily News* (Colombo), 8 June 1991, 17.

43. *"Nitara hiru eliya nisa kalu vana obe sama nävata susudu karaganne keseda?"* I have both Sinhala and English-language copies of this advertisement, which appeared in 1997, but I cannot determine the papers where they appeared or the dates because the photocopies came to me from the clipping files of an advertising agency. Similar advertisements also appeared on television.

44. For a treatment of the way the British visited their concerns about race on South Asia, see Susan Bayly, "Race in Britain and India," in *Nation and Religion: Perspectives on Europe and Asia,* ed. Peter Van Der Veer and Hartmut Lehmann (Princeton, N.J.: Princeton University Press, 1999), 71–95.

45. Casting agencies serve to provide modeling talent in Malaysia, but the advertising business in Sri Lanka is neither large enough nor profitable enough to make operating a casting agency viable.

46. The conservancy workers who traditionally have cleared the buckets from Sri Lankan latrines in coastal areas came from the Chakkliyan caste of South India. See Edgar Thurston, *Castes and Tribes of Southern India,* vol. 2 (New Delhi: Asian Educational Services, 1987), 2–7.

CHAPTER THREE

Local Ways of Being Foreign

Gehan Wijewardena's account of visiting his old secondary
school evokes a distinctive Colombo scene:

> A few years ago I attended a celebration of the 150th anniversary
> of my old school, which followed a quite rivetting game of rugby
> played between the school team and their long-time rivals. The
> celebration was males only, we drank expensive imported scotch
> out of plastic cups, listened to a rock band playing new versions
> of old tunes remembered from my childhood and watched the
> younger 'old boys' dance with each other.[1]

The younger 'old boys' dance with one another, the older 'old boys' look
on drinking scotch, and a rock band plays popular songs. How to characterize the event? The paradigm is the English public school, but the realization—scotch in plastic cups, rock band playing songs popular before
rock and roll reached South Asia, young men dancing with one another—
is Sri Lankan.

Viewed through the eyes of the generality of Sri Lanka's peoples,
of course, the scene is anything but Sri Lankan. Outside of some middle-
class venues, Sri Lankans do not drink scotch. Nor do they listen to rock
bands or dance with one another, no matter what the gender. Their reaction to people who do so is likely to range from bemusement to contempt,
regarding these practices as foreign, vulgar, and threatening to the local
way of life. The problem is that they are the local way of life for other Sri

Lankans, and they have been so for several centuries. In the past it may not have been scotch, but arrack, and the bands that have played Jim Reeves and Engelbert Humperdinck for the last thirty years were playing *baila* (a social dance of Portuguese origin) a hundred years prior to that. Three hundred years earlier they were playing the *caffirinyā* (another Portuguese dance). The local other follows a line of descent long enough to justify its claims to being both local and other.

That there are many Sri Lankas is old news to anthropologists rethinking the ethnographic project. Part of the discipline's self-reformation owes to concerns that the power to portray a way of life has historically been tied to systems of power that have dominated those same societies and epistemological misgivings that dehistoricizing social life denies not simply one of its characteristics but a constitutive one. The critique that links together both the political and epistemological complaints centers on the central trope of anthropological thinking. It argues that *culture* is a concept too powerful for its own good, that no society, however small or economically undeveloped, can be adequately represented by a set of propositions or coherent narrative account.[2]

Although they do not have the slightest interest in innovative forms of copywriting consistent with the changefulness and uncertainty of life, advertising executives also recognize several Sri Lankas. They begin from the more straightforward idea that there are two Sri Lankas, one found in Colombo and its hinterlands, and another found elsewhere on the island. The first is the Sri Lanka of people who countenance scotch and social dancing; the second is the Sri Lanka of people who do not. There are more Sri Lankas, to be sure, but dividing the society into two categories reiterates a distinction that advertising executives experience when they are at work, take a trip outside Colombo, or watch television. Their professional dilemma is as much political as economic—how to sell things to one Sri Lanka without alienating consumers in the other.[3]

When advertising executives say that Sri Lankans are traditional, conservative, restrained, and cautious, they have all Sri Lankans in mind, not just consumers who live in villages. In this context the market emerges as a single entity. Look at Sinhala and English newspapers for the same day and one finds a number of advertisements that appear in both languages—tires, motorcycles, Singer sewing machines, A. K. Gold House, Sony televisions, lottery tickets, Kandos chocolates, Ceylinco insurance, Lucite paint, water pumps, Bristol cigarettes, Sampath Bank, NEC, Bata shoes, Toyota spark plugs, army enlistments, Upali travels, Anchor yeast, Casio watches, Sisil refrigerators, motorcycle roller chains, and plumbing supplies.[4] Some English language advertisements appear in Sinhala papers or, more often, they appear as Sinhala advertisements with substantial amounts of English text, but the reverse occurs only sporadically. Television likewise runs a commercial in English and follows it with one in Sinhala, presuming viewers can shift easily from one to the other.

In other ways, what consumers buy sorts out relative to the place where they live. Colombo-dwellers purchase a disproportionate percentage of cellular telephones, they are more likely to carry-away their evening meals, and they use cosmetics and hair products unknown to most Sri Lankans. Advertisements that appear only in English—study in Australia at any of a variety of business colleges, visit the Taj Samudra lounge, buy soft furnishings such as curtains and upholstered chairs—suggest a cosmopolitanism that has a distinct regional expression.[5] For their part, rural Sri Lankans buy disproportionate percentages of batteries, bicycles and bicycle tires, certain kinds of soap such as Rexona, all varieties of arrack, sweets such as Dot, Merrigold, and Delta candies, Lux soap, and Sunlight laundry soap. They have practical reasons for buying the lion's share of hand tractors and herbicides. They are, in other words, two communities of consumption in Sri Lanka.

People who live in one locality see themselves represented in advertisements that try to speak to them by way of images that situate them now in one context, now in the other. Colombo—its street scenes, its daily practices, its human types—serves as a source of tropes and figures to reach either of these markets—consumers living in Colombo and village alike. Rural Sri Lanka is an equally fertile source of tropes and figures. It is not hard to imagine what symbolic loads each locality carries, because the colonial port city is linked to the West, commerce, social change, high levels of consumption, sophistication, evil, corruption, and foreign influence. Rural Sri Lanka has similarly contradictory associations—with tradition, history, and virtue on the one hand, backwardness and gullibility on the other.

The opposition between a colonial port city/national capital and the agricultural hinterlands that surround it appears all across Asia.[6] Sri Lanka simply represents the opposition in transparent form—a primate city with no equal supported by a society in which the great majority of Sri Lankans live. It is also a clear example of a place that has remained distinctively itself. Relative to other economic centers in Asia, Colombo has received only a small amount of in-migration from the countryside, maintaining a strongly felt distinction between the two regions. In the hundred-year period from 1871 to 1971, Colombo and its environs increased its share of the island's population only from 18 percent to 21 percent.[7]

When advertisers want to segment their audience, the most obvious strategy is to employ Colombo imagery to reach Colombo consumers and rural imagery to reach rural ones. But of course there are reasons other than the island-wide dispersal of newspapers, journals, and electronic media for not wanting to do so in every case. The simplest one is that the rural market is simply too big to ignore and growing rapidly. Cities such as Ratnapura and Matara, as well as many villages in the southwestern quadrant of the island have enjoyed unprecedented levels of prosperity in recent years because of remittances from overseas, employment in free-trade zones, and the growing strength of the gem trade. Absent these economic and social changes, advertisers have other motives to speak of one part of Sri Lanka in order to speak to consumers in the other part. A client may want to construct a product as sophisticated and sell it to rural consumers or reposition a product in such a way as to make it seem different from its competition.

The production of locality is not a process that began with the advertising business. The disposition to feel "at home" can be produced by ritual, but more often it grows out of routine, practical activities. That structure of feeling is less a natural occurrence than a social achievement. Building a house in a particular way or cultivating gardens and fields against a distinctive landscape creates a local form of subjectivity. When Appadurai argues that local subjects are made not found, he is not simply redescribing the concept of culture in phenomenological terms. Nor is he blurring the line between ideational processes and material ones. The ethnographic project depends on the same misrecognition as the production of the local subjectivities it wants to understand. Both assume that local context is the ground of existence, not its figure.[8]

By suggesting that all forms of belonging are produced, Appadurai's argument bypasses the discussion of cultural authenticity altogether. And by so doing, it allows me to approach advertising as a source of culture as much as an economic institution. The peculiar allure of the local does not prevent chasing down the historical origins of social practices and distinguishing the old from the new. But understanding locality as something achieved collapses the distinction between membership in a community of consumption as something that is produced and membership in a village community as a brute fact. In a similar way, insisting that locality as such is produced puts membership in larger forms of community, such as the nation, on a par with local forms. Instead of seeing nationalism as a distinctively imagined form of community, consider it a distinctively mediated one. In this cause, Appadurai redescribes Anderson's characterization of nationalism's genius—its success at using print capitalism to allow immense numbers of people who have never had face-to-face contact with

one another to understand themselves as a community—as "the efforts of
the modern nation-state to define all neighbourhoods under the sign of its
forms of allegiance and affiliation" (213).

It is hard to find a social formation that produced a sense of locality more formidable than the traditional Southeast Asian theater-state.[9]
And to that extent, putting the imagination to work for the sake of the
state is nothing new. But I want to concentrate on a recent transformation
of what can be imagined. Under the colonial state, public culture was centered in Colombo and consumed by people who also lived there. The focus
fell on metropolitan doings, both in Colombo and London. What marks
the production of locality in postcolonial states is the way the nation-state
takes the village—its inhabitants and their daily activities—as the center
of gravity of the state and the neighborhood by which all other neighbor-
hoods are defined. In Sri Lanka this process has involved more than focusing public culture on the peasantry as the moral core of the society. The
state has invested substantial resources in reproducing the smallholder way
of life.[10] As the state looks out on its constituents these days, the village has
become the neighborhood that counts.

The growth of radio broadcasting illustrates the state's involvement in that process. In 1924 Sri Lanka became the first British colony to
establish a broadcasting service, and programming reflected the colonial
state's interests.[11] Programs concentrated on Western gramophone music,
market and share transactions, road reports, general news, and weather.
Less than 10 percent of the broadcast day was devoted to Sinhala and
Tamil music. By the late 1940s funds were allocated to put a large number
of radio receivers in villages, and programs aired expressly for Sinhala and
Tamil rural listeners. But actually reaching most villages came only with
the democratization of Sri Lankan society in the 1950s and 1960s.[12] A
widely popular serial, *Tumpath Rata,* began to provide rural listeners a
practicum on how to be villagers. Throughout the 1980s and into the
1990s it followed the same monthly format—"the first week on a typical
rural village; the second on an event of cultural value; the third week on a
folk tale highlighting the villagers' creativity. The fourth week centered on
an illustrious personality whose life and career demonstrated distinct signs
of Sinhala culture." [13]

The transition from Westernized programs to didactic ones aimed
at rural listeners indicates the change in broadcast content; the dispersion
of radio service—first to the north-central province, then to the south and
Kandy—suggests the change in range. Government interest in new forms
of allegiance lay behind both changes. When Anandatissa de Alwis—no
longer Director of J. Walter Thompson, but Minister of State—inaugu-

rated radio service from Anuradhapura in 1979, he summarized the modernist view of the functions of radio. He said it had become an active way to disseminate information about development, give people of the region a way to communicate among themselves, and create rapport between the government and the people.[14]

Inserting the village at the center of popular culture has obvious implications for Colombo. It remains the entrepôt for foreign commodities and culture, not to say the national capital. It continues to be the home of the newspaper industry and the advertising business on which newspapers depend. Although radio signals are now broadcast from regional centers, it remains the center of the national service. It naturally became the venue for television production and broadcasting. In all of these contexts, Colombo is the source of cultural production, but only occasionally its object. The public culture that gets produced in Colombo is a culture that celebrates a tradition organized around the village, the temple, the irrigation tank, and ancient Anuradhapura, not the colonial port city. In a modern media regime, place no longer needs to be produced in place.

Radio serves as an example of the mediation that the electronic media create between different kinds of people. Given its visual component, television has been an even more powerful source for producing localities in Sri Lanka. It does so by celebrating government's role in representing the nation state to its public within the nation, villages, cities, the frontline conflict with a guerrilla army, and its interaction with the larger world.[15] Until recently, television has been equally much a government operation as radio, designed on the British pattern to serve the interests of the government in power and strengthen its authority.[16] Sri Lankans know the drill; they see television for what it is. The joke is to refer to the government television network, *Rupavahini*, as *Pujavahini* (waves of worship), mocking the way the network provides a steady supply of news pieces showing the incumbent government in a way that borders on worship. As with radio, the premise was that television broadcasting would serve as a tool for national development. Jayewardene initiated television with that understanding in 1978, including television along with the Mahawela project and the free-trade zone as instruments with which Sri Lanka could join the ranks of the developed nations. When he laid the foundation stone for the television broadcasting complex in Colombo, he said that his government hoped to develop the nation, "while preserving the ancient spiritual values—the *dharmistha* [righteous] approach to civilization—without giving up those traditions to which our people clung for 2,500 years." [17]

Television served as part of a larger consumption package in a way that radio had not. Both radios and televisions are consumer items, but television was a spectacular one, finally available after many years of import controls, even more seductive in its powers than radio, and widely accessible because of the establishment of easy available credit. But television was part of that consumption package in a second way. It was a commercial medium, exposing Sri Lankans to consumer advertising hugely more persuasive than anything most people had seen previously, advertisements that moved, picturing Sri Lankan society, its night spots as well as its villages, with the full force of 32 mm color. If the public sphere is the arena where European societies of an earlier time became aware of themselves as national entities, it is hard not to give similar status to the "endless spectacle" that television brings into the home, flowing from one program, one advertisement to the next, always as self-referential as the television screen itself, awaiting human attention.

The locality that Jayewardene most wanted to produce was the nation itself, and talking about protecting the *dharmistha samajaya* (righteous society) was talk about the nation. Its referent was the village, not to say a Sinhala village and one locked in the past, but rural Sri Lanka served as a metonym for the island as a whole. The goal was "national" development, its beneficiaries were people living in Colombo as much as the countryside. The entity that Jayewardene wanted to take its place among the developed nations of the world was not village Sri Lanka, however *dharmistha* it may have been, but the Sri Lankan nation. "While using the benefits of TV to achieve [development sufficient to place Sri Lanka among the developed countries], Government would also ensure that TV was used to promote the disciplines of a civilized nation—to cultivate the spiritual and cultural values of the nation." [18]

A Port City

Colombo's difference has historical origins. Before successive European powers—first the Portuguese, then the Dutch and British—made Colombo the center of political power and economic activity, Arab traders used the port to bring together maritime trade and domestic commerce. Ibn Batuta describes Colombo as being controlled by a wazir and ruler, "who has with him about five hundred Abyssinians." [19] He calls Colombo a Muslim town with two mosques and a Muslim cemetery. A Cufic inscription found in that cemetery dates the settlement to at least as early as the tenth century. [20] The city was constructed by cutting back jungle and filling marshland, and it was built with an eye to utilitarian solutions to urban problems, not to preserve any continuity with other settlements in the island or to dazzle the eye. Reverend James Selkirk, a Protestant missionary at the beginning of the British period, wrote that the most conspicuous building, next to the lighthouse, was the customhouse.[21] Colombo's most common architectural form was also utilitarian—the *go-down,* namely, a storehouse for goods.

In the early nineteenth century, Reverend Selkirk was struck by Colombo's confusion of people: "There are frequently, nay daily, to be seen there English, French, Dutch, Portuguese, Singhalese, Chinese, Parsees, Bengalees, Tamulians, Moormen, Malays, and Caffres, and each in a different dress," the local communities lined up without privilege among the others (5). The newcomers brought with them alien religions and practices. In the 1960s a Jesuit father described Colombo as "one of the most Catholic cities in Asia."[22] While churches occupy privileged places, historically important Buddhist monasteries are hard to find, and Hindu temples and Muslim mosques are not places one casually stumbles upon either. There are new Buddhist monasteries in parts of Colombo, but only a few such places, and they are often tucked away in out-of-the-way settings.

Although monasteries are few and far between, since Independence ceremonial Buddhist architecture has come to dominate many public spaces. An enormous Buddhist relic mound, held high above the ground by a concrete and steel tripod, stands near the entrance of Colombo harbor, a Buddhist image has been built facing City Hall in Viharamahadevi Park, and substantial Buddha-images now reside at important approaches to the Colombo Fort. Their centrality and insistent size marks the shift of political power to the Buddhist majority.[23] Buddhist practitioners have also reclaimed public occasions. Until 1970 Buddhist monks had never been ceremonially welcomed at Queen's House, then the residence of the Governor-General of Sri Lanka. Security concerns put Queen's House out of bounds for everyone these days, but monks are regular participants at ceremonial occasions.

Colombo's domestic architecture reflects both the building styles of the colonial period and the "American"-style houses of more recent days. Streets have been renamed after Sri Lankan historical figures, even though many people still refer to them by the colonial names—Prince Street, Turret Road, Wellington Crescent. All of these forces have made Colombo an alien place, an arena where foreigners and local people act in foreign ways. A Dutch Burgher historian reiterates the conventional wisdom: "Colombo is a city forced on the people of Ceylon in spite of themselves. It was never a creation of their own choice or making."[24] From my perspective, Colombo may be distinctive, but it is still the product of the people of Sri Lanka.

During the colonial period, the presence of European powers in Colombo made it a place where other newcomers could make a living. Portuguese rule left behind a substantial number of African troops as well as a smaller Portuguese community.[25] Dutch rule contributed a community of Dutch Burghers who had once worked for the regime as civil servants but came to be identified as *Vrijburghers* after they had left the Company's service. Portuguese and Dutch Eurasians have remained heavily concentrated in Colombo, although they sometimes moved beyond Colombo, settling in other urban centers. Dutch rule also brought Malay troops, who stayed on after the Dutch were driven from the island, serving the British as the Ceylon Rifles. Some migrated to faraway villages, such as Kirinda in Hambantota district, where they intermarried with local people.[26] Others settled in Colombo, retaining their distinctiveness, and often gravitating into particular professions, such as the police force.

Several groups of South Indian Chettiars became the primary source of credit for ordinary people, providing financial services that did not interest commercial banks, while also working as accountants and shroffs. Their distinctive dress—Ceylon or Colombo Chetty men wore a white jacket with a high collar, swooping hat, and immense gold earrings—made them striking figures in the urban landscape. Unlike other Chettiar communities, these people were Christians. They still are, and their conversion, as the community's account of their past shows, is a fundamental part of their self-understanding.

> In point of religion, all the earliest ancestors of the Ceylon Chetties—like the ancient Britons who worshipped Odin and Thor—were heathen, and worshipped deities like Kottavi or Aye, a war god like Murugan, a fish god like Ea of the Chaldees, a goddess named Minadtchy, & . . . But it must not be assumed that they were less deserving of respect, on the ground of religion; neither should *we* now discard the language of our forefathers (Tamil), nor refuse to accept what is beneficial in their customs and literature, although from our standpoint, we now possess the advantages of *hereditary* Christianity, consequent on the wise and fateful decision of our early Chetty converts, whereby we have the tradition of particular ways of thinking about things, particular standards of conduct which came to us when we were children, and shaped our

thoughts, and molded our characters, all under the influence of a
Society, of which CHRIST is the Life.[27]

Some communities made their peace with colonial power on the Chetty
model, and others did not. Dutch Burghers successfully weathered the
transition from Dutch rule to British. According to Brohier, at the beginning of the nineteenth century, Colombo had some fifty thousand residents, of whom perhaps three thousand were Burghers. Their small numbers notwithstanding, the community used the transition to English as the
language of government and commerce in 1801 "to greater advantage than
the larger communities in the Island."[28] Most Hindus kept on practicing
a religion centered on Murugan and Minakshi, while other Tamils con-
verted to Christianity, and many more learned English. Muslims did not
convert, although elite Muslims engaged in trade learned English. Immi-
grating from the Malabar and Coromandel coasts of India, other Muslims
became shopkeepers, jewelers, lapidaries, masons, and farmers.

By the beginning of the twentieth century, the island's import-
export trade was dominated by seven Bohra firms, a few Memnon traders,
and Parsis who arrived during the early part of the nineteenth century.[29]
One can only speculate on the reaction of other residents of the island to the
operations of a Tower of Silence in the Bloemendahl swamps for the dis-
posal of the dead.[30] Parsis were followed by Afghans, who became money-
lenders and enforcers. Even Sinhalas and Tamils who lived in Colombo
were marked as alien because of innovations in appearance, religion, social
practices, ways of making a living, and patterns of consumption. Nowadays, Colombo's difference is imagined in ways that respond to the civil
war in the north. A newspaper article reports that 1,500 Tamils move into
Colombo every week, pretending to be refugees, shifting about from place
to place to avoid official notice. For many Sri Lankans, Colombo is that
kind of place—unstable, dangerous, hyperbolic.[31]

Gananath Obeyesekere makes an argument that complicates these
images. The southwestern quadrant of the island, he argues, is the direct
descendant of the great hydraulic civilizations that once inhabited north-
central Sri Lanka. Colombo itself is not of much importance in the cultural
migration from the north, but the areas around Colombo are critical. The
primary shrines for the major guardian deities of Sri Lanka are located
there, as well as the cult of the goddess Pattini.[32] Many of the greatest
literary figures of the period that immediately preceded colonial domination came from the southwest. Obeyesekere speculates that Sinhalas moved
into Colombo and surrounding areas not because of the collapse of the

hydraulic civilizations of northern Sri Lanka, although that may have given them a push. They moved because of economic possibilities made possible by foreign trade conducted through the mediation of Arab traders.

Obeyesekere's argument challenges several popular conceptions— that Kandyan culture is more authentically Sinhala than forms of life characteristic of the southwestern quadrant, and that the movement to the southwest has no connection to the classical civilizations of the north. It also confounds the notion that Colombo and its hinterlands represent an artificial and alien development in the history of the island. Brohier's evaluation better captures the more common understanding of Colombo, but the irony is surely that this alien place evolved amidst part of the island that not only has not been marginal to the dominant social forms of Sinhala life, but has been the native place for several practices that derive from the island's earliest civilizations.

A Vocabulary of Derision

Colombo's difference has more recent sources. Some of its communities maintained close ties with India and elsewhere, creating economic and social connections to places beyond the island. People spoke a jumble of languages. The operations of trade and government required the work of translators, variously known as *dubāshā* or *tōlka mudali* (talking official), to negotiate the growing variety of languages. *Dubasha* is a *Hobson-Jobson* word and the product of the interaction of people and languages.[33] The most plausible derivation traces the word to the Sanskrit *dvibāshā,* meaning a person who speaks two languages; another traces the expression *dubasha* to the distinctive hats, *topi,* worn by men who worked as translators.[34] Still another derivation links the expression to "native" troops, who served the British and their predecessors. As much as translators, troops recruited from Africa or other parts of Asia inhabited a world that existed betwixt and between.[35]

A cognate term, *topaz* or *topass,* suggests local social distinctions. Roberts, Raheem, and Colin-Thome say that *topaz* refers to the offspring of marriages in the seventeenth and eighteenth centuries between Europeans and local people.[36] Viewed from afar, *topaz* was only one category in a taxonomy of people government authority wanted to identify and treat as different. The Dutch distinguished Dutch people born in Europe from those born in Asia, just as the British did with similar social types in India.[37] But the locally-salient distinction fell between Hollanders—wherever they were born—and Sinhalas and Tamils. On the one hand, the

Hollanders (or Burghers) were distinguished from native-born Sri Lankans, and on the other, Hollanders of long residence were increasingly people of the place, just as other Hollanders came to think of themselves as natives of South Africa.

All of these expressions—*dubasha, tuppahi,* or *topaz*—for people who did not fit snugly into either the dominant European community of the nineteenth century or the local population carry a negative connotation. Back in the late nineteenth century, Goonetilleke argued that *tuppahi* referred only to descendants of Portuguese men and local women, excluding the Dutch, whatever their descent, from the sting of this insult. Roberts, Raheem, and Colin-Thome say the word connotes "degenerate, contaminated, Westernized lifeways," whatever liminal community is being referenced.[38] Yasmin Gooneratne argues that *tuppahi* refers to the English-educated class, regardless of their racial origin or linguistic practice, tracing the expression to a time long before the rise of aggressively chauvinist politics in the 1950s.[39] These pejorative expressions put the burden not on local Europeans but on people who were at once like the indigenous population and yet not like it.

The most evocative figure is *kärapottä* (cockroach). The word gets used in a variety of ways, but generally it references someone who is different. Roberts, Raheem, and Colin-Thome treat it as the paradigm insult Sinhalas use to castigate Burghers, and they think the expression draws its power from its reference to discolored skin, as in the spotted appearance of some cockroaches. But Burghers use the expression, too, again seizing on the word's connotation of foreignness. Ignoring the self-reference of his words, Michael Ondaatje writes, "Ceylon always did have too many foreigners . . . the 'Karapothas' as my niece calls them—the beetles with white spots who never grew ancient here, who stepped in and admired the landscape, disliked the 'inquisitive natives' and left."[40]

What people of Portuguese, Dutch, and British extraction had to say about local people suggests just as much alienation. The British used expressions that ranged from the benign—"the natives," "villagers," and "Ceylonese"—to the racist. Leonard Woolf found one of the first Englishmen he met in Jaffna addressing Ceylonese as "black buggers" and "fat Jaffna harlots," and such expressions establish the low end of the range.[41] Roberts, Raheem, and Colin-Thome suggest that well-to-do Sinhalas referred to the generality of Sri Lankans as *godayā* (bumpkin) or *yakō* (demon; 13). Sri Lankan expressions for local people with European connections are equally contemptuous. A police sergeant told Roberts that "*tuppáhiä* was the worst thing one could call another *(ántima pahat deya),* and a worse insult than referring to someone as *geriyā* (eater of putrid flesh) or *sākkiliyā* (a Tamil caste that supplies conservancy workers in many Sri Lankan towns and villages; 18).

Generally, these expressions point to the moral behavior of the person being abused, but, more narrowly, they reference eating, drinking, making music, dancing, and promiscuous behavior. From a local point of view, social dancing—such as the *caffirinyā,* which came with the Portuguese by way of their African adventures and spread to the Dutch—and musical traditions such as *baila,* which came with the Portuguese and became urban Sinhala popular music, must have been quite shocking. But expressions such as *kana bona minissu* (eating-drinking people) textualizes the newcomer's reputation for finding pleasure in food and drink, ostensibly an unremarkable practice, but jarring in a Sri Lankan context. Nowadays Burgher authors reveal what must have aroused Sri Lankan feelings about Burgher ways. Ondaatje's *Running in the Family* recalls the boisterous doings of his well-to-do Burgher family as they ricochet about the island, often in a drunken state. Carl Muller's three-volume novelization of a Burgher railroadman's family presents a working-class variant on similar themes—dancing, drink, and obscene language, as well as sexual abuse.[42] In relating the exuberant behavior of a Burgher woman in Jaffna and his amorous adventure with her, Leonard Woolf picks up on these same themes.[43]

There has been continuing scholarly interest in the evolution of words such as *tuppahi* since Goonetilleke's 1889 article on its derivation, the more so in the last decade as scholars have searched for the origins of ethnic chauvinism and the growing estrangement of Sri Lanka's peoples. There has also been a steady supply of social movements and historical moments organized around this expression, its variants, and the tacit division between those who act in properly Sri Lankan ways and those who do not. By the 1950s Philip Gunawardena used the expression to refer to practices, not people, criticizing social forms that derived from Western contact. He assured voters that he was speaking not in a racist sense but a cultural one.[44] Losing none of its contempt, the term began to appear in Sinhala political discourse as a criticism of practices Gunawardena regarded as *misra* (mixed) and, because of their being mixed, degenerate.[45]

In 1970 I attended a political rally in a remote village in Sabaragamuva province. An Ayurvedic physician urged voters to keep Dudley Senanayake in office because of his love of country.[46] He attacked the SLFP for their unpatriotic actions and concluded by saying that "nowadays they are dancing *baila*" *(daen bailā natanavā).* When I heard that the opposition was dancing *baila,* I came to a complete stop. Why was dancing *baila* an insult? What did the reference mean in a political context? In retrospect I can provide my own analysis. Just as Philip Gunawardena attacked the Senanayakes in an earlier time for their *tuppahi* ways, the speaker went after Senanayake's successors for similar misdeeds. They were the ones dancing *baila* these days, ignoring the national interest. Dudley Senanayake was the patriotic alternative. He loved his country, he wanted it to develop, and he did not dance *baila*.[47]

That following alien practices can be an insult worse than being accused of eating putrid flesh, that a person's unpatriotic actions can be epitomized by his dancing a dance of colonial origin—these are insults that possess great power for people who see their way of life and their political interests threatened by forces outside of their control. A people with the longest entanglement with colonial domination in Asia, Sri Lankans have reason to worry about the enervation of local languages, literatures, dress, religions, naming practices, painting, music, architecture, and identity. For well over four hundred years, Sri Lanka has been economically exploited and culturally reshaped by European powers, and Colombo has been the chief venue of this influence, as well as its usual point of entry to the island. Not for nothing Colombo figures in popular perceptions of despair and threat. Consider how a nationalist writer weighed out the relationship between England and one's native village thirty years ago:

> Everybody, at least everybody who has normal feelings, likes
> his motherland and calls his home the country where he and his
> ancestors have been born and lived. But there are some of our
> people who talk of England as their home! "Next year we are going
> home." Such or similar phrases I have often heard from some of
> our people who have been grounded in the school of Thuppahi
> culture and who are in high positions today in the country. Some
> of these people could comfortably reach their original village
> homes close to Colombo by bus or rail for less than a rupee![48]

As Anglophilic as some Sri Lankans have been, few have had the resources or the inclination to maintain a residence in England. But for Sinhala nationalists, the more general threat has not been multiple residences but multiple loyalties.

E. Valentine Daniel's description of the Colombo elite evokes lives that seem hardly South Asian—"a Latin Club in Colombo that meets regularly to read Cicero or St. Jerome's letters, a bookstore in the capital that sells issues of the *Times Literary Supplement*, the collection of antiques, the connoisseurship of Western classical music and jazz, the [distinctive] organization of space in homes (especially living rooms and kitchens)." [49] British influence has reshaped space in Sri Lankan homes in ways Daniel has never seen in South India. The empty space of the South Indian middle-class home is replaced in the Sri Lankan equivalent by potted plants, carpets, and a density of furnishings that would look cluttered to an Indian. A government minister once told me of sitting in the Prime Minister's house listening to his grandson denounce the gathering force of Western values in Sri Lankan life. The minister thought to himself, "here is this boy, seated on a couch in a room with curtains, carpets, and paintings on every wall, oblivious to his having always lived in Westernized surroundings."

Few postcolonial societies show as many signs of Western traditions in music, art, literature, and theater. But cultural fundamentalists have been equally upset by the way everyday foreign practices drove out local ones:

> Why do most local merchants and shopkeepers name their establishments and shops only in English? Why do so many prefer to say good-morning and good-evening, when you have nice expressions in your own language for greeting each other? . . . I cannot understand why our people have such a great liking for being called Mr. or their women Mrs. . . . Another custom, unnecessarily imported, is the shaking of hands. Why not stick to your beautiful and respectful way of saluting with both hands raised? It has also the great advantage of being more hygienic than the constant touching or shaking of hands. [50]

Colombo serves as the subtext of Buddhadeva's complaints. Elsewhere in the island, shopkeepers do not greet customers in English, people do not insist on Western honorifics, and they do not shake hands.

Colombo Produced

The foreign attribute that most threatens many Sri Lankans is the English language itself. It is the *kaduwa,* the sword that allows some people to advance in life, clearing their way by hacking through others who have not mastered it. It gives its speaker immediate power. And it inverts the natural order.

> The question, often heard, "Is this person educated?" is to many people equivalent to the other question; "Does he know to talk,

read and write English?" If so, he is ranked among the educated. If this definition of education confining it to a more or less perfect knowledge of a foreign tongue were proper, then hundreds of English, German, French, Russian, and Chinese of excellent learning and refined culture must needs be styled uneducated, whilst many a cook or butler in Colombo would have a right to reckon himself educated.[51]

When economic opportunity is a scarce resource and when aspirations rise (as has been the case since Independence), access to English has implications that reach far and deep. It determines who is what—authentically Sinhala or otherwise—as well as who gets what. Those who are not authentically Sinhala are *tuppahi*.[52] But having English does not always ensure getting ahead, for working as a cook or butler is not a well-paid or prestigious job. Colombo suffers again on this count, inverting the class order of Sri Lankan life by giving the lowly—just because they speak English—the illusion that they are educated.

A quarter of a century has passed since Buddhadeva wrote those words I quote above. English is now back in favor and just as much the *kaduwa* of Sri Lankan life, and English-language names still speak volumes about cultural loyalty. Personal names provide fertile ground for parody:

> Queenie Hulankatura had problems with her name. It didn't quite synchronize. Her friends used to say that it was like the "ela haraka and the mee haraka" [a cow and a water buffalo]. . . . She knew a lot of others who had similar problems with their names. There was Trevor Hatarabage and Gavin Patakuda and Alston Nugawela and Shereen Koskottanna. Whenever [she] was to be introduced as an air hostess, she used the kaduwa name, Shereen. . . . But Koskottanna had its own uses. At times of war with neighbour Halparuwa, for instance, she used to proudly declare "api honda Sinhala Koskottanna umbala wage Halparuwo nevei dannavada" ("We are good Sinhala Koskottannas, not Halparuwas like you").
>
> When Douglas [her husband, Douglas Udabokkuwa] and Shereen used to go for golf, they had Dough and Sher proudly emblazoned on their golf bags, and everybody used to make way as if this was Arnold Palmer himself and his wife come to play golf at the Colombo Golf Club. But when they went to Sarachchandra's *Maname* at the Lumbini [theater] in the evening, Shereen used to make it a point to have Mr. and Mrs. Udabokkuwa proudly written on the programme.

When the culture editor of an uptown newspaper comes and addresses them saying, "Mr. and Mrs. Udabokkuwa, what do you think of Khemadasa's latest opera?" Shereen is in seventh heaven. Udabokkuwa fits this kind of occasion perfectly. . . . Just as everything was going all right and the culture editor was beginning to show his naked admiration from ear to ear, somebody shouts "Shereen Shereeeen, darling how are you? Why I didn't see you since the last time you served Kankung with pork on the AirLanka flight from Teheran."

Shereen's world suddenly collapses, and the culture editor walks away as if the entire Sarachchandra lineage had been grossly insulted.[53]

Struggles such as these—Shereen Udabokkuwa's attempts to exploit the authenticity her surname implies undone by her work as a stewardess, a given name such as Shereen, not to say a friend who makes a spectacle of their friendship—are alien to many Sri Lankan lives. But Shereen's story is not exclusively hers. Colombo is home to many people who live liminal lives. And those lives themselves play a part in the production of Colombo because localities are produced relative to the kinds of lives they support.

The *Jātika Cintanaya* (national way of thought) movement provides another example of the production of Colombo as a locality. Sri Lanka's most recent expression of popular anxieties about national identity developed at the initiative of Nalin de Silva, a mathematics professor at the University of Colombo, and Gunadasa Amarasekera, a novelist and cultural critic. By way of a series of publications and newspaper articles in the mid-1980s, de Silva and Amarasekera began to articulate a vision of an "indigenous way of thinking," a way of acting that could constitute the foundation for a Sri Lankan nation.[54] The animus of their writing has been twofold—the threat that Sri Lanka might be washed away by what they variously called "global culture," "Western *cintanaya*," or "Judaic *cintanaya*" and the consequent need to build a national ethos. For de Silva and Amarasekera, that basis has a single source, Sinhala Buddhist life as defined by Anagarika Dharmapala. "If that terminology," Amarasekera writes, "smacks of chauvinism, we could use a different terminology. . . . We could call it by another, nonpartisan name. But a change in terminology should not detract us from the truth, that this transcendent culture is primarily a product of the humane, civilized way of life of the Sinhala Buddhists of this country over the centuries."[55]

Inflammatory expressions such as "Judaic *cintanaya*" have only a small effect in places such as Sri Lanka, and the *Jātika Cintanaya* movement itself had minimal effect until a group of University of Colombo students—the United Science Students—tried to impose indigenous practices on campus. Where de Silva and Amarasekera spoke abstractly about the evils of aping Western ways, the Colombo students had policies, and they wanted them observed on campus. They prohibited social dancing, which had been the practice for several decades, and beat up a group of students who tried to stage a dance, sending one student to the hospital. They prohibited the sale of Coca-Cola, Fanta, and Sprite (while leaving Elephant House soft drinks alone and advocating local beverages such as tea instead), the wearing of short skirts by female students, and the use of English. Asked why they had beaten up students wanting to hold a dance, one *Jātika Cintanaya* student organized his comments around both new social practices and civil war: "These cabarets go against our culture. Today all we have are casinos and cabarets. Our country is at war, and we don't think that dances should be held on campuses. How can we at this time permit Ojaye [pop music] groups like the Gypsies to perform here and have dances. To drink, dance, and enjoy oneself is today morally wrong." [56]

University life, especially at Colombo and Peradeniya, throws together large numbers of students from provincial towns and villages with a small number of students from elite backgrounds. The students from provincial settings lack both English and economic support; elite students typically have both. Students from Colombo can live at home; students from away are left at the mercy of a university hostel system that can house only six hundred of five thousand students needing accommodation. One expression of these demographic forces is the practice of "ragging" or hazing undergraduates. The invidious effects of social class and the great difficulties many students face aside, the logic of dispute depends on a familiar figure—social dancing is unpatriotic. And when a civil war is underway, dancing, drinking Coca-Cola, and enjoying oneself are worse than unpatriotic. They are morally excessive. Colombo is the natural setting for thrashing out these issues, a place for students from near and far to contest what constitutes a properly local subjectivity.

Media and Mediations

Sometimes social forms play a relatively straightforward role in the production of a sense of locality. Other times whatever counts as "local" or "foreign," "acceptable" or otherwise is produced by association. The notion that *baila* is "foreign" derives from its origins in Colombo and the kinds of people who first danced it—the urban middle class, Burghers, and the inebriated. The foreignness of the practice also derives from its being social dancing. Despite its Tamil origins *kavadi* (an ecstatic dance traditionally performed by Saiva Hindus for the god Skanda) is not marked as foreign or alien, and it is on its way—in Kataragama, Kandy, and a variety of other Sinhala sites—to being absorbed as part of Sinhala tradition.[57] Its being danced in a decidedly nonurban and nonmodern setting such as Kataragama may account for its not being eschewed for its being "foreign."[58] Young men dancing *baila* is "foreign" by this logic, while the young Sinhala men and women dancing together in a procession (while cross-dressing) is not.

The different destinies of *baila* and *kavadi* demonstrate that society scarcely needs media to produce cultural practices marked for being "foreign" or "local." *Baila* was stigmatized long before the emergence of those media in Sri Lanka; however much *kavadi* has been appropriated by Sinhalas, the media have not had a hand in it. But when modern forms of media start to produce culture, the relationship between the local and the locally foreign becomes more unstable. The context in which forces work on these cultural categories grows wider; new forms of agency start to reshape the production of both the local and the foreign. The nation-state appropriates that distinction for the sake of legitimating itself, the media restate it daily in portraying the doings of a society too large to know itself directly, and the advertising business exploits it for the sake of getting the consumer's attention.

Fredrik Barth's now dusty study of ethnic identity bears on the distinction between the local and the foreign in a world where those categories interact with rising emotion.[59] Ethnicity, Barth writes, is not so much a set of cultural attributes or anything that arises autochthonously. It is a strategy that becomes relevant in dealing with other kinds of people. When people of two groups need to deal with one another, even when each group follows many practices in common, successful interaction may require finding cultural attributes that mark their respective differences. According to Sahlins's reading, Barth's argument has implications important for thinking about culture as such.[60] The fundamental one is that signs of "cultural distinction represent modes of organization rather than . . . traits in themselves" (414).

Recalling Barth's work serves Sahlins's efforts to undo the argument that culture nowadays is an otiose concept, especially so in a world where it has become a self-serving tool for nationalists, ethnic groups, and communities facing external pressure or possibility. When reduced to a thing, culture deserves scorn, but Barth suggests that cultural forms are better understood as processes or strategies. But what to make of Scots wearing kilts, Hawaiians, hula skirts, and other cases where cultural practices seem contrived purely for political and economic purposes?[61] To the argument that invented traditions are somehow different from authentic culture, Sahlins argues that traditions—not just the notorious cases—always derive from political and economic circumstances. But they do not arise willy-nilly. Human action is unconditionally chiastic: "a politics of culture entails the culturalization of politics."[62]

Because societies inevitably cope with threat and change in their own terms, the logic of cultural production—in precolonial, postcolonial, and extracolonial contexts—always works the same way. Confronted with a world that is ever more with them in the form of global culture and commodities, societies "would make some autonomy of their heteronomy. . . . what needs to be recognized is that *similitude is a necessary condition of the differentiation*."[63] Sahlins insists that the relationship of the local to the global has less to do with either resistance or surrender than "the differencing of growing similarities by contrastive structures." In other words, what Barth said thirty years ago about border conditions operates in an increasingly globalized world with modern media regimes because it is ever the case that signs of "cultural distinction represent modes of organization rather than . . . traits in themselves."

The contrastive structure that is more important than the distinction between the global and the local, the Western and the Sri Lankan, or the material and the cultural is the distinction between the local way of being foreign and the local way of being local or Sri Lankan (or Sinhala). The foreign in untranslated form enters Sri Lankan lives in some contexts, but the more important distinction lies onshore. Instead of drawing a line at the point where Colombo's harbor meets the island proper, the line gets drawn along the boundary where Colombo and its hinterlands blend into the rest of Sri Lanka. Colombo is a setting marked by local ways of being foreign; the rest of the island—the "real" Sri Lanka, the site of "authentic" culture—is marked by local ways of being Sri Lankan. Sahlins's argument that *"similitude is a necessary condition of the differentiation"* still speaks to the case, but local heteronomy is moved inland and parsed out in two forms—the locally foreign and the locally local.

One example will suggest how radio broadcasting transforms the epitomizing operations of cultural distinction. In 1928 the Ceylon Broadcasting Corporation asked one of the foremost Buddhist preachers of the time, Palane Vajiragnana, to sermonize on the air.[64] On the radio his preaching—in Sinhala—had novel effects, not only distributing a Buddhist sermon to listeners of all kinds, but also putting religion in a context where it stood out all the more because of the contrast with Western music and the evening news. Consider the innocence of the times: a Muslim attorney in Matara wrote a letter to Vajiragnana saying that the first thing he had heard on his new radio was the monk's hour-long sermon, and it was reward enough for having purchased it.[65]

Whether Buhari, the attorney, had been moved by the thrill of the technology or the humanistic content of the sermon, broadcast technology brought Sri Lankans together in entirely new ways. He was not likely to have heard Vajiragnana in his *bana sala* (preaching hall) at the Vajirarama temple, one hundred miles away in Colombo. He was not likely to have heard him preach in Matara either, had the monk paid a visit to a local *bana sala*. But the radio brought a Buddhist monk into a Muslim home. Writing from homes far away from both Matara and Colombo, several of the attorney's co-religionists subsequently complained in the press of Buhari's promiscuous listening habits, because the press had created another novel connection—between Buhari and his far-flung co-religionists. When Buhari heard the sermon on the radio and expressed his appreciation in newsprint, he entered a public sphere that put radio listeners and newspaper readers on a par. They had become a community of consumption. Buhari's co-religionists simply insisted on a contrastive structure to counter this growing similarity.

In the late 1940s when funds were allocated to put a large number of radio receivers in villages, and programs aired expressly for Sinhala and Tamil rural listeners, the production of culture took a new turn. "The boundary work," Sahlins says, "of culture-signs is a realization, in the social dimension, of their logical status as class names. Classes are inclusive and contractive, hence also exclusive. By the same token (so to speak), the classification is a moral judgement: what is so distinguished is good, and right to be so distinguished."[66] Where Buddhist interests saw sermonizing on the radio as a way to reclaim their place in the public culture of late colonial Sri Lanka, they could not have envisioned the consequences of broadcasting for listeners such as Buhari. Although boundaries need to be defended from both sides, each community had distinct ideas of what was at stake— for the Buddhists it was the Buddhist character of public life; for Buhari's co-religionists, proper Muslim behavior for radio listeners.

According to Benedict Anderson, newsprint functioned inadvertently in the production of national communities, turning readers into a league of anonymous equals.[67] Readers were brought into a single time and space not so much by virtue of the substantive content of newspapers and novels but through the regularity brought by the daily reading of a newspaper and the demotic voice with which papers and novels addressed their readers. They became fellow citizens for formal reasons—they came to share the same set of references, a succession of plurals. Those plurals—hospitals, prisons, remote villages, monasteries, Indians, Negroes—in the case of colonial Mexico (which is Anderson's example) occupy a bounded territory and common time (34–35). To this extent newspapers insinuated the nation into the lives of people whose national feelings were otherwise inchoate.

The problem with Anderson's argument for the imagined community is another unintended quality of the media, and the problem grows stronger as representation becomes more visual. The media cannot avoid a second succession of plurals—surnames, faces, language patterns, musics, costumes, and cuisines, as well as dances such as *baila* and *kavadi*—and these plurals serve as metonyms for still another set of plurals—religions, ethnicities, genders, social classes, and localities. The media create a world, and they can nationalize subjectivity in surprising ways. But in representing that world, media make present other identities that pull readers and viewers in contrary directions. The imposition of surnames itself is the nation-state's most innocuous discipline, but if Buhari had not had a distinctive surname, his enthusiasm for Buddhist homilies would not have become an issue for Muslim readers. Under electronic circumstances, all of these figures of identity become caught up in endless circulation, change, and opposition. And as the media become more visual, faces appear and dances come to be enacted—now with the play of movement and 32 mm color—naturalizing the boundary work of culture and making it all the more cunning.

NOTES

1. Book review, *Lanka Guardian* (Colombo) 14, no. 2 (15 May 1991): 27.

2. The critique begins with several articles published in James Clifford and George Marcus, eds., *Writing Culture* (Berkeley: University of California Press, 1986). A more recent set of critical evaluations appears in Sherry Ortner, *Fate of "Culture": Geertz and Beyond* (Berkeley: University of California Press, 1999).

3. For an account of a comparable phenomenon in India, see Arvind Rajagopal, "Thinking through Emerging Markets: Brand Logics and the Cultural Forms of Political Society in India," *Social Text* 17, no. 3 (Fall 1999): 131–49.

4. These advertisements appeared in the *Daily News* (Colombo) and *Divaina* of 16 May 1991. The day was arbitrary, but the advertisements of that date are representative.

5. Besides Colombo, that region might include an area bounded by Negombo in the north and Kalutara in the south, and then inland to, let's say, Gampaha, some fifteen miles to the east.

6. There are several sources for the sociological study of colonial port cities. One of the most theoretically-motivated is Anthony D. King, *Colonial Urban Development: Culture, Social Power, and Environment* (London: Routledge and Kegan Paul, 1976).

7. See Economic and Social Commission for Asia and the Pacific, *Migration, Urbanization and Development in Sri Lanka* (New York: United Nations, 1980). By the 1981 census, the population of Colombo itself had risen modestly from 562,420 to 587,647, but surrounding towns showed substantial population increases. The population of Moratuwa, for instance, rose from 96,267 to 134,826 in that same ten-year period (Economic and Social Commission for Asia and the Pacific, *Urbanization and Socio-economic Development in Asia and the Pacific* [New York: United Nations, 1993], 73).

8. Arjun Appadurai, "The Production of Locality," in *Modernity at Large* (University of Minnesota Press, 1997), 178–82. Appadurai argues that locality has an inertia, a naturalness that leaves the person who inquires about it no better able to recognize its operations than the actor. In the middle part of this chapter, I describe Colombo's history, risking the naturalistic fallacy that Appadurai points out (179). I do so advisedly, wanting to lay out the forces that motivate Sri Lankans' understanding of Colombo as a figure.

9. The classic sources are S. J. Tambiah, *World Conqueror and World Renouncer* (Cambridge: Cambridge University Press, 1976); and Clifford Geertz, *Negara* (Princeton, N.J.: Princeton University Press, 1980).

10. Mick Moore, "The Ideological History of the Sri Lankan 'Peasantry,'" *Modern Asian Studies* 23, no. 1 (1989): 180.

11. C. L. Pujitha-Gunawardana, *This Is Colombo Calling* (Nugegoda: Perali Publishers, 1990), 19.

12. Although by the late 1940s there were radio programs expressly for Sinhala and Tamil rural listeners, broadcasts were "seldom if ever received outside a very limited range of between 20 to 30 miles around Colombo" (Nandana Karunanayake, *Broadcasting in Sri Lanka: Potential and Performance* [Moratuwa: Centre for Media and Policy Studies, 1990]: 217).

13. Nandana Karunanayake, *Radio Broadcasting in Sri Lanka: Significant Dates and Events, 1921–1990* (Moratuwa: Centre for Media and Policy Studies, 1990), 65.

14. Nandana Karunanayake, *Radio Broadcasting in Sri Lanka,* 61.

15. For the few Sri Lankans able to afford a satellite dish, television produces a global order of locality, just as shortwave radios and foreign newspapers and journals had for a few Sri Lankans at an earlier time. Satellite dishes make it possible for Sri Lankans to watch broadcasts from Moscow, St. Petersburg, Delhi, Madras, China, Indonesia, and Malaysia, as well as CNN, the World Service of the BBC, MTV, and Star TV. Because satellite equipment costs some Rs 50,000 (US $900), the number of buyers is very small. In India where satellite transmissions are delivered by cable companies, the revolutionary impact of new orders of locality is worth contemplating. As of 1991, there were some 100,000 cable viewers in Delhi and more in Bombay ("TV Comes in a Dish, and India Gobbles It Up," *New York Times,* 29 October 1991, A4).

16. Ranggasamy Karthigesu, "Television as a Tool for Nation-Building in the Third World: A Post-Colonial Pattern, Using Malaysia as a Case-Study," in *Television and Its Audi-*

ences, ed. Phillip Drummond and Richard Paterson (London: British Film Institute Publishing, 1988), 306–26. Karthigesu argues that while the "colonial model" (as opposed to the "metropolitan model" of the BBC or an "independence service model") guided media policy in Pakistan, India, Malaysia, and Sri Lanka, in time propaganda objectives in these new nations evolved in the direction of the Soviet and East European broadcast systems, using electronic media to serve the interests of the political party in power, not simply a tool for government propaganda (307–9).

17. "TV for National Development, Says President," *Daily News* (Colombo), 5 March 1980. A fuller discussion of Jayewardene's neologisms *dharmistha* and *dharmistha samajaya* (righteous society) can be found in Steven Kemper, *The Presence of the Past* (Ithaca, N.Y.: Cornell University Press, 1991), 161–93.

18. "TV for National Development," *Daily News* (Colombo), 5 March 1980.

19. Ibn Batuta, *Ibn Battuta: Travels in Asia and Africa,* trans. H. A. R. Gibb (London: Darf Publishers, 1983), 260.

20. Alexander Johnston, "A Cufic Inscription Found in Ceylon; with a translation by Rev. Samuel Lee," *Transactions of the Royal Asiatic Society* (Great Britain and Ireland) 1 (1827), 545–48.

21. James Selkirk, *Recollections of Ceylon* (London: J. Hatchard and Son, 1844), 4.

22. S. J. Perera, *Historical Sketches: Ceylon Church History* (Colombo: Catholic Book Depot, 1962), 70. Some 20 percent of Colombo's residents were Catholic.

23. Gananath Obeyesekere saw signs of this architectural transformation some thirty years ago: "Religious Symbolism and Political Change in Ceylon," in *The Two Wheels of Dhamma,* ed. Gananath Obeyesekere, Frank Reynolds, and Bardwell Smith (Chambersburg, Penn.: American Academy of Religion, 1972), 58–78.

24. R. L. Brohier, *Changing Face of Colombo* (Colombo: Lake House, 1984), 2.

25. Portuguese Eurasians suffered discrimination relative to Dutch Eurasians in Sri Lanka, and skin color seems to have played some part in maintaining that distinction. See McGilvray, "Dutch Burghers and Portuguese Mechanics," 242–46.

26. See Leonard Woolf, *Growing* (New York: Harcourt Brace Jovanovich, 1961), 45.

27. Antony F. Ascrappa, *A Short History of the Ceylon Chetty Community* (Colombo: Catholic Press, 1930), 42; italics and capitals in original.

28. Brohier, *Changing Face of Colombo,* 58.

29. Kumari Jayewardena, "Some Aspects of Class and Ethnic Consciousness in the Late 19th and Early 20th Centuries," in *Ethnicity and Social Change in Sri Lanka* (Colombo: Karunaratne and Sons, 1984), 80.

30. Brohier, *Changing Face of Colombo,* 56.

31. "1500 Tamils Are Settling in Colombo Every Week," *Divaina,* 25 August 1999.

32. Gananath Obeyesekere, *The Cult of the Goddess Pattini* (Chicago: University of Chicago Press, 1984), 5–10.

33. According to *Hobson-Jobson, dubasha* derives from Hindi and Tamil, and means "a man of two languages" (Henry Yule and A. C. Burnell, eds. [New Delhi: Munshiram Manoharlal, 1968], 328). *Hobson-Jobson* defines *topaz* or *topass* as a "name used in the 17th and 18th centuries for dark-skinned or half-caste claimants of Portuguese descent, and Christian profession," adding that other derivations, such as ones deriving the word from the Hindi word *topi* (hat), were "often in the minds of those using the term, as its true connotation." This second derivation receives some corroboration, *Hobson-Jobson*

says, from "the fact that Europeans are to this day [c. 1886] often spoken of by natives (with a shade of disparagement) as topeewalas or 'hat-men,' but also in the pride commonly taken by all persons claiming European blood in wearing a hat" (933).

34. The nineteenth-century scholar William Goonetilleke puzzled over the word *dubash* and its derivative *tuppahi* in an article written at an early moment in the rise of Sinhala nationalism ("Dubash and Tuppahi," *Orientalist* 3 [1888–1889]: 212–13). He says it refers to a person who speaks two languages, but adds that it was also a term of contempt referring to offspring of Portuguese men and local women. In other words, the expression had acquired a pejorative sense before the end of the nineteenth century. I take a later article (R. C. Temple, "Topaz-Topass," *Ceylon Antiquary and Literary Register* 7, no. 4 [1920]: 210–17), as evidence of continuing interest in a philological issue made important by social tensions that grew during the first three-quarters of this century.

35. There are still small communities of people of African descent living in Sellankandal in Serambiyadi in Puttalam District. They practice Catholicism and have intermarried with local people. See "These Others, Called Kaffirs," *Sunday Times* (Colombo), 4 May 1997.

36. Roberts, Raheem, and Colin-Thome, *People Inbetween,* 42. Roberts, Raheem, and Colin-Thome suggest that another pejorative expression for Dutch Burghers, namely *kärapotta* (cockroach) may have derived from a Portuguese word, *carapuca,* for a cap worn in the sixteenth and seventeenth centuries by Asian converts to Catholicism in India and Sri Lanka (3, 8). In the early period of intercultural contact, headgear of all kinds figured imaginatively in the interaction of Europeans and South Asians in disproportionate ways. See Arjun Appadurai, "Consumption, Duration, and History," in *Modernity at Large,* 74.

37. The British categorized people of European parentage on both sides who had been born in India as "domiciled Europeans," distinguishing them from both Europeans and Anglo-Indians. British officials treated domiciled Europeans as only slightly preferable to Anglo-Indians, tainted by too much association with India and having many of the disagreeable qualities of Anglo-Indians (see Lionel Caplan, "Creole World, Purist Rhetoric: Anglo-Indian Cultural Debates in Colonial and Contemporary Madras," *Journal of the Royal Anthropological Institute,* n.s., 1, no. 4 [December 1995]: 759 n. 7).

38. See chart I, between pages 14 and 15.

39. "The English-Educated in Sri Lanka: An Assessment of Their Cultural Role," *South Asia Bulletin* 12, no. 1 (1992): 30 n. 22.

40. Michael Ondaatje, *Running in the Family* (New York: Norton, 1982), 80.

41. Leonard Woolf, *Growing,* 48.

42. Carl Muller, *The Jam Fruit Tree* (New Delhi: Penguin, 1993); Carl Muller, *Yakada Yaka* (New Delhi: Penguin, 1994); and Carl Muller, *Once Upon a Tender Time* (New Delhi: Penguin, 1995).

43. Woolf, *Growing,* 67–68.

44. Reggie Siriwardena, "Jathika Chintanaya or Multi-Culturalism," *Dana* 15, nos. 5 and 6 (1990): 4.

45. The target of Gunawardena's abuse was not simply Westernized Sri Lankans or the UNP. Gunawardena's expression, according to Roberts, Raheem, and Colin-Thome, referenced his arch-enemy, Doric de Souza, himself a Marxist like Gunawardena, but the son of Armand de Souza, a journalist who migrated to Sri Lanka from Goa (Roberts, Raheem, and Colin-Thome, *People Inbetween,* 17).

46. Kirindagala Amerasekera, UNP political rally, Udamulla, Balangoda, 6 May 1970. A Sinhala friend once said that only illiterate people dance *baila,* adding that what he found most offensive about the practice was not the dance itself, but the two-line stanzas that dancers sing, ridiculing others with vulgar language.

47. I attended that political rally to learn more about local politics and came away having heard only about national figures such as Dudley Senanayake. Mick Moore has also noted Sinhalas' striking familiarity with leading political figures and dependence on the state, coupled with the weakness of local politicians and institutions (*The State and Peasant Politics in Sri Lanka* [Cambridge: Cambridge University Press, 1985], 180–81).

48. Asoka Buddhadeva, "Ceylonese in Danger of Losing Their Values," *Tribune* (Colombo), 24 May 1970, 10.

49. E. Valentine Daniel, *Charred Lullabies: Chapters in an Anthropography of Violence* (Princeton, N.J.: Princeton University Press, 1996), 48.

50. Asoka Buddhadeva, "Ceylonese in Danger of Losing Their Values," 7.

51. Asoka Buddhadeva, "Ceylonese in Danger of Losing Their Values," 7.

52. When I have asked informants whether it is possible for a Tamil to be *tuppahi,* the answer has always been no.

53. A. Rajpal, "A Rose by Any Other Name Sucks," *Island* (Colombo), 11 November 1991, 3.

54. De Silva's best-known publications are *Jathika Sanskitiya Saha Chintanaya* (Colombo: Chintana Parshadaya, 1991) and *Mage Lokaya* (Dehiwela: Mudanya, 1992), although his political opinions appeared regularly in Sinhala newspapers and magazines in the 1980s. Amarasekera's writings on the subject are found in a series of articles in the Sunday *Island* (Colombo), that appeared in the wake of Reggie Siriwardena's Doric de Souza Lecture of 1990, although he himself traces his thinking to a series of Sinhala pamphlets he wrote in the 1970s. It is worth pointing out the middle-class origins of both de Silva and Amarasekera—the former, a professor of mathematics. and the latter, a dental surgeon.

55. Gunadasa Amarasekera, "Jathika Chinthanaya: What Does It Mean?" *Dana* 15, nos. 5 and 6 (1990): 7.

56. Kalpana Isaac, "Jathika Chintanaya Acolytes Rub It In," *Sunday Observer* (Colombo), 19 May 1991, 21.

57. A suggestive example would be the way *kavadi* dancing has been incorporated into a Buddhist procession in an out-of-the-way village in Sabaragamuva province (Jonathan Spencer, *A Sinhala Village in a Time of Trouble* [Delhi: Oxford University Press, 1990], 58–69). Two of Spencer's informants told him that *kavadi* had no place in a Buddhist ceremony (59).

58. See, for instance, Obeyesekere's treatment of the Sinhala appropriation of all of the rituals associated with the god Kataragama ("Social Change and the Deities: The Rise of the Kataragama Cult in Modern Sri Lanka," *Man,* n.s., 12 [December 1977]: 377–96.

59. Fredrik Barth, introduction to *Ethnic Groups and Boundaries,* ed. Fredrik Barth (Boston: Little, Brown, 1974), 9–38.

60. Marshall Sahlins, "Two or Three Things That I Know about Culture," *Journal of the Royal Anthropological Institute,* n.s., 5 (1999): 399–421.

61. The relevant source is Eric Hobsbawm and Terrence Ranger, *The Invention of Tradition* (Cambridge: Cambridge University Press, 1983).

62. Barth, *Ethnic Groups and Boundaries,* 417.

63. Sahlins, "Two or Three Things," 411; italics in original.

64. Nandana Karunanayake, *Radio Broadcasting in Sri Lanka,* 7. Vajiragnana's career is treated in H. L. Seneviratne, *The Work of Kings: The New Buddhism in Sri Lanka* (Chicago: University of Chicago Press, 1999), 53–55.

65. Pujitha-Gunawardana, *This Is Colombo Calling,* 29. Ven. Vajiragnana also gave a 30-minute talk on "Caste and Class Distinction," causing N. M. Perera to object in a speech he gave in the State Council. Perera's discomfort suggests another sort of boundary work, in this case among religion, social status, and politics.

66. Sahlins, "Two or Three Things," 415.

67. Anderson, *Imagined Communities.*

CHAPTER FOUR

The Sri Lankan Advertising Business

Although Portuguese and Dutch colonial regimes tied Sri Lanka to the their economies, the British had the advantage of nineteenth-century industrial technologies for extracting and processing coconut, rubber, and tea, and they did so with great efficiency. Ever since then the import-export sector has been dominated by British agency houses, brokering the relationship among the tea and rubber estates, shipping lines, and commercial interests in London. Agency houses appointed the executive staffs to estates, established financial and agricultural policy, bought produce, and sold it at auction in Colombo and London. Eventually those houses came to trade in retail products and thus they also served individual customers, themselves linked in various ways to government and the chief export industries.[1] This part of the economy was marked by a market orientation, the generation of surplus, and the use of capital in organizing and increasing production. Left to itself, the other part of the island's economy—the local, rural, peasant or subsistence sector—was characterized by low levels of consumption, high rates of savings, and underdevelopment.[2]

Depending on exports and imports had negative effects on Sri Lanka's economy coming and going. The emphasis on coconut, rubber, and tea made Sri Lanka vulnerable to the vicissitudes of world demand, and while exporting generated profits, they were seldom put to uses that developed the rural sector of the economy. The import business, by contrast, was profitable and steady, giving the entrepreneurial class little reason to develop other forms of business.[3] These economic structures were established long before advertising entered Sri Lankan life, but they also had their effect on the volume and nature of advertising expenditure. To this day newsprint emphasizes unlikely products—rain pipes, spark plugs, motorcycle roller chains, and plumbing supplies—that can be advertised at relatively low rates because of the weakness of the market for the home furnishings, clothing, scent, watches, shoes, and so on that dominate Western print advertisements.

The boom and bust character of an economy tied to exporting agricultural commodities had further effects. Although the Korean War caused a boom in rubber prices, the balance of trade became a grievous problem as the 1950s, 1960s, and 1970s unfolded, leading to austerity programs and import controls. Expensive foreign goods were either replaced by locally-made equivalents, as in the case of biscuits and batteries, or they disappeared altogether from people's lives. To the present moment the economic contraction that occurred in the 1960s and 1970s has shaped people's attitudes toward consumption and government. The state explained import controls with economic arguments—we simply cannot afford to import things now. First we develop our economy on our own, then we import. But government also explained its policies by reimagining human needs as such. Once needs were redefined, consumerist practices—distinctive packaging, product choice, advertising—could be reduced and foreign exchange saved. Both the Sri Lanka Freedom Party and the United National Party, according to Anandatissa de Alwis, came to think there was no other way:

> At one of the early meetings held in the hall of the Chamber of Commerce, a very distinguished theoretician of the Government of that time . . . said why do you want marketing? After all people want soap, that is true. But why do you want different kinds of soap, why do you want to make the choice so complex, after all soap is intended to wash either clothes or the human body or utensils or what have you. If there is a functional soap that will do this, why must you put a name on it, why must you put a perfume on it, why must you wrap it in all kinds of different styles, why must you have beautiful women in the advertising, why must you have hoardings [billboards], why must you have competitions, why don't you have a big barrel and put this soap into the barrel and keep it in a shop, surely everyone will know it is soap, and he said, "can you, this country afford the luxury of having so many different kinds of soap . . . ?"[4]

Those choices marked a defining moment in the recent history of Sri Lankan consumption practices—Sri Lanka was poised between the proliferation of marketing and advertising conventions that dominate the modern world and a "barrel" model deriving from the unspoken logic of the small shops that carry on business in Sri Lankan villages and towns.

For several centuries, such shops have sold varieties of rice and other cereals, chilies, onions, and dried fish, and those foodstuffs are put on offer in the same form as they are shipped—in barrels, bags, or arrayed on wooden trays. Today barrels and such are joined by metal cans and bottles, containing commodities such as dried milk, cooking oil, and kerosene. Provision shops are the primary venue where Sri Lankan consumers have encountered regional flows of food—rice from Sri Lanka, South India, China, and Burma, Bombay onions, Maldive fish, Masoor dhal, and more recently tinned goods from Europe and Australia. They were not the only places where people in towns and villages had contact with the world economy—most towns also have had tea shops, textile outlets, shops that sell building materials, and appliance shops. But the provision shop is the place where people—from inhabitants of the smallest village to shoppers at open-air markets in Colombo and Kandy—shop regularly. It offered choices, but choices limited to things such as varieties of rice. Packaging was whatever was necessary for shipping, and advertising gratuitous.

What the provision shop was to the local sector of the economy, Elephant Cold Stores was to British families and well-to-do Sri Lankans. Trade there was also straightforward. Through the first half of this century, the economy of Colombo was centered on a colonial elite of some twenty thousand people or so, of whom some five thousand had credit privileges at Elephant House. Once a month the woman of the house would be driven to its cold stores, where she would restock her pantry—five pounds of lamb, ten pounds of chicken, ten pounds of sausage, a case of Orange Barley—and move onward. The same company also delivered dairy products and carbonated beverages to her house. At small shops along Galle Road, she would purchase English tinned goods, toiletries, and sweets, leaving the purchase of fruits and vegetables to a servant who walked to a nearby market as the need arose.

In this world of steady consumption, businesses had little variety to sell and little motivation to advertise. In the words of the first manager of what became Sri Lanka's leading newspaper:

> "Advertisers felt [in first years after World War I] that they were conferring a favor by advertising in a newspaper. To many of them money spent on advertising was money thrown down a drain. The

> Pettah [the area of Colombo where dry goods, fruit and vegetables, hardware, and gold businesses are located] shops, especially, took years to learn the value of press advertising. The large British business houses were the hardest to tackle. They were content to advertise in the newspapers owned by Europeans."[5]

When advertising appeared, it was confined to tombstone ads, largely unmotivated by any desire to increase sales, and directed toward the small number of Sri Lankans who read English-language newspapers and were, in a local historian's words, "not very consumption-minded" in any case.

Newspapers had a material interest in advertising, but the colonial elite—Sri Lankans as much as British expatriates—regarded it as crassly American in much the way Europeans did at home. One of the founders of the advertising business in Sri Lanka characterized the colonial attitude toward the very idea of advertising as fixed on not only vulgarity, but intrusiveness into the natural order of things. Like advertising in general, that presumption was marked as American. He made the point by recalling an editorial he had read long ago in the *Manchester Guardian* in response to the Marshall Plan's suggestion that the British could restart their economy more quickly by using the tools of marketing: "Before the war the Americans treated us as a nation of shopkeepers. Now they want to tell us how to run the shop."

In quick order he told me a story that made the same point. In the early days of advertising, one of his peers had approached a large British agency house in Colombo in hopes of interesting management in advertising their sandalwood soap on the radio. He had been repeatedly turned away—never able to overcome resistance to advertising's crudeness and banality—until he decided to stop denying these qualities and exploit them. He strolled through the firm with a guitar in hand, singing and strumming a jingle he had composed about sandalwood soap. His singing got the attention of every clerk in the office. But it also attracted the concern of the British office manager, who rushed forward and informed him that he was intruding in a place of business, not a cabaret. "You've seen how effective my singing has been here," the prospective ad man responded, "imagine the impact on radio." The firm took him on, and, in this case, "capitalism's love song to itself" literally began with a song.

AGENCIES, MARKETS, AND HISTORY

The advertising profession proper had its origins in the 1950s at a time when the Commercial Service of the Ceylon Broadcasting Corporation had just begun selling air time for advertising. That historical coincidence suggests how capitalism and culture came to be organized in Sri Lankan public life in the face of new technologies and an insistent outside world. Commercial radio carried Western popular music and love songs from Indian movies, and advertising spots by Sri Lankan standards had a similar brashness. The first Director of the Commercial Service, Clifford Dodd, was a fast-talking Australian who made Radio Ceylon South Asia's most popular station, renowned across the subcontinent for its Saturday morning broadcasts of rock and roll music.

The dominant newspaper of the period objected to the impropriety of commercial advertising during radio programming, saying that the public was content with the National Service of the Ceylon Broadcasting Corporation, which carried no advertising. Because Sri Lanka inherited a huge broadcast tower left behind from Lord Mountbatten's stay on the island during World War II, the Commercial Service of Radio Ceylon not only advertised foreign things, it beamed its signal across South Asia.[6] The Indian government was itself offended, complaining that the CBC's commercial broadcasts, especially the Saturday rock and roll programming, diverted their own listeners from India's cultural and educational programs.[7]

By the very logic of broadcasting—a model taken from the British example—commercial radio developed apart from, and in opposition to, the National Service of the Ceylon Broadcasting Corporation. Both were government owned, and both were initially directed by foreigners— John Lampson was Director-General of the National Service from 1949 until 1952; Dodd was director of the Commercial Service from 1950 until 1960. Neither man, by all accounts, had much knowledge of, or interest in, Sri Lankan culture. But the two services developed in very different ways. One served commercial interests associated with the larger world; the National Service presented the sermons of Buddhist monks and the work of local singers and musicians, sometimes recently rescued from neglect. Inadvertently the British model of broadcasting reinscribed the distinction between capitalism and culture. On the one side, capitalism, foreign things, and advertising; on the other, local culture without commercial interruption.

When S. W. R. D. Bandaranaike came into office in 1956, ordinary Sri Lankans—teachers, farmers, small merchants, and Ayurvedic physicians—rushed into the life of the nation. Although born to the most well-placed family of the colonial elite and educated at Oxford, Bandaranaike made the Sinhala language, culture, and Buddhism political issues. The masses had been invited into history, but the invitation written in Sinhala characters. Although the state had provided a rice-ration before

Bandaranaike came to power, he and his wife—who followed him in office after his assassination—spent increasing amounts of money in support of rice and cloth rations, medical care, and education through the university level—laying the foundation for Sri Lanka's position today as a society with a high quality-of-life index, even while remaining one of the twenty poorest countries in the world.

Because of investments made in those years, the island's literacy rate nowadays has reached 90 percent, life expectancy is seventy years, and the number of infant deaths per thousand births is twenty-five. Those figures put Sri Lanka on a par with Malaysia and Chile, both countries with per capita GNP figures five times higher.[8] The growth of the private sector, by contrast, was stunted. State-run enterprises established monopoly control in industries that required substantial capital investment—cement, steel, auto and truck tires, plywood, sugar, paper, chemicals, fats and oils, ceramics, mineral sands, and leather. Trying to control prices, Mrs. Bandaranaike's government fixed a maximum price for some products. When companies such as Singer found they could not make a profit within those limits, they began to make a lower-quality sewing machine with parts imported from India. A book published by the Ceylon Chamber of Commerce to celebrate its 125th anniversary described the condition of private enterprise as "cabined, cribbed, and confined."[9]

Even before the draconian controls of the 1960s, the emphasis on rural Sinhalas, the growth of state enterprises, and creeping austerity made the Bandaranaike years an unlikely time for a transnational advertising firm to set up for business in Colombo.[10] In Colombo Grant Bozell found an advertising market without serious competition and a place with potential for economic growth. It also found a market where it had to invest only US $1,000 to set up shop. In quick order Grant's was joined by two other firms, Stonach and J. Walter Thompson. Although small, these firms created a new profession by their example. The local firms that followed their lead were often started by people who worked for these firms or had some such connection to them.

From the first, the situation was transnational and contradictory—the most heavily advertised products were manufactured in England, and the advertising techniques used to sell them came from America. Several of the retired executives I have gotten to know talk about their debt to Vance Packard's *The Hidden Persuaders* or *The Status Seekers*. Books that carried a cautionary message in the West became formulas for selling in Sri Lanka. The first generation of advertising executives read Packard for straightforward advice on writing compelling advertisements and exploiting social aspirations. At the same time, the political balance was tilting in the direction of rural Sinhalas, who tended to be big savers and small consumers.

Even after public culture shifted toward the countryside, the advertising business continued to aim most of its messages at the middle class, investing its resources in English-language print advertisements that could be read by the kind of Sri Lankans with income to spend on appliances, luxury goods, travel, and toiletries (see fig. 3).

In the years before there were advertising agencies as such doing

FIGURE 3. Imagined consumers for the Bridges de-luxe Neonic drill (*Community*, 1962, no. 4).

business in Sri Lanka, there was advertising in inchoate form. Some companies got their artwork done in India, and those advertisements were placed in local papers by local offices of global companies, such as Shell and Horlick's.[11] The British agency houses had small advertising staffs and placed print ads directly in local newspapers. When international agencies began to recruit people, they looked to the advertising and art departments of local newspapers and the advertising staffs of these agency houses. Reggie Candappa, who became manager of Grant Bozell, had worked previously as the director of the art department at the Lake House Group of Newspapers. Before he took a job with Candappa, Anandatissa de Alwis had also been employed at Lake House, where he worked on the editorial staff.

Besides this continuity, there was a technological reason for the advertising business to concentrate its energies on advertising in newspapers and journals. Television came only in 1978, and Sri Lanka lacked facilities to process and edit advertising films. As a result the few advertising films that were locally made had to be sent abroad to be set to a sound track and trimmed to size before they could be shown at a movie theater.[12] Waiting for the feature, moviegoers saw a series of advertising slides projected on the screen for thirty seconds. The first urged parents to ensure their children's health by serving them Bovril or Marmite [British sandwich spreads that have been sold in Sri Lanka since the early part of this century]. Thirty seconds later Bovril yielded to a slide praising the virtues of Kist brand Passion Fruit Cordial. Even on the silver screen, advertising had a textual quality.

Into the late 1970s print prospered by lack of competition. It still consumes over half of all advertising expenditures, with television taking 27 percent, radio 10 percent, and point of sale advertising 9 percent. The contrast with the United States, where television receives some 80 percent of advertising expenditures and newspapers get 3 to 4 percent, suggests the Sri Lankan emphasis on newsprint. Advertisements were not only textual, they were didactic and reading-intensive. Ovaltine and Horlick's entered the Sri Lankan market as gifts one carried to a hospital to help a relative recover his or her strength (see fig. 4). Convincing consumers that a mother should invest in a pricey dietary supplement required written instruction.

Advertisements had an innocent and straightforward quality. For several decades Elephant House used the same slogan for its soft-drinks— "So much more in every bottle"—meant to remind consumers of a literal truth: Coca-Cola was sold in 300 milliliter bottles; Elephant House products, in 400 milliliter ones. In those days, Coke was the paradigm of a

FIGURE 4.   A text-heavy pitch for Ovaltine as nutritional supplement and "value
for money" (*Ceylon Daily News, Vesak* Annual, April 1955).

foreign product. "Coke you can place in a rushing brook," the director of
a photographic studio once told me, "but you cannot do that with Portello
or Orange Barley. It will not work." Local soft drinks, by her account,
could not sustain the unlikely background. They look preposterous bathed
in running water. Better to sell local soft drinks by celebrating their economy or their healthfulness. Advertisements for foreign products sought to
evoke elegance, and sophistication, and sometimes just their difference.

    Before J. R. Jayewardene's election in 1977, the most striking
quality about advertising was its noneconomic character. Advertising was

not consumer driven. Companies advertised because it had become the thing to do, and it made the company visible even if it did not increase sales. One local brewery advertised its products despite the fact that the firm was already producing as much beer and ale as it could. It wanted only to improve its reputation. If European faces showed up in print ads for Sri Lankan firms, those faces suggested sophistication, which in turn, the reasoning went, would have the same benefit for the company—improving its reputation. When Sri Lankan faces appeared in advertisements, they often got there by way of personal connections. Executives asked friends to model.

Reducing tariffs on imports, privatizing government enterprises, encouraging foreign investments, cutting back government programs, and bringing a huge hydroelectric and irrigation project to completion in seven years rather than fifteen, Jayewardene tried to do everything in a hurry. The advertising business began to grow by some 20 percent a year. Firms began to hire a few Sinhala copywriters, and some began to emphasize their ability to construct advertising in the so-called "local idiom." The largest accounts, most global accounts, and the largest fraction of the business all told continued to be directed at English-language advertising. But advertising executives began to think of those advertisements too as being written in the local idiom—written in such a way that they made consumption plausible to rural consumers as well as urban, the young women who nowadays have income because of their work in free-trade zones, and students who read English although it had not been their first language.

Just as establishing transnational agencies during the Bandaranaike years ran against the grain, the explosion of advertising during Jayewardene's administration had its contradictory moments. Ethnic violence against Tamils became more and more of an issue, culminating in the pogroms of July and August 1983. For the advertising industry, ethnic conflict had economic implications, but few strategic ones. Having never addressed much attention to Tamil consumers (beyond a small number of advertisements written for Tamil publications) before 1983, agencies had less reason to do so after the Tamil market became that much smaller. Advertising agencies simply adjusted to the fact that Jaffna was increasingly not part of the national economy.

In 1987 the chief executive of J. Walter Thompson addressed the Sri Lanka Institute of Marketing on advertising in a crisis situation. Suggesting ways that marketers could cope with the consequences of civil war in the north and east—the downturn in the economy caused by a swelling military budget, the collapse of the tourist trade, and lack of confidence in the future—she stressed the relationship between marketers and advertising agencies, largely ignoring Sri Lankan consumers. Don't panic, know your product and your consumer, never forget that your brands are your major assets, exploit hard times don't deny them, avoid an automatic price reduction, find your market and advertise to it, and treat your advertising agency as a true partner, not as a supplier.[13]

Where the colonial port city had been the zone of interaction between the outside world and Sri Lanka for five hundred years, the open economy linked up the global system of economy and culture with the Sri Lankan countryside in a much more direct way. Trade and television still radiated out from Colombo, but suddenly televisions appeared in village homes and new commodities in provincial shops. A free-trade zone put young Sri Lankan women in garment factories run by East Asian entrepreneurs, and those women went back to their villages and towns with money in hand and an evolving sense of themselves as women and workers.[14] Even more portentously, Jayewardene accepted a gift of television transmission facilities from the Japanese government. During his time in office in the late 1960s Dudley Senanayake had turned down an offer from West Germany for black and white broadcast facilities. When Jayewardene accepted the Japanese offer ten years later, television broadcasting arrived in a sophisticated form.[15] Sri Lankans would be able to watch both Western and local programming, and the Japanese would be able to sell television sets.

So would the new East Asian owners of the Singer corporation. What historically had made Singer a profitable global business was its efficient network of shops spread across the countryside. In Sri Lanka, it used that network to act on the knowledge that remittances from Sri Lankan housemaids and chauffeurs in the Persian Gulf and wages earned by free trade zone workers had put unprecedented amounts of wealth in villages and towns. Remitted income was not only disposable, it was disposable by a spouse left with great independence. A family could buy a sewing machine from a nearby shop (and get it serviced there), and they could do so in provincial towns, not just major cities. They could buy a television, videocassette player, or refrigerator outright, or they could use Singer's installment facilities. Meantime, Singer began to sponsor the world's most widely viewed program of the time, *Dynasty*. First arrange for the easy credit encouraged by the open economy, buy a television set, and then watch a glamorously costumed melodrama such as few Sri Lankans had ever seen. Individualism and its cinematic representation, in other words, arrived hand in hand.

For advertising agencies, the problem was learning how to advertise products and services to large numbers of Sri Lankans in smaller cities and villages while holding onto an established market of middle-class consumers. Ask an advertising executive about those circumstances, and he starts out speaking of the local idiom. But soon he moves on to the Sinhala idiom. Among the one hundred agencies that now do business in Colombo, only one, Vashicara, specializes in Tamil-language advertisements. At other agencies, when an English-language advertisement is translated into Tamil, the translation is done by a Tamil copywriter—once described to me as a Tamil "scholar," suggesting just how arcane the task was understood to be—who travels between agencies and does translations on the spot. There are advertisements in Tamil publications aimed specifically at Tamils, but no one in my experience refers to a "Tamil idiom" as a parallel expression for protecting local proprieties.

When radio broadcasting came to Sri Lanka, no code for conduct was established, because broadcasters were assumed to know the limits of good taste. But television was different. The medium itself seemed to invite advertising that put men and women together in casual, if not threatening, contexts, exploiting the cuteness of children, and ignoring local decencies. Instead of worrying about the growing alienation of Sinhalas and Tamils, executives worried about giving offense. But they also began to develop a sense of themselves as independent actors, willing to stand up to clients when they proposed advertising that stepped over the limits of good taste. No longer simply "agents," they began to think of themselves as consultants—on matters of business strategy as well as standards of good taste. The director of one Colombo agency has a framed drawing of a human backbone on the wall of his office. The caption reads: "Backbone—you cannot run an agency without it." [16]

As the number of agencies and the volume of annual billings skyrocketed across South Asia, advertising began to advertise itself, celebrating the profession and announcing the need for talented people.[17] Other agencies wrangled "gray" advertising from local newspapers, recounting their activities in promotional articles. They spoke of advertising as part of a sentimental education for consumers being brought into the national economy: "This meta-education . . . serves multiple functions, but the main one is to identify the interests of the advertising industry, and the media generally, with that of the people and the nation. In the most brilliant of these ads, private, consumer concerns are effectively linked to the rhetoric of freedom and democracy, with the advertising industry seen as the broker of this auspicious union." [18]

The rhetoric of freedom and democracy has been made stronger by reference to economic development, drawing another parallel between nation and consumer. The advertising business, by its own account, mediates the relationship—invoking the nation as the object of loyalty and telling consumers that their own prospects are tied to the state's development.

> One of the most significant indicators of a country's economic activity and progress is afforded by the state of its advertising industry. . . . The consumer also is made a participant of this prosperity. . . . This may be called a "virtuous spiral." Advertising performs a dynamic role for the strengthening of industry and the educative aspect of advertising assumes a wider perspective than the mere advocacy of the virtues of a particular product when it introduces among the ideas publicized the aim as well to spread knowledge and understanding among readers of matters of tremendous importance to the national and even international welfare, like the conservation of natural resources and protection of the environment from pollution.[19]

The individual's economic prospects are joined to the nation's, the writer insisted, and government must look after both. It would do so by paying more attention to children, the living figure of personal development and the future beneficiaries of national development, once achieved. These tropes represent advertising rhetoric in full spate—freedom, economic development, and the future, embodied in the person of the child.

In a 1980 meeting, the leading advertising firms established a professional organization, the Association of Accredited Advertising Agencies, and used that body to prepare a code of ethics in advertising.[20] The idea of an advertising code has transnational origins, and the Sri Lankan code closely resembles standards put into place earlier in other Asian societies. Drawing up a code of ethics derived from people's growing awareness that advertising was a profession. But it also responded to advertising people's sense that advertising, especially television advertising, was reaching people beyond the capital city: "advertisements should not contain statements or visual presentations offensive to the standards of decency prevailing among those who are likely to be exposed to them. . . . Advertisements should not be framed as to abuse the trust of the consumer or exploit his lack of experience or knowledge."[21]

The code also urged that advertisements should not play on fear, exploit superstitions, or condone acts of violence or illegal activities. Nor should they mislead customers about a product or service, misuse research results, exploit statistics or scientific language, or confuse the distinction between editorial material and advertising. Comparative advertising was acceptable only when done fairly, and packaging that resembled that of another manufacturer was forbidden. Finally, advertising agencies were urged not to address or portray young people in ways that might harm them.

This regard for children was more fully expressed in the industry's involvement in public service advertising that directs its attention to women and children. These advertisements gave the advertising industry another way to align itself with the interests of the nation. Sometimes the projects were sponsored by international agencies and sometimes by the national government. In both forms, public service advertisements typically speak to women about their children. One childhood disease project sponsored by UNESCO featured Neela Wickramasinghe, a well-known playback singer who contracted polio as an infant before a vaccine was available. The Sinhala advertisement reads, "Mother, it is the same devil who brought tears to her eyes [Neela, shown crying] who would make your child a victim if you happen to delay even a moment. He would make your child a cripple *(angavikalā)*. If your child is to be saved from this dreadful disease, go to the nearest Government Children's Clinic to receive free polio injections." [22]

The agency that advertised the childhood immunization campaign—Grant Bozell—won a regional prize for it, the Max Lewis Memorial Award at the Fifteenth Asian Advertising Congress in Bangkok. Another Sri Lankan agency, Phoenix, had won an earlier award for its campaign for the Ministry of Plan Implementation on the recovery of agricultural credit. Working with transnational organizations, nongovernmental organizations, and ministries, agencies found a source of business that tied the profession to the national project. At the same time, membership in the Asian Federation of Advertising Association gave the business a status commensurate with their colleagues in the more developed economies of Asia. To this extent, Sri Lanka gained a measure of recognition among other Asian advertising executives in ways consistent with the character of the national economy—a poor country with remarkably high standards for literacy, infant mortality, and life expectancy. Sri Lankan agencies distinguished themselves, in other words, for their ability to construct skillful advertisements in the public interest, not for a particular commodity.

The Bangkok meeting provided an occasion to screen a video presentation of Colombo's best work, "A Heritage in Communication." [23] The video began with a Kandyan drummer blowing a conch, a call to worship sometimes heard at temples, then asserting that modern advertising has emerged seamlessly from a tradition of communication in Sri Lankan society. A map metonymizes the island's 2,500-year history in one image, before a group of Buddhist monks are heard reciting the *Tun Sarana* (Triple Gem, the invocation of values to which Buddhist laypeople commit themselves) just as the voiceover says

> "Buddhism plays an important role in the culture of Sri Lanka. Agriculture is the way of life. Traditionally it has been an agricultural nation, and even today this is the main means of livelihood for 74 percent of the people. The sea that surrounds the verdant island offers livelihood to coastal dwellers [in quick order the viewer sees a fish vendor, children taking a sea bath, a man water skiing, and a couple dining in a beachfront restaurant]. The people of Sri Lanka are charming, friendly, and young, nearly half of them are under nineteen years. . . . The majority, about 74 percent, are Sinhalese Buddhists, about 18 percent are Tamil Hindus, living mostly in the north and east, and among the other people are the Moors, the descendants of Arab traders, the Burghers, who are the descendants of European colonists, and the Malays, each with their own distinctive cultural differences. . . . The rate of growth has risen rapidly in recent years due to liberalized economic policies, creating a rush of consumer products. . . . Colombo . . . is a bustling city. Supermarkets are springing up everywhere, stacked with every conceivable commodity, while a brisk business goes on in open-air markets. How does the businessman in Sri Lanka reach a market made up of such differing rural, urban, and ethnic lifestyles? In olden days Sri Lankan monarchs sent out men with drums to convey their message to the nation. Surprisingly these old traditions still continue.[24]

As the scene dissolves from the round leather head of a *bera* drum to the molded plastic of a radio speaker, the viewer hears the rapid beat of a drum and "This is the Sri Lanka Broadcasting Corporation," read by the announcer who daily delivers that tagline at the start of broadcasting. Those elisions—from imposing the "nation-form" on the ways Sri Lankans traditionally made a living, to fishermen hawking fish alongside middle-class people vacationing on the beach, and on to traditional means of proclamation and their modern-day appropriation by radio—build a context in which advertising is both a part of the past and an essential service in a society with "such differing rural, urban and ethnic lifestyles."

Linking advertising to the past, to culture, to the future, and to the nation-state itself has motivations that figure in many markets—doing so naturalizes a practice that is alien, invasive, seductive, and often criticized as dangerous. In the Sri Lankan case, it makes doubly good sense because the advertising business hit some very low points in the early 1970s. The business's entanglement with capitalism, the larger world, and consumerism made it intrinsically suspect in some quarters of Sri Lankan society. But two incidents left the impression that advertising was guilty of a worse kind of complicity. In 1971 one of the first agencies with global connections, International Advertising Services, went bankrupt. Its collapse left newspapers and national radio carrying some three million rupees of the agency's debt, the backwash of an industry that had grown in the 1960s before financial circumstances—brought on by foreign exchange troubles, the cancellation of import quotas, the shift of emphasis from private enterprise to state corporations, and price controls—created cash flow problems for a large number of agencies.

Something more scandalous happened that same year. When Anandatissa de Alwis left J. Walter Thompson in 1966 to become Permanent Secretary to the Minister of State, he was replaced by William Thompson, an American sent out from New York to manage the Colombo agency. During the election campaign of 1970, the official newspaper of the Sri Lanka Freedom Party, *Sirilaka,* accused Thompson of being a CIA agent. He sued the editor, but withdrew the case after Mrs. Bandaranaike took office, and things returned to normal until late in 1970. Without explanation, Thompson decamped for Bangkok, handing over the keys to his bungalow and car to his household staff and leaving without explanation.[25] Whatever conclusions Sri Lankans drew about Thompson's guilt, the profession did not profit from the incident. Against this background, Jayewardene's election gave the industry two opportunities—one, to take advantage of the accelerated economic activity that came with Jayewardene's open economy and, two, to rehabilitate itself as a legitimate business with no antinational connections.

ARTICULATIONS

In 1997 there were some one hundred advertising firms doing business in Colombo, a number that has risen from eighty in 1993. All are located in Colombo, and range from six transnational agencies to firms that handle a single client or occupy some small place in the market such as handbill advertising. The largest firms employ upward of 120 people; the smaller ones consist of one or two persons. A few of the firms are long-lived, but many are less than a decade old. Of the one hundred firms, six are affiliated with transnational agencies—McCann-Erickson (American), J. Walter

Thompson (American), Lintas (British), Bozell (American), Bates (American), and Ogilvy and Mather (British-American). Each of these agencies has had a changeful relationship to the outside world. The local partners who are now principals at McCann-Erickson were until recently affiliated with Grant Bozell, although in the mid-1970s they entered into affiliation with another transnational agency, Kenyon and Eckhardt. The firm now has a nonequity relationship with McCann, keeping the Grant name first on the firm's new nameplate—Grant McCann-Erickson. Depleted of staff, the Bozell office has been rebuilt by the firm's office in New York.

Because of its political problems, J. Walter Thompson has shifted its affiliation between the transnational firm and Hindustan Thompson in Bombay; Lintas entered the market only in 1994, striking a partnership with executives who had worked previously at J. Walter Thompson and Unilever; and Phoenix recently established a nonequity affiliation with Ogilvy and Mather. In the 1970s and 1980s Phoenix was the local firm that made the most of its ability to speak "the local idiom." It now does so in league with a transnational British-American agency. There are three more recently arrived global firms. Bates has entered a partnership with a local agency, Strategic Alliance. Gray has brought an Indian staff to Colombo to place ads in various print sources, and the Indian firm Mudra has affiliated itself with a local firm, Masters.

These firms control well over 70 percent of the advertising market.[26] They bring an array of global accounts into the market. McCann-Erickson represents Agfa, Cathay Pacific, Coca-Cola, Nestlé, Perfetti, Recket and Colman, Unilever, UPS, and the World Gold Council. J. Walter Thompson represents Kodak, Ford, Kellogg, Kraft Foods, Motorola, Nestlé, Pepsi, Philips NV, Unilever, and Warner Lambert. Lintas represents some of Unilever's accounts, which is to say that one transnational firm employs three local agencies. One represents Unilever's soap products, another its foodstuffs, and so on. Phoenix represents B.A.T., Eveready, and Goodman Fielder.[27] Gray has one major client, John Player. When global flows of commodities reach Sri Lankan homes, these are the firms that reconfigure them for local consumption.

J. Walter Thompson represents Kraft foods in Sri Lanka, and their relationship exemplifies the relationship between a global producer and a global agency working in Sri Lanka. Kraft's main product is cheese, not a product one associates with South Asia, but middle-class Sri Lankans acquired a taste for cheese long ago and serve it to children and guests. Kraft cheese is sold in slices as a niche product (because it is quite expensive) and in block form (in the blue box that used to be seen all over Asia). In dealing with their agency in Colombo, Kraft is insistent on how they want their cheese represented, which comes down to two variables—product values or attributes and technical values, which is to say the high quality of the advertisement itself. For cheese, the product attributes are health and love. When their advertisements are seen in Australia, the mother says, "When I look into those blue eyes, how could I give him anything less than Kraft?" Elsewhere in Asia, "brown eyes" replaces blue; in Sri Lanka, "beautiful eyes" evokes the same sentiment. For such a client, the agency does not have to do much but make local changes and maintain quality.

In the early 1990s the product categories that received the largest amounts of advertising expenditures were lotteries, banks, and insurance (all three of which are markets dominated by government enterprises), followed by housing, powdered milk, confectioneries, soft drinks, agricultural chemicals, analgesics, and food products.[28] Automobiles, cosmetics, and beer hardly figure in the advertising market, which concentrates instead on products within the reach of most Sri Lankans. In the middle of a half-hour program, prime-time television viewers get up to ten minutes of commercials. If each runs for thirty seconds, viewers can be exposed to commodities that range from Ceylinco Insurance, Keel's sausages, Nespray dried milk, Atlas Professional Pens, Edna Chocolates, Supremo razor blades, Vick's Cough Drops, Dulux paint, and Coca-Cola to Sunlight soap. For the few who can afford them, cellular phones offer the imaginative possibilities made possible by leaping beyond the Sri Lankan telephone system. For most Sri Lankans, cellular phones are simply beyond imagination.

Because transnational firms have a reputation for market research and high-quality advertisements, they usually win the most profitable local accounts. Many global accounts enter the local market without competition. They are tied to a certain transnational agency. By this logic Phoenix, for instance, represents Eveready in Sri Lanka because Ogilvy and Mather—with whom Phoenix now has a partnership—represents the brand elsewhere. In the same way, McCann-Erickson represents Coca-Cola and J. Walter Thompson, Pepsi Cola. In advertising parlance, they are "clubbed up." The rest of the market is shared by ten or so medium-sized firms and some eighty smaller ones. Competition has caused different agencies to radiate into different parts of the market. Phoenix has a majority share of lottery advertisements, besides doing the advertising for the United National Party in recent elections.

When accounts are not tied to transnational agencies, they attract the attention of various agencies that want to represent the product. Senior executives of an agency pitch an account by selling themselves to clients and drawing on their social connections. One of the defining features of a developing market, I think, is that executives spend a disproportionate amount of time keeping clients happy. Agencies make an annual proposal to their clients at a five-star hotel, showing them "where they want to take the product" over the next year. In the year that follows, they meet with clients on a frequent basis. In hiring new employees, agencies are interested in personable people who can provide client service much more than people with creative imaginations.

Agencies also compete by claiming to offer distinctive service. Before it went out of business, Zenith stressed its desire to cooperate with clients, working with them as partners both in advertising their products and services and in other ways. Because it was a small agency, it did not do its own market research, but it tried to operate as a partner with its clients, "hiring the services of consultant market experts and commissioning market research."[29] Impact House of Advertising stresses its point-of-sale competence by citing an example meant to be taken literally and metaphorically. The firm's chief executive worked for Unilever in the past, stacking Sunlight soap in food shops all across the island. The agency can rightly claim that it understands market conditions from its director's own experience.[30]

The advertising profession's annual ceremony honors the most creative advertising work done in the previous year. The group has gathered at the Oberoi hotel, eaten dinner together, and everyone has turned their attention to the dais, where awards are being announced. There is exuberant cheering among the staffs of Grant Bozell and J. Walter Thompson. A wave of sound spreads out from one set of tables, followed by a wave from elsewhere in the ballroom. The Grant people yell, "We've got the best," and the Thompson people respond, "We've got the most," referring to the gold, silver, and bronze *ola* awards (prizes named for the palm leaves that Sri Lankans once used for preserving Buddhist texts and medical traditions) given in recognition of the best advertising campaigns. The Thompson side went on to win twenty-five, and Grant Bozell, sixteen. An executive looks across the ballroom and says, "For a moment I thought I was at the Royal-Thomian [Colombo's two elite secondary schools] cricket match."[31] His comment referred to the cheering, but it might as well have characterized the crowd itself. They are people who attended the best private schools on the island and who played cricket or watched it, and they are the kind of Sri Lankans who cheer at public ceremonies and make raucous fun of their own enthusiasm.

As early as the 1950s there were cries for advertisers to employ local advertising talent, and the people who have come to occupy senior positions in Colombo firms have been to an overwhelming degree local people, not expatriates.[32] But they have come from a narrow range of Sri Lanka's society—the Colombo middle class—and like the advertising business in India, they are English speakers. When Anandatissa de Alwis gave talks about advertising, he quoted Western popular thinkers of an earlier generation—Vance Packard and Rudolph Flesch, who wrote *Why Johnny Can't Read.* He made references to Aldous Huxley, Ernest Hemingway, Voltaire, and Franklin Roosevelt.[33] His peers in the business have traveled in Asia and Europe. Many have children living in the West or doing university degrees there. Some have green cards, allowing them to reside in the United States.

Looked at more closely, the narrow origins of advertising executives are often even narrower. A number of executives have entered the business because they had a close relative already working in an advertising firm—the president of de Alwis Advertising today is Anandatissa de Alwis's nephew; Neela Marikkar runs the agency her father Reggie Candappa started. For outsiders who aspire to executive positions, the virtues necessary for entering the business turn on the ability to speak English and handle clients. Clients by and large speak English and they give their advertising business to agencies run by people who also speak English. The capacity for handling clients is directly related. However important its product, this is a service industry. A woman who runs a Colombo agency indicated that the two qualities she looks for in hiring new people are patience and politeness.

What appears to have little to no influence in determining who is recruited into the business is the kind of street smarts that characterize advertising in Western countries and Japan.[34] Male executives in Colombo do not sport ponytails or earrings; they do not wear exuberant ties, suspenders, or tee shirts under sport jackets. What men sport are white shirts and conservative neckties. Male and female employees alike dress in a restrained way, although some agencies are more casual about how employees come to work than others, and creative people dress more informally than executives. When I asked an executive whether he considered a job candidate's knowledge of Sri Lankan popular culture a virtue, he said that a new employee can learn everything he or she needs to know about popular culture on the job. The most important quality is the capacity to serve clients, and to that end, dressing properly, speaking English, and being personable are critical, not knowledge of youth culture or the world beyond Sri Lanka and not high imagination.

There are a number of creative people in the advertising business who have reputations for producing striking advertisements. In a few cases, they produce work that is distinctive enough to be recognizable as that person's work. But their work is recognizable to knowledgeable people in the advertising business, not the public. A few advertising executives have reputations of an order sufficient to make them known beyond the advertising industry. One of the founders of the advertising business, Anandatissa de Alwis, served as J. R. Jayewardene's Minister of State, giving him an international reputation.[35] But there are no media figures such as the star copywriters (Japanese, *kopii raitaa*) who win public acclaim in Japan for their ability to write advertisements elegant in their sparse use of language, their ability to capture Zen qualities in a thirty-second commercial.[36] In a business that increasingly trades on its visuality, the people who create advertising in Sri Lanka are themselves invisible.

Growing at 15 to 20 percent a year, the advertising market has expanded so fast in the last two decades that employment prospects for newcomers are very good. A university degree is an advantage for someone with hopes of rising to an executive position, but having a degree is far less important than good English and social skills. A creative director with the ability to use computer graphics really stands out. Chances for promotion are also good, and talented people frequently get hired away from their agency to work for another agency or a client. Some of the people who are in the greatest demand—account managers and creative directors—have held five jobs in the space of a decade.

This is a small world—there are probably less than two thousand people who make a living in the business—and the people who have reputations have leverage and mobility. The creative director of a global agency once told me about the way he had reconstructed the advertising for a particular painkiller. As the conversation progressed, he revealed that he had also done the advertising for the brand he was now working against, as well as a third, less-popular painkiller. In other words, one creative person produced—not at the same time, but over a period of several years—advertising for the three largest analgesics on the local market.

Compensation levels for the middle 1990s suggest the range of salaries in the business. Graphic artists earned Rs. 3,000 to 10,000 a month (Rs. 50 or so = US $1.00); a middle level executive, Rs. 10,000; copywriters, Rs. 12,000; and top executives, Rs. 40,000. The disparity between the artists who produce the color drawings and the executives is striking, and the same is true of the disparity between technical people who make television advertisements and executives. Accredited agencies also draw a 15 percent commission from newspapers, magazines, radio, and television billings. The principals in a firm share in the net profits of the agency that derive from commissions and advertising fees, which is to say that they have an additional source of remuneration. It can be very handsome. The US $60 a month that a beginning graphic artist earns means that he or she commutes to work by bus, while the executive travels in his or her own car.

Workers are distinguished from managers by social distance as well as income. As a group, executives are the descendants of that class of middlemen who made a living in the colonial capital when the British and their interests ruled the island. Of the several hundred executives who manage advertising firms, Burghers and Catholics are overrepresented. A tally of the people who managed Colombo's agencies in the late 1950s— Gerry and Herbert Jayasinghe, Associated Advertising Services; Tim Horshington, International Advertising Services; Anandatissa de Alwis, J. Walter Thompson; Reggie Candappa, Grant Advertising; Cyril Massillamany, Masters; Oliver Perera, Metropolitan; Kingsley Wickremeratne, Wicks; and R. Bulner, Group Publicity—suggests that pattern began at the beginning of the profession.[37] Nowadays women manage a number of agencies.

My comments about the disproportionate number of Burghers and Catholics notwithstanding, ethnicity is less important than it might be. First and foremost, advertising executives are Westernized Sri Lankans. They live in and around Colombo, where all agencies are located, and if intermarriage is any indication, advertising executives find religion and ethnicity less important than most Sri Lankans. To this extent, the social composition of the advertising business resembles the social world Michael Ondaatje evokes far more than that of the people who read and view advertisements. Despite his attention to a small, generally prosperous Burgher minority who traced their descent to Dutch colonists, the world of Ondaatje's ancestors was peopled by Sri Lankans who were the children of intermarriages among Sinhalas, Tamils, Burghers, Dutch, and British. Ondaatje's father identified himself as Tamil. Asked by the British Governor about his ethnic identity, one of his parents' friends threw up his hands and said, "God only knows, your excellency."[38]

From the point of view of graphic artists, what distinguishes executives from themselves is language. Other differences—place of residence, taste, material advantages—are important, but language is decisive. Executives wield a *kaduwa* (sword). That sword is the ability to speak English, the instrument that kept the majority of Sri Lankans at a disadvantage from the early nineteenth-century until Bandaranaike's election in 1956. English is now taught in a wider variety of schools, and the government makes an effort to reach out to Sri Lankans whose families have not traditionally been English speakers. But speaking English is still the instrument that allows one to cut through life's difficulties, to find a well-paying job, to get on with life—and only a small fraction of Sri Lankans have it. To this extent, the organization of the advertising agency replicates the pattern of Sri Lankan society—a small elite of English speakers dominates an enormous majority of people who speak the two local languages.

AGENCIES AS SITES OF PRODUCTION

The front door of the J. Walter Thompson office in Colombo is approached by way of a portico edged by a reflecting pool where turtles and tropical plants hold forth. The reception area is done up with elegantly-carved Indo-Portuguese furniture of the kind that often finds in well-to-do homes. Brassware, Dumbara pillows, and large lithographs of colonial figures—the Colombo Chetty with upstanding collar and giant earrings, the Kandyan chief, the Buddhist monk with talipot fan—further domesticate the feel of the place. The largest, most professional, and most global of Colombo's transnational agencies has the most local feel; it has been artfully organized for just that effect. But generally, advertising offices are functional spaces. They do not sell themselves by way of architecture or ambience. Sitting in the air-conditioned offices of an agency in Colombo, one could just as well be sitting in an advertising office in Rio de Janeiro or Seoul. Men and women mix freely in a way that is quite unlike most other Sri Lankan contexts. One midsize agency has produced four marriages in recent years.

Colombo agencies emphasize the creativity of their creative director, and that makes such people the hottest commodity in the advertising business. The most successful agencies tend to be run by men and women who started out as creative directors and who continue to exert control over the creative work of the office. Many of the long-lived agencies, large and small, are firms that have had a former creative director at the helm over most of the lifespan of the business. As the Chief Executive Officer of the firm, their presence guarantees the quality of the work. They may spend most of their time interacting with clients and soliciting new business, but the assumption is that their being in charge means that individual accounts will receive the same high quality creative input as when the CEO was doing creative work full time.

Such is the case at Phoenix, where Irwin Weerackody insists that his creative director and account managers know what he wants done with the brands they represent. They learn his style, and when an advertisement appears that violates that style, he lets the employee know of his discomfort. Weerackody makes the same point in another way, speaking of his serving as the creative director of his agency for the last twenty years, even though other employees have carried that job description over that period. What a client receives by hiring a transnational agency is a creative director known for doing interesting work. The cost is high and the service uncertain. What a client, typically a local client, gets by hiring a local agency is lower overhead and solicitous service.

In many cases the advertising that a local client requires is largely informational—he wants an advertisement saying that his new hydraulic pumps have arrived and are on offer from Thursday. That kind of work hardly requires a creative director, and in midsize and smaller firms, creativity has less of a place than trust and attention. Smaller firms offer much more of a partnership with their clients, sometimes doing "ghost" shopping and informal market research. A client calls his agency to complain about the advertising. He is not selling any of the ceramicware he has put on the market. "It must be something wrong with the ads because I have offered a twenty-five year warranty!" Without identifying himself, the account manager calls around and asks what other suppliers are offering, eventually discovering that ceramicware in Sri Lanka is routinely sold with a lifetime warranty.

Because of the heavily print-oriented character of the advertising business, many creative directors started off as journalists, and many of their inclinations continue to be literary in nature. They read novels as a pastime, some write them, and they see writing copy itself as a literary endeavor. But they are creative in ways that have little to do with literature. One is a jazz pianist who performs on the weekends in Colombo and occasionally in five-star hotels in the Persian Gulf. Another is a painter who has been working in oils for forty years. He recently had a retrospective exhibit of his works, which sell for enormous prices. A third is an amateur landscape architect and gardener who has designed his own compound around a waterfall and exotic species of flora and fauna, including parrots, Java swallows, and monkeys.

These avocational interests reflect the social distance that separates creative directors not only from the generality of Sri Lankans but even from most middle-class people. But the important point is not so much that the people who create advertisements are not representative of the people who consume them. That distance raises the prospect that advertisements justified in terms of their having been constructed in the local idiom are forms of cultural production. What creative directors do is less a reflection of local ways of thinking and being and more a simulacrum of it. But when I say simulacrum, I do not mean that culture produced by advertising practice is inauthentic. The same thing Michel Foucault says of the author—that he or she functions as "the principle of thrift in the proliferation of meaning"—could be said of the creative director, copywriters, and graphic artists who run an advertising agency.[39] The culture that advertising produces is new and motivated by commercial interests, but it follows as logically from cultural forms that precede it as any other cultural production.

I was talking to a voluble, warm, and enterprising creative director who had just started his own firm. Over a period of ten years or so, he had worked for eight different firms, including two intervals working for an agency in Oman. Now he was running his own firm out of his apartment, but doing well enough to expand into the second-floor apartment above him, attract a large number of accounts, and hire sixteen employees. Having won an award from the Sri Lanka Institute of Marketing for his creative work for his only client at the time, he then landed an account from a foreign producer of fertilizer and was skillfully trying to position the product. The price of fertilizer in Sri Lanka is fixed by what local manufacturers charge, which at that time was Rs. 150 a bag. His client was getting Rs. 5 more. "Why?" I asked. His reply: "They know that they can get it, and foreign products are better, no?"

Pradeep had won the account by telling the firm to leave the fertilizer out of the advertising altogether. Fertilizer is fertilizer, and, what's more, none of it is interesting. He urged putting the product in an environmental "zone of display." His Korean clients liked the environmental connection and suggested a tree-planting scheme to counter the implication that fertilizers might have damaging consequences for the environment. They even offered a jingle to be used in the advertising, "To grow our rice and feed our nation, let's plant a tree at every station." An upscale clothing redistributor, Odel, had been making an environmental pitch, and this fertilizer campaign would pick up on the growing fear that economic development was undermining the careful balance of Sri Lanka's ecology. Pradeep told me that Sri Lankans see building houses and fertilizing paddy fields as a serious threat. He intended to use Buddhism to call attention to the issue.

I asked him how he knew that would work. Did he run focus groups? Distribute questionnaires? He said that in Sri Lanka he did not have to do so. This is a small country. It costs the same amount of money to run an ad as to do a focus group. So a firm might as well run the advertisement. I asked the same question again. How can he be sure that anyone is listening? Print advertising is relatively inexpensive, but surely an advertiser would like to know whether it was likely to persuade anyone. He said two things in response. The first was that his advertisements had offered a free environmental decal to anyone who wrote for it, and he got lots of requests from Sinhalas. The second was that he knew what Buddhists are like, and they are born conservationists. For them, a message about conservation has religious significance. Knowing that Pradeep was Roman Catholic and Tamil, I kept wondering about how he could justify those assertions.

Buddhists believe in living in harmony with nature. They do not kill animals or eat meat, he said. They are minimalists who believe in balance. For them, there is no sin in suicide. If a person takes her own life, the only fault is that she takes bacteria with her. Since Buddhists believe in karma, suicide hurts no one but oneself. The individual is responsible to herself lifetime after lifetime. An advertisement about saving the environment is bound to hit home with such people. I was stunned by his misunderstanding of Buddhism, assuming that a sophisticated man would know better.[40] But the misreadings are instructive. The Buddhist tradition has not had any great interest in ecology, although for quite other reasons Sri Lankans have lived in harmonious ways with their environment. Sinhalas fish, and although the butchering of animals in Sri Lanka is not often done by Buddhists, in my experience the great majority of Buddhists eat some variety of meat, fish, or eggs. Moreover, Buddhist religious thinkers insist that suicide is wrong. If it is not a "sin," it is certainly an abhorrent act with serious moral consequences. And as for Buddhists being "minimalists," I see no evidence for that in the past or the present.

These ideas represent an outsider's picture of the religion, to be sure, but they also show unmistakable signs of New Age Buddhism, now adrift in the global cultural economy. A person as cosmopolitan as Pradeep knows about a local religion not by engaging it directly but through the worldwide circulation of ideas about Buddhism as a religion of vegetarianism, ecological concern, economic restraint, and personal balance. I have heard other creative directors say similar things about Sinhala Buddhists of earlier times living in spiritual harmony with their natural environment. But when they make the connection between Buddhism and the environment, they do not reflect what exists now or even what was present in the past and is now dissolute. They reproduce in commercial form a Buddhism that comes from E. F. Schumacher.[41] The potent connection is not putting fertilizer in a "zone of display" associated with the environment. It is putting Buddhism there. At some point in the future, Buddhists may well begin to see some connection between their religion and their environment, and advertising may have had some hand in drawing that connection for them.[42]

NOTES

1. Sources on this important element of the colonial economy include "Agents for Whom?" *Logos* 14, no. 3 (August 1975); S. B. D. de Silva, *The Political Economy of Underdevelopment* (London: Routledge and Kegan Paul, 1982); and Geoffrey Jones, *Merchants to Multinationals: British Trading Companies in the Nineteenth and Twentieth Centuries* (Oxford: Oxford University Press, 2000).

2. The relationship between these two parts of the economy in Sri Lanka has been thoroughly, if inconclusively debated. See Donald Snodgrass, *Ceylon: An Export Economy in Transition* (Homewood, Ill: Richard D. Irwin, 1966); S. B. D. de Silva, *Political Economy of Underdevelopment;* and Asoka Bandarage, *Colonialism in Sri Lanka: The Political Economy of the Kandyan Highlands, 1833–1886* (Berlin: Mouton, 1983).

3. H. N. S. Karunatilake, *Economic Development in Ceylon* (New York: Praeger, 1971), 36.

4. Anandatissa de Alwis, *Some Ideas on Communication: Speeches by the Hon. Dr. Anandatissa de Alwis,* ed. Tilak Ratnakara (Colombo: Department of Information, n.d.), 44. De Alwis's remarks were made in a speech to the Colombo Lions Club in 1983; his reference to the distinguished theoretician appears to refer to Mrs. Bandaranaike's administration in the early 1960s or 1970s.

5. Quoted by H. A. J. Hulugalle, *The Life and Times of D. R. Wijewardene* (Colombo: Lake House, 1960), 112.

6. Before the British went home at the end of the war, they offered those facilities to the newly independent country at concessionary rates. The Sri Lankans declined, correctly assuming that, failing to get a response to their bargain-basement offer, the British would be forced to simply abandon the broadcast tower.

7. Nandana Karunanayake, *Radio Broadcasting in Sri Lanka: Significant Dates and Events, 1921–1990,* 46. Sir Edmund Hillary listened to Radio Ceylon on his ascent of Mt. Everest.

8. United Nations Development Programme, *Human Development Report 1994,* 16.

9. Ceylon Chamber of Commerce, *The Story of Economic Development in Ceylon* (Colombo: Colombo Apothecaries' Co., 1964), 4.

10. A concise and convincing argument for the way elite interests and the state have favored the Sinhala peasantry can be found in Mick Moore, "The Ideological History of the Sri Lankan 'Peasantry,'" *Modern Asian Studies* 23, no. 1 (1989): 179–207.

11. Elmo Leonard, "Advertising Vital in a Free Economy," *Island* (Colombo), 17 April 1988.

12. Reva and Soma, "Why Ceylon Lags Far Behind in Film Advertising," *Times* (Colombo), 1 May 1969.

13. "How to Advertise in a Crisis Situation," *Daily News* (Colombo), 26 May 1987.

14. See Caitrin Lynch, "The 'Good Girls' of Sri Lankan Modernity: Moral Orders of Nationalism and Capitalism," *Identities* 6, no. 1 (1999): 55–89. An instructive parallel can be found in Aihwa Ong, *Spirits of Resistance and Capitalist Discipline: Factory Women in Malaysia* (Albany: SUNY Press, 1987).

15. I have been told on several occasions that Senanayake had his first encounter with television broadcasting while in Washington, D.C., recovering from surgery for stomach ailments. Having seen a steady flow of American television, he decided that Sri Lankans could survive without broadcasting.

16. I suspect that the avowed independence of Sri Lankan advertising agencies represents a local appropriation of a Western conceit, namely one deriving from Bill Bernbach's insistence from the late 1960s onward on artistic privilege and his willingness to "fire" clients who disagreed. See Thomas Frank, *The Conquest of Cool: Business Culture, Counterculture, and the Rise of Hip Consumerism* (Chicago: University of Chicago Press, 1997), 58–59.

17. "Going Our Way?" *Daily News* (Colombo), 8 February 1988. The advertisement's text explains exactly what the Phoenix agency was looking for:

    You are the type of young person who feels at ease in any company—you like people and people just naturally like you.

    You like to communicate, discuss and debate ideas logically and in their correct sequence.

    English is your forte and although you are not equally qualified in Sinhala, you enjoy speaking it.

    Maybe, you have collected a degree in Sociology, Mass Communication or Economics, down the line.

    Or you prefer to go on, in the university of experience, satisfied in the knowledge that you are learning as you go along.

    Above all, you are not—repeat, not—a clockwatcher. In which case, you are going our way, and can qualify for membership in our team.

    The work can be exacting, but if you are the right person, we make it more than worth your while.

    If you think you are the kind of person we want, apply within 7 days with copies of certificates and bio-data.

18. Arjun Appadurai and Carol A. Breckenridge, "Buying the Nation: Advertising and Heritage in Contemporary India," typescript, 4.

19. Lionel Daniels, "Advertising and Living Standards," *Daily News* (Colombo), 12 September 1986.

20. "Code of Ethics for Advertising," *Island* (Colombo), 8 August 1984.

21. "Ad Agencies Form Association," *Observer* (Colombo), 4 September 1980.

22. *Lankadipa* (Colombo), 28 October 1990.

23. "Sri Lanka Elected Countrymember at AdAsia Bangkok '86,'" *Daily News* (Colombo), 25 July 1986.

24. "A Heritage in Communication," video produced by Tele-Cine Limited for the Association of Accredited Advertising Agencies, Sri Lanka, 1984.

25. What made the incident more scurrilous to Sri Lankans was the departure to Bangkok several days earlier of a married woman who worked at J. Walter Thompson and who had been romantically linked to Thompson. "JWT—The Sword Hangs over Advertising," *Ceylon Observer* (Colombo), magazine edition, 2 February 1971.

26. Minoli de Soysa, "Sri Lanka Ad Firms Sell with a Rural-Urban Mix," Reuters World Service, 20 December 1994 (available from Lexis-Nexis).

27. "'AAI' Picks Next Major Marketers," *Advertising Age,* 18 September 1995, I33–I43. Grant Bozell has recently reestablished its office in Colombo. It handles Chrysler, Samsung, and Scott Paper.

28. "Asian Media Guide," *Advertising Age,* 8 November 1993.

29. "Zenith Advertising Celebrates 31st Anniversary," *Daily News* (Colombo), 18 December 1987. When the Kumaratunga government came to power, Zenith quickly went out of business.

30. "New Advertising Agency Firmly on Track," *Daily News* (Colombo), 13 March 1990.

31. Chitra Weerasinghe, "Lanka's Ad World Celebrates the Best and the Brightest," *Daily News* (Colombo), 2 August 1988. Royal College and St. Thomas are Colombo's premier secondary schools. Their names suggest their origins.

32. "Use Local Talent, Advertisers Urged," *Daily News* (Colombo), 22 February 1957. As against Southeast Asian cases, the small size of the market and the underdeveloped character of the retail business in Sri Lanka made hiring foreign talent unlikely.

33. *Anandatissa de Alwis, Some Ideas on Communication: Speeches by the Hon. Dr. Anandatissa de Alwis,* ed. Tilak Ratnakara (Colombo: Government Press, n.d.). De Alwis cites Franklin Roosevelt as a frustrated advertising man, quoting Roosevelt to this effect: "If I were starting life all over again, I am inclined to think that I would go into the advertising business in preference to any other" (4).

34. See Frank's discussion, *Conquest of Cool,* 35, 111–15.

35. As the Member of Parliament from Kotte and holder of several ministerial positions— Tourism and State—Anandatissa de Alwis became a public spokesman for Jayewardene's administration. See Anandatissa de Alwis, *Collected Speeches of Dr. Anandatissa de Alwis,* ed. Tilak Ratnakara (Colombo: Government Press, n.d.).

36. See Marilyn Ivy, "Critical Texts, Mass Artifacts: The Consumption of Knowledge in Postmodern Japan," *South Atlantic Quarterly* 87, no. 3 (Summer 1988): 431.

37. Percy Colombage, "25 Years of *Observer* Advertising," *Observer* (Colombo), *150 Years Supplement,* 3 February 1984, 41.

38. Michael Ondaatje, *Running in the Family,* 41. *Ontacci* is a Tamil title.

39. Michel Foucault, "What Is an Author?" in *The Foucault Reader,* ed. Paul Rabinow (New York: Pantheon Books, 1984), 118.

40. See Mary Evelyn Tucker and Duncan Ryuken Williams, *Buddhism and Ecology* (Cambridge, Mass.: Harvard University Press, 1997).

41. See, for example, *Small Is Beautiful: Economics As If People Mattered* (New York: Harper and Row, 1973), especially 50–58.

42. A parallel case in India is the melding of yogic traditions with German nature cures, transforming a South Asian practice fixed on the otherworld to one interested in physical fitness and treating bodily ailments.

CHAPTER FIVE

In the Local Idiom

Sri Lanka is an outlier in the global system of advertising and commerce, but it is not simply a node or a choke point in that system. When commodities and culture reach the island (or Mongolia or Tonga, for that matter) local purposes do not simply disappear because new possibilities have arrived. Some possibilities are absorbed without remainder, but many more are reinterpreted, misunderstood, resisted, innovated on, or otherwise fitted to the local scheme of things. As Burke shows in an African case, the people of Zimbabwe took Unilever products and used them in ways their makers could scarcely imagine.[1] They applied margarine to their bodies just as they had traditionally used butter for softening their skins. Starch marketed for pressing pants and shirts they ate. Local agency is not always dramatic, but it is always present, no matter how often forgotten by commentators worried about the prospect of a world of sameness.

The kind of agency that interests me here is the interpretations that advertising executives make whenever they construct advertising in the local idiom. This is a distinctive kind of agency—the agency's agency—not the consumer's innovation on a commodity's usual function, but the activity of a modern profession located in a colonial port city, working in collaboration with transnational corporations, government ministries, global institutions such as UNESCO, as well as local businesses and the people of the place. Approaching the advertising agency as an ethnographic site may seem unlikely, but the interstitial place of advertising agencies that makes them unlikely also reveals the coevality of subject and object, the global and the local, and structure and practice.[2]

The reinterpretation of a global campaign constitutes one example of advertising done in the local idiom, but there is a more local form of local idiom advertising, and it amounts to a much larger share of the total volume of business that advertising firms do. This kind of local idiom advertising appears in several contexts: when advertising agencies, both global and local, attempt to position local products (as in the case of locally made cream crackers competing against foreign brands), link up consumers in the countryside with those in the city (surely the default-value motivation of most marketing schemes), or domesticate a product that has a long entanglement with colonial power and practices (of which banking is the proximate example). All call on creative directors to find means to create a specifically local kind of subjectivity. The convention in Sri Lankan advertising discourse is that doing so requires mastering "the local idiom."

Local idiom advertising, especially in this second sense, carries two different but related senses. When people talk about the local idiom in a general way, they mean that set of local decencies which they attempt to observe when writing copy and constructing visuals. Sri Lankans are offended, the reasoning goes, when they see physical contact between men and women or children challenging their parents. Knowing the idiom avoids these mistakes. When creative directors talk about the local idiom in a more specific way, they have in mind advertisements that appeal to Sri Lankans as Sri Lankans, drawing on tropes that make claims on their national identity. Through a process that is circuitous and gradual, what advertising executives say about their society becomes generative knowledge, the production of a locality, and the process whereby Sri Lankans invent Sri Lanka.

COSMOPOLITAN KNOWLEDGE AND SRI LANKAN SOCIETY

On my definition, an ethnographic account that depends on a person's reflection on his or her own society represents a folk ethnography.[3] What follows is a folk ethnography in a stronger sense of the word—an account of how Sri Lankan society works constructed from the point of view of businesspeople who have a professional stake in that knowledge. Advertising executives are people who have not only earned their views, they have sold them. They make a living from selling their understanding of what

Sri Lankans are like, and they have ready opinions about the nature of Sri Lankan society, as ready-to-hand as a Buddhist monk's opinions about the way this life is linked to the next or a homemaker's views about which curries are best served together. Yet advertising people come by these views in distinctive ways. Their views derive from neither traditional institutional schooling (as in the example of Buddhist monks) nor less formal modes of learning (as in the homemaker's case).

Advertising people acquire some of their knowledge about Sri Lankan society from simply growing up in Sri Lanka, being formally educated, and having adult engagements that range from reading to conversation. But what is distinctive about those views is what they have learned from practicing their profession. They pursue a business that keeps them in the company of foreign clients and Westernized Sri Lankans, but their livelihood requires their speaking to and for the generality of Sri Lankans. Their position makes them cultural brokers as much as folk ethnographers, and because they receive regular feedback about their ability to recognize affinities between certain commodities and certain consumers, they are self-conscious about their role as modern day beachcombers.

What creative directors say about Sri Lanka often sounds a lot like what academics, journalists, bureaucrats, and many middle-class Sri Lankans say. When they assert that Sri Lankan society is made up of mainly Sinhalas and Tamils, that Sri Lankans are disproportionately young, and that the life expectancy of the island's peoples is now upward of seventy years, it is hard to disagree. These claims are neither counterintuitive nor obscure. It is also hard to take those assertions seriously as ethnographic knowledge. There is something equally suspect about such assertions posing as disciplinary or professional knowledge. Not being different from cosmopolitan understandings of the same issues, these claims to knowledge seem hardly worth talking about.

Until the 1980s ethnographic accounts have followed a distinctive trajectory. They explicated systems of categorization—cosmologies, social divisions, edible and proscribed foods—that run counter to academic understandings of those same phenomena. South Indian Smartha brahmins, let's say, believe that onions are sexually stimulating and never allow onions to enter their kitchens. Food scientists discount the idea that any foodstuff has such properties, but those Smartha ideas have value to the ethnographer because they are linked to a way of life organized around such concerns. That argument seems so harmless, so well-intentioned as to need no support, but it hides an assumption that is worth scrutinizing. A "way of life" by this approach gets defined by its difference. In Alfred Gell's nice phrase, anthropology has approached its subjects as if "sane but enchanted."[4] A society did not have a "way of life" unless its people were living their lives in a way different from life in the North Atlantic industrial states.

To this extent, otherness as such was the unspoken rationale for the ethnographic project. Critiques of these ethnographic conventions have pointed out the consequences of implicitly searching for difference— namely the tendency to exoticize, reify, and isolate its objects in time and space. Those critiques did not say anything about what was lost by not thinking about "ways of life" in a more generous way, but that orientation gave the ethnographic record an awkward asymmetry. People such as advertising executives who believe that Sri Lankans are disproportionately young certainly drop out of the ethnographic record because entertaining such a view hardly makes one "enchanted." And as more media and commodity flows enter lives lived in places such as Sri Lanka, it becomes increasingly difficult to resist popular cant about a world of sameness.

Newer conventions of ethnographic writing sidestep the perils of reification, exoticization, and decontextualization by making several moves. One is to insist that ethnographic knowledge is the product of a particular time and place, made possible by the way the ethnographer enters the scene. The extreme example is Kevin Dwyer's *Moroccan Dialogues,* which reproduces conversations between Dwyer and his one-time landlord, the Faqir, as they chatted through the summer of 1975.[5] A second strategy is to replace the dominant informant with a series of voices, however discordant, as Vincent Crapanzano does in *Waiting.*[6] A third is to dispense with the actor's perspective altogether, replacing it with a set of images, voices, or intensities none of which has any particular privilege and all of which lack any fixed order.[7] The postmodern turn in ethnographic writing has several virtues, but the one pertinent here is the concern to represent difference without rendering individual societies as windowless monads.

I have never been anything but an outsider in all of the times I have sat in advertising agencies, but I was less of an alien there than I have been when talking with astrologers or sitting in Buddhist monasteries and asking questions of monks. Watching graphic artists work, having a conversation with an executive, or making a telephone call, I could be mistaken for an employee or a client. Sometimes I was treated less indulgently than a client, quickly ushered from a busy office when a deadline was looming or a delegation of Japanese clients arriving. I always had trouble scheduling appointments to see people, because advertising executives are busy people. On the other hand, I have been asked whether I would be interested in a short-term job as an account manager and once became an

"American talent" by recording a radio commercial for a supermarket in Colombo.

All disclaimers made about the constructed nature of the knowledge that derives from ethnographic interviews, it would be disingenuous for me to say that working in advertising agencies entailed meanings that had to be meticulously negotiated, asymmetries of power managed, and the distance between self and other bridged in the same way as when I have done other fieldwork. All of those forces were present, to be sure, and I could cite examples of conversations that were undone by questions about good faith and confidentiality or shaped by my being who I am. But those forces were hardly central to the project. Relative to what got said and what did not, the power-laden, dialectical aspects of human interaction have counted less in this project than my membership in the cosmopolitan world I share with people in the advertising business.

I did not set off to do this project because of an interest in a particular kind of fieldwork, but I took what was given. How many ethnographers can get on their Netscape browser and fire off a question to an informant halfway around the world, get a response in short order, and rethink the project accordingly? The virtues of cyber-ethnography aside, sharing a common world reduces the enormous space—both geographical and phenomenological—between where I live and where I do anthropology.[8] When I talked with a creative director, he might tell me about his experiences trying to find a place to live with his growing family in Colombo, and I would tell him about how an American finances a home renovation. It is easy enough to treat what advertising executives say without exoticizing it, because most of their representations derive from the cosmopolitan world I inhabit as much as they do.

Ethnographers who have suggested the importance of treating ethnography as an occasion for producing a shared text that develops in conversation argue that it is by focusing on the dialogue between ethnographer and informant that they capture the play of discourse—namely the way talk produces moments in which one can see "the other as us."[9] Surely another way of coming to understand "the other as us" is to consider conversation in another sense, namely the conversation between cultures that proceeds quite apart from ethnographic encounters. Advertising is a highly imagined part of that conversation, an implacable force that the conventional wisdom assumes is turning others—people who live in non-Western places—into us—people who live in the North Atlantic nation-states. I obviously do not believe that such is the case, but submitting advertising to ethnographic scrutiny is one way to understand the intricate balance by which the other becomes more like us while keeping its distinctiveness, and sometimes finding new forms of it.

To borrow Clifford Geertz's language, "whatever use ethnographic texts will have in the future . . . will involve enabling conversations across societal lines—of ethnicity, religion, class, gender, language, race—that have grown progressively more nuanced, more immediate, and more irregular. The next necessary thing . . . is to enlarge the possibility of intelligible discourse between people quite different from one another in interest, outlook, wealth, and power, and yet contained in a world where tumbled as they are into endless connection, it is increasingly difficult to get out of each other's way."[10] To this extent, what follows is a kind of ethnography warranted less by epistemic currents in the anthropology profession than changes in a world where we can no longer "get out of each other's way." The trick is to recognize forces that link together lives the world over while insisting that otherness is less a matter of lives lived in isolation than making, scrutinizing, and contesting claims about identity and difference.

I will try to avoid reifying advertising executives' points of view, but I need to point out that all actors stand on a Möbius strip of interpretation. I can resist reifying what advertising people say generally by moving down to the testimony of individuals, there to treat what those individuals say as if an entity—stable over long periods of time and free of context. Doing so, I reify matters at a lower level. Of course those individuals themselves reify when they make generalizations about Sri Lankan society, speaking of it as if it were stable over long periods of time and free of context. To the extent that I have to fix what advertising executives say, I mark that shortcoming off to the perils of representation, assuming that I need to follow my informants' lead for two reasons. On the one hand, I want to be true to what they say, and on the other, I want to speak generally at some points, while sticking to cases at others.

TRADITIONAL AND CONSERVATIVE

Conceived of as a market, a society appears with certain attributes thrown into high relief. In the case of advertising executives talking about their market, the central assumption is that Sri Lankans are traditional and conservative. Constructing advertisements in the local idiom entails honoring those qualities. Their reading of Sri Lankan society sounds a good deal like what academics of an earlier time said about the place. But where anthropologists working on Sri Lanka concentrated on practices—caste, kinship, marriage rules, dietary categories, and temple organization—implicitly defined as traditional, these practices have little to do with what advertising executives mean by traditional or conservative. Speaking about Sri Lankan society relative to the interests of a transnational profession that wants to sell people a variety of modern goods and services, they begin by saying that Sri Lankans are slow to change and easily put off.

At bottom what they mean by these expressions is that Sri Lankans know what is proper behavior. A "traditional" society is a society that has clear ideas about how, let's say, a young woman ought to act—as opposed to a married woman—or, to choose a contrast at another level of abstraction, a Sri Lankan person ought to behave. A "traditional" society is also a "conservative" society because it wants to preserve those practices. It knows how to proceed into the future because it is clear about its past. Unlike the examples of Singapore, Malaysia, and Indonesia, neither the state nor the advertising profession has made an effort to portray Sri Lanka as a collectivity of ethnic communities or to invoke a rhetoric of unity in diversity. Sinhala culture—its past, its practices—is Sri Lankan culture, and Sinhala practices are the practices under conservation.

Even so, there are complications in portraying Sri Lankan tradition when it is reduced to Sinhala culture. One is the weight of four hundred years of colonial domination, crushing a great deal of what had been the local way of life before the arrival of the Portuguese and making easy markers of local identity hard to find. What counts these days for national dress for men—the white *kamisa* (the long cotton *kurta* of north India) and *sarama* (the sarong constructed from unsewn cloth)—was put to use in the 1930s and 1940s and is worn only by certain men and on certain occasions.[11] *Āriya sinhala* (Aryan Sinhala) or "national" dress has its uses for politicians. For advertising purposes, showing a man in national dress driving a new car makes him look more like a chauffeur than the car's happy owner.

A second problem is determining what parts of the Sinhala past qualify as tradition. Some practices are clearly unsuitable—the polyandry that was practiced in Kandyan society, the gritty exertions of women husking coconut fibers, and the hypermasculine life of fishermen. The best guide to what characterizes Sinhala tradition is the vision of tradition and the past that began with the late nineteenth- and early twentieth-century emergence of Protestant Buddhism, a Buddhism that the reformer Anagarika Dharmapala formulated and propagated. Dharmapala reacted to missionary Christianity by conceiving of Buddhism as a privatized and internalized religion.[12] He "protestantized" the Buddhism of his day, but he also "embourgeoised" it by propagating his concerns about the proper behavior of ordinary people in everyday contexts. Dharmapala told Sinhalas how to address one another, how to behave on buses and trains, how to keep small change in piggy banks, and how to use the lavatory.

Gombrich and Obeyesekere call these rules a "code for the emerging Sinhala elite," concluding that Dharmapala's "condemnation of peasant manners is based on Western notions of propriety." [13] The irony of his attempt to rally Sinhalas against Protestant domination in late nineteenth century Sri Lanka was its ambivalence. On the one hand, he reviled the European presence in Sri Lanka and celebrated local culture, but on the other, he had distinctly ugly feelings about not only local minorities but also the generality of Sinhalas. By reimagining Buddhism in ways that were marked by their Victorianism, not to say, their Europeanism, Dharmapala produced a new set of local pieties. And although his audience was Sinhala and Buddhist, the moral and hygienic qualities he celebrated have come to define bourgeois sensibility ever since, among minorities as well as the Sinhala majority.

Television advertisements are adept at smuggling in innovation and difference in the name of tradition. Those innovations make advertising talk about Sri Lankans as "traditionalists" that much more complicated. Village maidens appear on the screen in cloth and jacket, namely the idealized feminine dress of village life. Sometimes they wear the long-sleeved, embroidered white cotton blouse that developed among Low Country caste groups under colonial domination. No Kandyan woman wears the jacket, and even in the Low Country, only a fraction of women do so, and they are not young. But the young women portrayed on television stride down a village lane, exposing quite a lot of their legs, scandalous behavior for a village woman of any age. If this is tradition, it is tradition evoked to catch the eye, not to represent a known way of life.

Other parts of Sinhala life cannot be appropriated for commercial purposes. A creative director told me about an inspired idea he had for selling disposable razor blades. He envisioned a television commercial in which a child approaches a Buddhist monk at the end of the rainy retreat season when laypeople offer new robes, soap, umbrellas, and foodstuffs to monks as *dana* (a religious, merit-making gift). The child would give the monk a disposable razor, his sly smile suggesting that he knew the monk would use the razor to shave his head. My mind raced to commercials I had seen of Catholic nuns, medieval monastics, and Tibetan monks in commercial "zones of display." But of course, he said wistfully, I cannot do it. It is too much. Exploiting the physical person of a monk, making light of his tonsure, and suggesting that a monk is one man who really needs a good razor violates people's sense of what is appropriate.[14]

Ask an advertising executive what makes Sri Lankan society "conservative," and he will likely speak less of any particular way of life than a wariness of change for its own sake and a keen sense of what is vulgar and base. Advertisements respect these values by portraying women and children as well as the relationship between men and women in formal ways. Vulgarity has more to do with certain relationships among people than clothing styles, furniture, or any part of the material world. One gets a sense of what people consider vulgar when advertising people draw a distinction between what is acceptable in India and in Sri Lanka. In India, an advertisement can show a person sneezing or offending another with bad breath. One cannot do so in Sri Lanka. To speak the local idiom entails understanding what Sri Lankans find too bodily and overly personal.

Portraying banking products in a context that recalls the distant past has several virtues. It bespeaks a historical moment of great achievement and a time when Sri Lankan society could thumb its nose at the Western societies that would dominate Sri Lankan life during the long colonial period.[15] The island's ancient capitals, Anuradhapura and Polonnaruwa, are places with a past—settled out in relic mounds, moonstone steps, carved gatekeepers, and lotus baths—that can be pictured. In this context even Buddhism acquires a bleached-out character. A relic mound (dāgaba) is a Buddhist monument, to be sure, but it also transcends the religious connection by way of its archeological importance. It is the past. It is tradition. The pastness of the past, its impersonality and diffuse iconicity, means that a relic mound can be appropriated for advertising a bank (while a monk's physical person cannot be used for selling razors or banking products).

Talking about how the advertising business positions banks, I asked an executive whether there had been banks in Anuradhapura.[16] For a moment he had a blank expression and then, to his credit, began to think about what banking must have been like in an agricultural society in which foreign trade was dominated by mercantile communities who were tied more to the two major seaports than to Anuradhapura. For advertising purposes, it hardly matters where or how banking was done in ancient Sri Lanka. For advertising executives, there had to have been a Bank of Anuradhapura. What persuades is continuity between something that existed then and something that exists now. By the same token, it does not matter that the same bank that advertises itself as the successor firm to banking in Anuradhapura also celebrates its having facilities for international banking as well as ATM machines in all of its branches.

Tradition can be exploited in a second way that also follows a historical rationale. When Vanik Bank set up to do business in the early

1990s, advertising it faced several problems—it was a new bank in a market that already had seen the establishment of several other merchant banks and it was foreign owned. Its agency placed a set of four advertisements in Sinhala newspapers, such as *Dinamina,* that ran over four consecutive days (12–15 July 1994). Taken as a set, the advertisements suggested continuity with a past that happened to have been a progressive past. The first spoke of the original bank in Sri Lanka—forgoing any claim on Anuradhapura—the Bank of Kandy. It was founded by two enterprising *(niyāmika)* men, Jeronis and Lewis Pieris, bankers to the coffee business in its early days. Now Vanik Bank, the advertisement rushing to its conclusion, is establishing other innovative services—leasing, bill discounting, financing, and fund management.

The same logic was repeated in subsequent ads featuring Nattukottai Chettiars—"When the Bank of Kandy was closed around 1930, there was no accepted banking system for some time. But there existed a system where individuals were granted loans . . . a group of 556 members of the Nattukottai Chettiar community"—and William Thompson—"a London businessman who established the Bank of Ceylon in 1841 to serve the planting industry." All four ads end with a tag line: "A pioneer service for the future." This theme gets enunciated fully in the final advertisement, focused exclusively on Vanik Bank, which "faces the twenty-first century . . . just like earlier banks were born to cater to the demands of their respective eras." Where the advertising for a similar bank might have simply celebrated its innovation and technology, in this case a bank announces innovations that emerge from a tradition of progressive change.

When Seylan Bank opened its branch in a small town known for woodworking, its agency ran ads that invoked tradition in a third way. The headline read, "Now Moratuwa's unmatched Craftsmanship feels Seylan Bank's Warmth" (*Daily News,* 1 June 1990). The text explained, "Moratuwa . . . a town of open hospitality and charm is also known for its exquisite craftsmanship [the photo to the side depicts a woodcarver, tools in hand, seated in front of an elaborately worked door]. The grain is so indelibly etched in what is produced in that town, so rich in talent as is its national heroism [*sic*]. Seylan's banking service must surely combine to lay the bedrock to build further on Moratuwa's talents and aspirations. . . . Seylan Bank, The bank with Heart." Looking to local culture rather than history, the advertisement emphasizes the organic relationship between banking and the traditions—woodworking, hospitality, and strong ethnic feeling—of one town.

Vanik Bank emphasizes that it is as forward-looking as earlier banks (which also were started by foreigners, recasting a colonial social formation as a virtue, not a problem). Seylan Bank makes the claim that the opening of any branch bank invites—we are not simply doing business in this town, we have a natural, almost physical relationship to the people of the place. Even when tradition establishes the "zone of display," some themes are always close at hand. The bank is a warm place. The bank has a heart. It wants to join its customers as a partner. The idea of tradition figures in all of these assertions. Bank and customers are coparceners in a tradition that has a determinate trajectory. It was there in the past, and it is sure to become richer, both economically and culturally, in the future.

If the artifacts of a common past—tanks, relic mounds, distinguished bankers, and carved wooden doors—substantiate Sri Lankan "tradition" in a way that lends itself to the visual and rhetorical needs of advertising practice, being "traditional" and "conservative" enters advertising talk in a parallel way. Because Sri Lankans have inherited a cultural tradition, they have shared expectations about how to behave. They know when one steps over the line. One thing people regard as offensive is advertising that criticizes. When the Sri Lanka Broadcasting Corporation drew up a copy code for television, that code spelled out what radio practice implicitly assumed: it is wrong to criticize another product or to draw unfair comparisons.[17] In principle, advertising could play a small part in Habermasian rational-critical discussion; that it does not do so is more an expression of local sensibilities quite separate from advertising than of the corruption of public discourse.[18]

In its privatization campaign of the early 1990s, the government put up for sale the Puttalam Cement Corporation, which controlled upward of 90 percent of the domestic market. The economic potential of a near monopoly over a commodity that was hugely profitable and for which demand is expected to grow by 10 percent a year when the north and east are rebuilt gives economic force and high emotion to a mundane product.[19] Nor is it a trivial issue in a society that equates tradition with a particular ethnic identity. Sri Lankan forces, including the journal *Ravaya,* opposed selling off the Puttalam Cement Corporation for a variety of economic and moral reasons. But the ranking monk of one of the monastic establishments in Kandy went straight to the heart of the matter, insisting that "the minorities were enjoying better privileges than the indigenous people of the country."[20]

The successful bidders for the Puttalam Cement Corporation were not, in fact, people of a local minority community but Pakistani investors, the Tawakkal Group of Companies, which purchased the Puttalam Cement Works in 1993. Having paid Rs. 2.03 million to the Sri Lankan government through a leveraged buyout, the Tawakkal Group sought to recapitalize itself by issuing public shares.[21] The firm's advertising agency suggested an advertising campaign emphasizing tradition and the past. Just as the engineering genius of Sri Lankans was visible in the construction of Yoda Ela (a gigantic tank that supplied paddy fields around Anuradhapura with irrigation water), and just as the Ruvanväli säya, the great relic mound at Anuradhapura, raises the same questions as the pyramids—"How could any ancient society have build anything so large?"—so Puttalam Cement is the heritage of modern-day Sri Lankans.

One of the Pakistani buyers liked the strategy; the other wanted to emphasize price and profitability in announcing the share issue. Their account executive argued that Sri Lankans could not be approached that way, implying that what might work in Pakistan would not work in this market. Sri Lankans, he insisted, need to be approached carefully; they must be addressed in the local idiom. But consider what occurs when cement is put in this historicizing "zone of display." The profit-seeking basis of the enterprise yields to tradition, and the Pakistani ownership of this commodity is joined to the ancient builders of irrigation tanks and relic mounds.

Recall the advertisement for a milk product centered on a little girl drinking a glass of milk. She tells the camera, "Mother thinks I drink milk because it is nutritious. Actually, I drink it because it tastes good. Don't tell Mother!" The skillful part of the advertisement was the girl's being both self-possessed and shy, sharing a small secret with the television viewer—Mother has her reasons for giving me milk; I have mine for drinking it. The advertisement did very well, but it also provoked a backlash. Some viewers thought it stepped over the line, making a virtue of fooling one's mother, and then whispering about it in public. The standard that the Sri Lanka Rupavahini Corporation invoked was the code that prohibits advertisements that tend "to subvert or disparage law and order, adult authority, or moral standards."[22] According to the creative director who made the commercial, it might well have won a prize for creativity at the AdAsia convention when other advertising executives saw it, but it offended local sensibilities.

When advertising executives call Sri Lankan society "traditional" or "conservative," they clearly do not mean that this is a society trapped between an ancient order marked by sumptuary privilege and another historical moment in which fashion, consumerist attitudes, and advertising enter people's lives. Being "traditional" means not forgetting how a child properly treats her parents. But the expression also carries a technological referent. I once had an executive tell me that Sri Lankans were "traditional" because of the late arrival of television technology. In this sense, "traditional" means behind the times or not technologically savvy. In India, he said, an advertising agency can employ twenty-five different shots in a thirty-second commercial. In Sri Lanka, viewers cannot absorb more than seventeen. Visual literacy aside, on my view, the social forces that lead advertising executives to speak of Sri Lankans as traditional and conservative have more to do with the effects of colonialism and low levels of discretionary spending.

Advertising needs to "naturalize" or "domesticate" commodities marked for being foreign. Finding a place for some commodity entails finding a way to connect those goods and services with "tradition." One executive said that he constructed advertisements by imagining what would make his uncle proud. I asked him why he thought of his uncle, and he said that Sinhala was his uncle's first language but not his own. What made his uncle proud? Scenes of irrigation works, Buddhist places, and inscriptions. They remind him of Sri Lankan tradition. What makes the analogy powerful is not just that it evokes a past that Sri Lankans take seriously. Putting a commodity in a "traditional zone of display" mitigates its foreign character, and doing so is especially important in the case of banking, which, until recently, has been a thoroughly foreign practice. In the case of banking, calling on "tradition" also has a technological resonance. Those monuments had to be built or dug, and doing so required skill and innovation, allowing the advertiser to connect credits cards and ATM machines as skillful modern innovations to structures built several thousand years ago.

But the strength of this analogy can overpower some commodities. "Tradition" works for large, institutional products, of which perhaps banking services are the paradigm case. It can hide the foreign ownership of a cement corporation. It works less well, for example, for paper products, writing instruments, and beauty aids. These products have less affinity for tradition, and—in the words of a creative director—can be overpowered by it. One can say that beautiful ladies throughout Sri Lanka's history have used aromatic herbs for their skin. Nowadays, one advertisement reasons, they use sandalwood soap, but that evocation of the past recalls tradition on a small scale—the tradition of skin care—not the capital-letter tradition of a pristine state with large monuments.

SELF-RESTRAINT

Advertising talk about tradition meshes neatly with talk about the restraint of Sri Lankan consumers. The two notions have an elective affinity for one another, but self-restraint has direct implications for behavior. On the one hand, self-restraint means consumption-restraint because consumption has at best a checkered status in Sri Lanka (not to say South Asia in general); on the other hand, self-restraint entails emotional control. When people in the business invoke the "local idiom," their examples often illustrate a reserve, a propriety that distinguishes Sri Lankan consumers as a group. Sometimes Sri Lankan consumers are distinguished as being "traditional," or one kind of Sri Lankan is set off from others because they are more "tradition-minded." In the same way when talk turns to "self-restraint" or any of its synonyms, difference is not far away, and it is usually cashed out at the level of the nation-state: "Filipinos are sentimental, but Sri Lankans are more self-restrained," or "Sri Lankans would never tolerate the Coca-Cola advertising you see elsewhere; it is tasteless, no?"

There are counterexamples of communities and of individuals where consumerist attitudes prevail and where buying and using things are pleasurable activities in themselves, acquisition is tied to self-identity, or extravagance treated as virtue. Sri Lankan fishermen, for instance, lead lives that are anything but restrained.[23] They work hard, take serious risks, make a windfall from their catch or nothing at all, and when they have money they spend it. But advertising executives are not thinking of fishermen when they speak of self-restraint—another example of the disparity between the ethnography of Sri Lanka and the way advertising executives approach their market. The disparity between this figure of self-restraint and entirely unrestrained consumers such as fishermen also suggests the ironic calculus that links advertising to consuming. Lots of commodities are purchased by enthusiastic consumers to whom advertising never speaks.

Self-restraint has sources that range from economic necessity—this is a subcontinent where many people live at subsistence levels—to religion and culture. The center of South Asian religions and cultures is a tradition of asceticism and self-abnegation that has influenced over two millennia of South Asian history. But advertising does not trade on those regularities. It does not speak of poverty and it does not aim its pitch at the poor. In Sri Lanka religious figures appear occasionally in commercial contexts, but advertising draws on the "Protestant" parts of the tradition—those parts marked by propriety and middle-class restraint—and then only in highly constrained ways.

A Hindu priest arrives at a festival house to celebrate a young boy's initiation as a student; Buddhist pilgrims finally reach a historically-important Buddhist temple. These "zones of display" serve the interests of advertising in the diffuse way "tradition" generally provides, using religious figures for their expressive qualities. A clear example comes from a print advertisement for Sampath Bank. Just above a line drawing of a Kandyan temple painting showing a set of domestic scenes appeared a Pali quotation from the Buddha. The English translation appears below: "Set aside one-fourth of your income for sustenance, two-fourths for investments. Save the remaining one-fourth for a rainy day." [24] What recommends this advice is not what is said but who said it—following the Buddha's words to the letter sets standards for thrift that become even more unrealistic when compared with the 60 percent of income the average Sri Lankan spends on sustenance nowadays.

Because food is life's greatest expense for most Sri Lankans, food is both heavily advertised and the object of serious feeling. The fruits, vegetables, meat, and fish that people buy at the local bazaar are not advertised, but branded goods—from tinned milk products to cream crackers and soda—constitute one of the most heavily advertised parts of the consumer market. Showing food in advertisements needs to respect local canons of restraint. In the early 1990s the Singer Corporation ran a television advertisement featuring a small boy sitting cross-legged in front of a Singer refrigerator. He dreams about the good things to eat safely kept inside. The door opens and the viewer sees shelves heavy with more food than most Sri Lankans will ever find in their larder. When the Premadasa government came to power, its Minister of Cultural Affairs had the advertisement pulled from the airwaves because he found it inspired unrealistic expectations in a poor country.

Advertisements for gold, by contrast, provoke no opposition. Whether seen on television or in print, gold jewelry can be advertised without issue because gold plays a central role in dowries and a family's savings for Sinhalas, Tamils, and Muslims alike. Food provokes thoughts about self-restraint; gold does not. It is a part of life properly understood. As sareed ladies shop in the gold shops along Sea Street in Colombo, beggars regularly appear on the pavement. A shop assistant rushes out and hands a coin to a person in rags before his customers are discomfited. The contrast strikes the outsider as acting out the inequality of Sri Lankan life, but what affects Sri Lankans is more likely to be the extravagance evoked by displays of food.

Meat advertising draws an inordinate amount of attention. Consider this turn in government policy in 1993.

> A ban on meat advertising on television, soon to be extended to radio, has signalled the new rise of puritan politics in Sri Lanka, writes Lucien Rajakaruna in Colombo. The right-wing United National Party government has also halted the import of films carrying a PG or adult rating in an alleged bid to safeguard the

country's youth from corruption and violence. Both moves have been ordered by the Ministry of Information and Cultural Affairs, headed by Loku Bandara, a professed vegetarian and a strong opponent of Western values. Bandara claims that meat advertising creates an "un-satisfied demand" among large sections of the population who cannot afford it. However, others believe the government's actions have more to do with attempts to please extreme Buddhist opinion than concern for the poor. Sections of the Buddhist clergy have always opposed the sale of meat.[25]

To the extent that meat, especially branded meat products marketed by agency houses, provokes feelings about a range of issues—violence, corruption, Westernization, "unsatisfied demands," and vegetarianism—it is a foodstuff with symbolic power. But that is not the end of it. "The government decided to ban meat advertisements on television," according to a government spokesperson, "because it feels that poorer classes might feel inferior when they see meat products which they cannot afford to buy."[26] By that logic, television could carry no advertising of any kind. The issue that lay behind government concern in this case, however, was another aspect of the symbolic power of animal flesh—pork's capacity to inflame Muslim feelings. The meat in question was sausage, which comes in a variety of forms in Sri Lanka—beef, chicken, and fish, as well as pork. But when sausage is advertised without qualification, it is assumed to be a pork product, and a government with known and essential ties to Israel does well to listen to Muslim complaints.

Soda advertisements offend as many Sri Lankans as meat advertisements. Coke and Sprite advertisements made for Asian television markets have a kind of youthful exuberance and spontaneity that must make sense to their makers in Singapore. They strike Sri Lankan television viewers as explicitly sexual. A pair of teenagers exchange glances, take long draughts from their bottles of Sprite, and dive into a body of water. Taking the plunge has no overt sexual reference, but many people react to its subtextual meanings—male and female in very little clothing take joint action and disappear together into the water. Compared to the advertisements that Westerners view, the dive is tame stuff, and that is just the point. Even when advertisers have adjusted their advertising to Asian standards, they have not gone far enough for Sri Lankan consumers.

Sri Lankan advertising people have told me that Sri Lankans are "more objective" and "more rational" than Westerners and "we have more willpower" and thus fewer alcoholics. Little evidence was offered for either generalization, and some people framed these assertions as intuitions or arguing points. Whether these self-conceptions represent simply the advertising business or pertain in some way to Sri Lankans in general, they indicate the way some agencies think about their audience. One account manager surmised that Sri Lankans were not really consumers at all in the Western sense of the word. Sri Lankans obsess over price and value, the man went on, and we expect too much of products so that we end up criticizing products for not living up to our expectations. Is this how a modern consumer acts? Is this a consumer that can be persuaded by advertising that emphasizes anything but the quality and price of a commodity?

The need for emotional restraint in making advertisements works at cross-purposes with the rhetorical and visual strategies that characterize advertising practice in Western settings. As in other markets, advertising puts commodities in the context of family life, surrounding that which is for sale with a social setting where nothing is properly for sale. Even advertising aimed at Asian Americans presents family life in distinctive ways. When mainline American families are shown, they are portrayed as a group of individuals, each with his or her agenda. Asian-American advertising portrays the family as a commune, the focus of everyone's life.[27] The same emphasis on the group characterizes Asian advertising in general. In Sri Lanka the family is central, but overt signs of affection are inappropriate. Expressions of intimacy, solidarity, and familial love are private matters or simply not done. By one advertising woman's account, advertising in the Philippines shows lots of affection and feeling. Sri Lankans would find such advertisements unrealistic and alien.

The same executive said she had recently done an advertisement for a nutritional supplement, emphasizing the supplement's benefits for health and strength. As his mother looks on, her son races with a group of boys. He wins the race, and she smiles demurely. The multinational firm that hired the Sri Lankan agency to produce the advertisement could not understand the lack of emotion. Surely the mother should be jumping up and down during the race and hugging her child afterward. Sri Lankans, the creative director insisted, would find the tone just right. The child who wins the race knows his mother is proud of him by the look on her face. The mother, of course, wells up with pride and affection, but she does not project it. Family affection needs to be part of the scene, but it also needs to be constructed idiomatically.

Sri Lankans invest heavily in their children, spending substantial amounts of their incomes on education and health. Indonesians, another creative director said by way of contrast, spend more on shampoo than toothpaste, a distinction he meant to epitomize choosing appearance over health. Sri Lankans buy toothpaste for its cavity-fighting qualities, not its cosmetic ones. In the matter of selling toothpaste, the well-advised agency makes nothing of the ability of toothpaste to mask bad breath. Sri Lankans do not want to turn on their televisions and find sneezing. They do not want to see one person reacting to someone else's bad breath. Colgate toothpaste can be sold in India this way, he said. In Sri Lanka it cannot. Buying toothpaste, for that matter, is a family purchase. Whoever buys toothpaste chooses a brand that is good for the family's health, not to satisfy any individual's preferences.

I came across advertisements in a handful of cases that struck me as violating conventions about family values overriding individual interests and emotional restraint. One was aimed at young women, and introduced a line of dresses available at three shops located in upscale shopping malls in Colombo (see fig. 5). Sri Lanka is not a society with much of a fashion tradition, and this advertisement makes only a gesture at talking up these clothes as fashionable. Instead it lays out the connections between individualism and what one wears. Alongside three pictures of an attractive young women with unrestrained hair, wearing three outfits from the Liza Danelle collection, the tagline reads "Liza Danelle is for the 'girl' in you." [28] The text draws the connection between individuality and expressivity:

> You're the type who is elated to walk in a drizzle, you love life, people and simple pleasures. You love to cry at soppy love stories— and cuddle-up in bed on a cosy afternoon. You are overwhelmed at the sight of a rainbow . . . and feel touched when you see an old man's wrinkled face break into a smile. You sing your head off in the bathroom . . . and pick wild flowers as mementoes . . .

The reaction of the generality of Sri Lankans to the prospect of being elated to walk in the rain, cuddling up in bed during the afternoon, and singing one's head off in the bathroom is hard to imagine. But this is culture being produced, not transmitted.

The Liza Danelle ad is a Sri Lankan interpretation of a cosmopolitan social formation. Its success notwithstanding, it is tasteful and at least plausible. The ads that strike Sri Lankans as wholly implausible come directly from Western sources. A striking example is what appears to be an American advertisement for Goya perfume, an inexpensive scent made in the West and sold in Sri Lanka. The television advertisement begins from the visual point of view of a man riding up an escalator. He sees an attractive woman descending on the opposing escalator. She does not see him, but he is so stunned by her beauty that he runs off to a flower stall at the corner, purchases a bouquet, and runs back to give her the flowers. She is surprised, smiles brightly, and the perfume company's logo appears on the screen. There is a market for whimsy and grand gestures in Western societies, where the Goya advertisement was made. Sri Lankans react to the advertisement by thinking that the man has taken leave of his senses.

Hygiene products make many television viewers anxious. The television copy code proscribes advertisements for depilatories, and indi-

FIGURE 5.   Signs of a fashion system motivated by Western expressive figures—from rainbows to cuddles (*Island* [Colombo], 1 December 1991).

cates that advertisements for "body deodorants, mouth washes or anti-septics may be accepted for advertising if the presentation copy is tastefully done."[29] Advertisements for condoms and sanitary napkins appear in the press, but they are constructed very carefully. At first advertisements did not show the product or mention a brand name. But creative directors have "brought the public along slowly, so that we can mention brands and show the wrapped product." Television spots for sanitary napkins make men nervous, according to advertising practice, and ones for condoms are constructed to make them appear to be medicine. Because cosmetics are tied to glamour and self-expression, they must be approached indirectly and smuggled into many Sri Lankans' consumption regimes.

Few commodities pose as many problems for advertising as cosmetics. The proliferation of free-trade zones has put considerable amounts of discretionary income into the hands of young women. The problem is that those young women live at home under the authority of their parents—and their fathers in particular—who view cosmetics in terms not of self-expression but of promiscuity. And cosmetics cannot be naturalized by being put in a traditional setting or a village one. The imagery of the Anuradhapura period is simply too strong and constructing cosmetics against a village background alienates the principal market, young women who work in Colombo and other cities. Reaching women who live in villages, while holding on to those who cannot imagine themselves in relation to such places, requires ingenuity and indirection—focusing on facial close-ups, flowers, flames, and women whose appearance is attractive but unmarked by signs of either village or city life. The creative director who invented this formula says these advertisements have the "*sidevi*" look, modern enough to reach urban women, innocent enough to keep a village woman's father from objecting when he discovers his daughter's wearing scent or pressed powder.

There are very few so-called personal indulgence products in Sri Lanka within the reach of ordinary people. Over and above their utility, cellular telephones are one example, purchased for reasons of status and indulgence, but far too expensive for most consumers. Clothing qualifies as an indulgence product, but clothing is tied more to style than to brand names and makers' marks. In the Sri Lankan market, Lux soap exemplifies a personal indulgence product—branded, slickly packaged, and expensively advertised but associated with an everyday need. The soap is uneconomical because it wastes away quickly, which means that no one is likely to buy it without good reason. Lux advertising—"Beautiful women the world over use Lux soap"—depends on beautiful faces of all hues and shapes. When a woman purchases a bar of Lux soap, she makes a consumption decision with at least some implications for beauty and individualism. But using a particular brand of soap is an inconspicuous form of indulgence, not to say a fairly inexpensive one.

In Zimbabwe Lux soap has been marketed as a tool for cleanliness, and in turn civilization.[30] Its advertising in Sri Lanka took a different course by exploiting its own transnational character and telling women that nine out of ten film stars use Lux, as do beautiful women the world over. Unilever gave up the film star campaign when it became too expensive, feeling that buying endorsements was a seedy business. Images of film stars still appear in some Lux ads, although the "nine out of ten" claim has dropped away, and Lux advertising has tried to retain the accent on elegance without the known faces. In the African case, advertising emphasized the hygienic qualities of soap, taking a tutelary tone through the final years of colonial control. Sri Lankan advertising is no less tutelary, emphasizing the soap's ability to condition the skin. But Lux stands out in the Sri Lankan case as a rare example of celebrating beauty and glamour directly. Generally products that have some connection to enhancing one's appearance forgo that claim and speak instead of health.[31]

Since Anandatissa de Alwis wrote the well-known advertisement in colloquial Sinhala for Dagenite automobile batteries in the 1960s, there has been some advertising making use of everyday speech forms. But he did not start a trend. Colloquial speech needs to be appropriate to the product. In de Alwis's advertisement, a taxi driver praised the starting power of his Dagenite battery, and part of the appeal of the advertisement was the very idea of a taxi driver, as opposed to a trousered gentleman, speaking about such things. Colloquial speech is not appropriate for Lux, a product that tries to connect women's aspirations to a faraway world of beauty and sophistication. The major agencies maintain photo files of character actors, and such models appear in television commercials on occasion. But there is no tradition of any magnitude of eccentric characters, no Robert Morley, no little old lady asking, "Where's the beef?" The models who appear in television and print advertisements tend to be young and attractive, they appear in familiar contexts, and they avoid slang. Buying a personal indulgence product means casting one's lot with such people.

Caution

Advertising frequently conveys content with a tutelary tone—in Western countries and places such as Zimbabwe as much as Sri Lanka. Unless the advertising depends entirely on atmospheric effects, consumers have to be given reasons to buy a product. The tendency toward giving instruction increases in places where many consumers are being exposed to a new commodity. In developing countries where companies are trying to sell products such as soap or vegetable oil to people who are thrifty and cautious, advertisements are even more likely to be didactic. Prakash Tandon describes the way his boss at Unilever convinced Indians to replace ghee with Unilever's vegetable oil, Dalda, in the 1940s. Indian consumers tested ghee by rubbing it on their skin, smelling it, and then putting it on their tongue. Tandon says that Harvey Duncan, the Englishman who was his superior, organized the new advertising around

> his discovery of the smell-feel-taste test as its theme, repeating itself through every medium he used, demonstration stalls, newspapers, leaflets, films, girls visiting homes. He built gay little stalls on pneumatic wheels with colourful canopies. The cook stood with a table in front of him displaying the tins, and made simple sweets while the demonstrator talked to the crowd. After a while they folded up and pushed the stall to the next prominent street corner. He also built motor vans with a large replica of the round tin on the chassis and a [demonstration] platform at the back. . . . Duncan then produced a Dalda film and his first cinema van. The film had all the ingredients of an Indian picture: song, dance, pathos, humour, social uplift, march of time, coincidence. In 1,200 feet it depicted the story of a father who had got his daughter satisfactorily engaged, but could not afford to cook the wedding feast in pure ghee.[32]

Faced with financial ruin, the father begins to despair until a young relative arrives—shortly after having seen one of Duncan's demonstration vans—suggests Dalda, and the celebration goes forward.

Tutelary advertising is advertising that does more than celebrate a product's virtues. It teaches consumers how to consume. Sri Lankan advertising executives characterize local consumers as being as cautious as Indians who test oils three ways before making a purchase, and dealing with caution requires instruction. Sri Lankans are not slow to change, one man told me, but they never forget price, durability, and value. The concern for value, in turn, means there is a good measure of local agency even when advertising seems to be instructing an innocent consumer. Advertisements instruct, but consumers choose. Why advertising executives might emphasize the consumer's agency is no mystery. Advertising's self-understanding sees its productions as moving but not overpowering. Advertising must be able to persuade to justify itself, but the profession's sense of civic responsibility requires making a lot of the consumer's independence.

A product may appeal to consumers because it offers values that the maker had not imagined. Empty Dalda tins are good for a variety of uses—from scooping water as part of a Persian wheel to storing cereals and spices.[33] Sri Lankan manufacturers produce toothpaste and shampoo in sachets, reducing the size in order to bring the cost of an expensive product within the reach of ordinary people. But Sri Lankans see another benefit. A person taking a bottle of shampoo or a tube of toothpaste to the well to bathe will share, and would be expected to share, with others. No one would be offended, however, if a person with a 50 ml sachet of Sunsilk shampoo did not share; it is known to be a single-use container. But the thrifty Sri Lankan consumer can use it sparingly and keep the remainder for another time. To this extent, Sri Lankans have taken downsizing to an extent that manufacturers have not intended, and manufacturers have unintentionally given people a subtle way to economize by not sharing.

An environmental scientist interviewed on Sinhala radio was asked whether a poor country could afford to worry about the environment in the same way developed countries do. What prospects are there for recycling in a place like Sri Lanka? The scientist replied that recycling could be as efficient in an underdeveloped economy as a developed one, but Sri Lanka already has environmentally sound practices in place just because it has not developed rapidly. "We don't need to recycle bottles," he concluded, "we already have a more efficient practice. We refill them." Beer and soda bottles simply get returned to the place where they were first bottled and filled again. The economy is friendly to the environment because many of its distribution practices have not changed since the days of British colonial rule. Practices such as recycling that look minimalist to Western environmentalists looks gratuitous to consumers who are environmentally responsible because of the scarcity of their means and the slow development of the local economy.[34]

People who pay for bottles and carefully return them to the shop and people who get several uses from a 50 ml sachet are consumers who approach larger capital purchases with appropriate deliberation. Advertising executives often choose village settings to visualize thrift and rationality. Even when the product is one that sells just as much in urban areas, the village stands for tradition in not only the senses I have been discussing—propriety and restraint—but also thrift and good sense. Laundry soap get advertised on television by having a young man encounter a young woman on a path that runs between paddy fields. He asks her whether she is wearing a new saree blouse. She replies that it is an old blouse but she washes it in Sunlight soap.

Batteries are advertised by way of a scene in which an elderly man walking along a village pathway is blinded by a flashlight. He speaks in Sinhala, and his language reanimates the connection between the local idiom and caution. He tells the little girl with the flashlight that the light is like a fireball in his eyes, and she replies that it is only her Volta batteries. They are bright but not new. Both advertisements argue that old possessions can be kept new by carefully marshaling one's resources—washing a saree blouse with a particular laundry soap or using a particular brand of batteries. Advertisements, in other words, speak to a public that is already making purchases in a cautious way, and they celebrate the consumers' good sense. By being tutelary, these advertisements also contribute to "the production of locality," creating a sense of belonging—to Sri Lanka as much as to a village—by entirely modern means.

Selling things to cautious consumers entails providing them with reasons. Some come in the form of rationales that emphasize tradition or suggest how one can be properly restrained while buying a particular product. Another rationale is the more tutelary advertisement that shows how the product is meant to be consumed in explicit, almost patronizing ways. Advertising executives do not use the expression "tutelary"—my gloss for what they do talk about in an *ad hoc* manner—when they lay out the case for a product in a straightforward, narrative advertisement. Some part of their insistence on consumers being cautious and requiring rational persuasion I take to be an interpersonal effect—between Sri Lankans and the inquiring ethnographer—based on wanting to avoid my presumed suspicion that Sri Lankan advertising seduces consumers by employing the same strategies that Western advertising exploits.

Sri Lankans see their share of straightforward, rational advertising, emphasizing price, quality, and benefits. All societies do. But local circumstances invite a disproportionate amount of it. I have been given several explanations about why Sri Lankan advertising relies on this approach. Most often I have heard tutelary ads attributed to the high level of education in Sri Lankan society. Other Asians may buy toothpaste for reasons of personal appearance; Sri Lankans are better informed and buy it for reasons of health. Claims about glamour can be made in atmospheric, aspirational ways. Claims about health, by contrast, need to be supported by argument. But conceiving of Sri Lankans as rational and cautious is also a tacit presupposition that influences the way advertising people construct their public.

Even commodities that might be positioned by emphasizing their capacity to create freedom and leisure pretty much concentrate on the product itself, emphasizing its efficiency much more than the benefits of that efficiency. Singer makes an ironing contraption, for example, which sells at a price (Rs. 12,790 or US $64 in 1997) that restricts its appeal to Sri Lankans who are likely to employ servants. In my terms, the advertisement is tutelary, giving the consumer a straightforward description of how the appliance is meant to be used, not an account of the benefits of using a contraption that reduces ironing time by 50 percent. As figure 6 shows, the product's virtues are celebrated not by emphasizing the leisure that its use provides—only one of the four small images shows the housewife enjoying a moment of rest, and then she is shown at home chastely reading a magazine. The emphasis falls, rather, on the product itself and its ability to save time. "Surface area of the Press is 10 times the area of a regular iron," the advertisement contends, placing efficiency and time saved on a

FIGURE 6.   Ad for an expensive ironing device (*Lanka Monthly Digest,* December 1994).

par with other virtues—special features such as temperature control and safety.

At the margin, there are Sri Lankan advertisements that celebrate the ephemeral. The Liza Danelle "For the 'Girl' in You" advertisement takes the pleasures of the moment to a high level—of walking in the rain, an afternoon's snuggle in bed, and the sight of a rainbow or an old man's smile. But it stands out because few advertisements make much of whimsy, spontaneity, or self-indulgence.

What constitutes advertising knowledge about the local market is not a set of abstract propositions. It consists in a set of *ad hoc* inferences about what has worked in particular situations. As a consequence, one strategy may contradict another, as do appeals to reason on the one hand and appeals to tradition on the other. Sri Lankans spend a substantial amount of their incomes on milk powder. Even though most milk powder is used in the tea consumed by adult family members and guests, milk powder is associated with health, nutrition, and the needs of growing children. Anchor dominates the market, profiting from its association with foreign production. The paradox is that there are so few milk cows in Sri Lanka that Lakspray, the locally owned company, has not been able to produce milk powder without importing milk from abroad. Lakspray is made from imported milk products that are processed in one of the largest and most sophisticated milk powder plants in Asia, while Anchor gets its milk from Sri Lankan dairies. But the perception remains—Anchor is foreign and as clean, hygienic, and nutritious as the huge Swiss or New Zealand cows one sees in their advertisements. Lakspray, people think, is made locally.

It would be reasonable for Lakspray to fight back by emphasizing its locality. "Sri Lankans have enjoyed dairy products," let's say, "since the days of ancient Anuradhapura. Now they enjoy the healthful benefits of Lakspray." But in the early 1990s, Grant's began to construct Lakspray advertisements around price and quality. It flirted with the idea of showing cows walking off a freighter onto a quay in Colombo harbor, but chose a campaign that emphasized price and value. The massive cows on Lakspray packages are clearly foreign. But the argument itself spells out the case in rational terms, never mentioning that Lakspray is made locally. Under these circumstances, the advertisement uses rational argument to counteract the local perception that foreign is better. In doing so, it ignores the fact that the locally owned company uses foreign milk in its product, and the foreign company uses local milk.

Tutelary advertising is advertising's response to the perception that

Sri Lankans are cautious consumers. But which Sri Lankans—urbanites or villagers, English speakers or Sinhala and Tamil speakers—are addressed by tutelary advertisements depends on the commodity and how the advertising agency understands its audience. When Grant Bozell did the advertising for UNESCO's antileprosy campaign, it approached its Sinhala advertisements very differently from its English-language advertising. The agency assumed that Sinhala speakers have more "shame" about leprosy and could not be reached by a straightforward explanation that the early signs of leprosy can be treated. It would be difficult for a person to ask another person—a family member or a friend—whether they might have the early signs of the disease. As a consequence, the agency chose to shock people into action by displaying striking photographs, playing on the fear of parents, and urging them to act "before it is too late." The English-language text of the same advertisement is more informational, speaking of symptoms and concluding with the good news that leprosy is treatable.

The executive then suggests a counterexample. When he sells Singer refrigerators in English-language advertising, he makes a quality-of-life argument: a mother can make treats for her kids and save them in the refrigerator until they come home. The advertisement conveys the mother's love for her children, acted out by way of her taking time to make them snacks, which a refrigerator allows her to store. When the same executive sells the refrigerator to Sinhala speakers, he sells it as five cubic feet of refrigerated space. He sells it as an investment, which means that the advertising is heavy on facts, making the Sinhala advertising more tutelary than the English-language advertising. Regarding leprosy, English speakers get information, while Sinhala speakers get a mood. For refrigerators, the reverse is true: English speakers are given atmospheric reasons to buy; Sinhala and Tamil speakers are given instruction.

In none of these oppositions do the advertisements evoke tradition. They are making arguments. Take action on the first signs of leprosy because otherwise bad things will happen to your children. Take action because leprosy is curable. Buy this refrigerator because it will allow you to become the mother you want to be. Or buy a refrigerator because it can be resold in the future without depreciating very much. Even advertisements that create moods create them by making arguments, not by atmospheric effects alone. Perhaps the long domination of print advertising sustains the tendency toward advertising that gives reasons, but it continues in both print and electronic media. Sri Lankans, another executive told me, are intelligent consumers, largely indifferent to the origin of the product as such. There are exceptions—Coke and Levis were his examples—but nationality does not attach itself to most products. Sri Lankans are offended by advertisements that suggest the need to rebel against parents or that a man can win the girl of his dreams by buying something. Those kinds of foreign products need to be domesticated by being placed in the right context. Sometimes that context is tradition, but other times it is the web of reasons.

How to characterize these characterizations? Early on in this chapter I suggested they constituted the disciplinary knowledge of a profession situated between the global system of commodities and local consumers. The question is how advertising executives understand those consumers. They hardly think of Sri Lankans as "sane but enchanted." Nor do they approach their market as people who are swayed by fashion, who consume for the sake of consumption, and who watch advertisements for entertainment. There are Asian societies in which people encounter both print and electronic advertisements that are considerably more atmospheric and allusive. By contrast, people in the advertising business approach Sri Lankan consumers as motivated by the claims of tradition, propriety, and economy. When consumers themselves speak, as they do in chapter 7, they depend even more on the web of reasons.

NOTES

1. Timothy Burke, *Lifebuoy Men, Lux Women: Commodification, Consumption, and Culture in Modern Zimbabwe* (Durham, N.C.: Duke University Press, 1996).

2. The ethnographic tendency to treat faraway places as trapped in a historical moment distinct from the observer's is discussed in Johannes Fabian, *Time and the Other: How Anthropology Makes Its Object* (New York: Columbia University Press, 1983).

3. I need to make a distinction between folk ethnographers (persons who systematically or otherwise reflect on the nature of their own society's culture) and native ethnographers (anthropologists who practice ethnography on their own society). Lila Abu-Lughod discusses native anthropology in her essay "Writing against Culture," in *Recapturing Anthropology*, ed. Richard Fox, School of American Research Seminar Series (Seattle: University of Washington Press, 1991), 137–62.

4. Alfred Gell, "Newcomers to the World of Goods: Consumption among the Muria Gonds," in *The Social Life of Things*, ed. Arjun Appadurai (Cambridge: Cambridge University Press, 1986), 114.

5. Kevin Dwyer, *Moroccan Dialogues* (Baltimore: Johns Hopkins University Press, 1982).

6. Vincent Crapanzano, *Waiting* (New York: Random House, 1985).

7. Examples include Michael Taussig, *Shamanism, Colonialism, and the Wild Man: A Study in Terror and Healing* (Chicago: University of Chicago Press, 1987); Smadar Lavie, *The Poetics of Military Occupation: Mzeina Allegories of Bedouin Identity under Israeli and Egyptian Rule* (Berkeley: University of California Press, 1990); and Anna Tsing, *In the*

Realm of the Diamond Queen: Marginality in an Out-of-the Way Place (Princeton, N.J.: Princeton University Press, 1993).

8. Sri Lanka has been in the world news recently when its embassies around the world were besieged by a deluge of e-mail messages sent by the Tamil Tigers, who intended to sabotage the embassies' capacity to communicate with the outside world. I'm not sure this campaign deserves to be called cyber-terrorism, but whatever it is called, it is balanced by this example of cyber-ethnography.

9. See, for instance, Stephen A. Tyler, "Post-Modern Ethnography: From Document of the Occult to Occult Document," in *Writing Culture: The Poetics and Politics of Ethnography,* ed. James Clifford and George Marcus (Berkeley: University of California Press, 1986), 122–40.

10. Clifford Geertz, *Works and Lives* (Stanford, Calif.: Stanford University Press, 1988), 147.

11. See Eric Hobsbawm and Terrence Ranger, *The Invention of Tradition* (Cambridge: Cambridge University Press, 1983); and Richard Handler and Joyce Linnekin, "Tradition, Genuine or Spurious," *Journal of American Folklore* 97 (1984): 273–90.

12. Richard Gombrich and Gananath Obeyesekere, *Buddhism Transformed: Religious Change in Sri Lanka* (Princeton, N.J.: Princeton University Press, 1988), 202–40; and H. L. Seneviratne, *The Works of Kings: The New Buddhism in Sri Lanka* (Chicago: University of Chicago Press, 1999), 28–36.

13. Gombrich and Obeyesekere, *Buddhism Transformed,* 215.

14. I have seen actors assuming the role of monks in television dramas and situation comedies, such as *Kopi Kade,* and these appropriations of a traditional and respected social type struck me as pushing the limits of propriety. A monk himself would never act, and actors portray monks as characters incapable of moral fault. But television viewers are insulted sometimes by the very idea of an actor's representing a Buddhist monk ("Actors Preaching 'Bana,'" *Daily News* (Colombo), 9 October 1991).

15. A fulsome passage in a pamphlet from the end of the colonial period suggests the sentiment, "when the rude barbaric ancestors of the British nation were dying their bodies with woad and covering their nakedness with leaves of the forest, the Sinhalese were living in prosperous cities and enjoying the benefits of a splendid eastern civilization" (John Senaveratne, "The Past Might and Glory of the Sinhalese Nation," pamphlet [Colombo: Lorenz Press,1939], 2).

16. To position a product is to construct it in a way that distinguishes it from its competition, giving it a brand identity. To reposition it is simply to alter the way the brand is understood relative to others.

17. Sri Lanka Rupavahini Corporation, *Sri Lanka Rupavahini Corporation Code of Advertising Standards and Practices* (Colombo: Government Press, 1985), no page numbers.

18. Jürgen Habermas, *The Structural Transformation of the Public Sphere,* trans. Thomas Burger (Cambridge, Mass.: MIT Press, 1989), 181. Where once individuals consumed culture in quiet places by reading literature and treatises on politics—later to talk in coffee houses, literary salons, and "table" societies about what they had read—Europeans of Habermas's time consumed it in social settings, giving those cultural forms no further discussion. With that change, the motivation for rational communication was lost, and the public sphere reduced to a "platform for advertising."

19. See "Cement: The Concrete Mess," *Sunday Times* (Colombo), 19 November 1989.

20. "Foreign Companies and Non-Nationals Acquiring Our Lands—Asgiriya Maha Nayake," *Island* (Colombo), 21 May 1994.

21. "Puttalam Cement Plans Public Share Issue of Rs. 850 m," *Observer* (Colombo), 3 October 1994.

22. Sri Lanka Rupavahini Corporation, *Sri Lanka Rupavahini Corporation Code of Advertising Standards and Practices,* no page numbers.

23. R. L. Stirrat, *On the Beach: Fishermen, Fishwives, and Fishtraders in Post-Colonial Sri Lanka* (Delhi: Hindustan Publishing, 1988).

24. *Daily News* (Colombo), 9 May 1990.

25. "Meat Gets TV Chop," *Observer* (Colombo), 25 July 1993.

26. "Sri Lanka Bans Television Meat Ads," Reuters News Service, 19 July 1993 (available from Lexis-Nexis).

27. "Targeting Asians," *Far Eastern Economic Review,* 21 January 1993, 41.

28. *Island* (Colombo), 1 December 1991.

29. Sri Lanka Rupavahini Corporation, *Sri Lanka Rupavahini Corporation Code of Advertising Standards and Practices,* no page numbers.

30. Burke, *Lifebuoy Men, Lux Women,* 17–62.

31. Facial soap reveals more complicated calculations. Two of the faces that once appeared most regularly in print advertisements for Lux were Malini Fonseka, a now-faded movie star, and Rosie Senanayake, a beauty queen-become-mother and television spokesperson. What recommends using film stars goes beyond their beauty and recognizability, because Sri Lankans assume they lead a life marked by glamour, personal independence, and luxury. When the United Nations Family Planning program established a birth-control project in Sri Lanka in the 1970s, a leading advertising executive suggested using Malini Fonseka to sell birth control the same way she had been selling soap: "In my busy career, there is no time for an unwanted pregnancy. That's why I choose birth control." His suggestion was dismissed by other creative directors. Film stars can do testimonials for soap, but their reputation for decadence and promiscuity makes them absolutely wrong to personify any commodity with moral implications (Steven Kemper, "Culture and Consumption in the Sri Lankan Advertising Business," [paper presented at the Social Science Research Council Conference, "Advertising, Consumption, and the New Middle Class in India," Monterey, Calif., 18 April 1991]).

32. Prakash Tandon, *Beyond Punjab* (New Delhi: Thompson Press, 1971), 122–23.

33. See Tandon, *Beyond Punjab,* 122.

34. Plastic bottling has arrived in Sri Lanka, and television now portrays plastic as the figure of modernity. The agency that produced television commercials for Pepsi Mega bottles began by making an invidious distinction. A Sinhala housewife, hair tightly knotted at the back of her head and wearing a saree, encounters a 'smart housewife' whose appearance suggests she is a Burgher. She wears her hair loose and is seen in jeans and tee-shirt. She is driving a car; the Sinhala shopper comes on foot carrying her empty bottles with her. The "smart housewife" shows her the modern, up-to-date alternative—buy soft drinks in plastic and toss the empty bottles away.

CHAPTER SIX

Banking and Belonging

Advertising people employ "the local idiom" in a second sense—in constructing advertisements that sell things to Sri Lankans by making claims on their identity as Sri Lankans. In this chapter, I move from a large number of examples centered on practitioners' perceptions of a set of virtues—respect for tradition, conservatism, self-restraint, and caution—to a campaign built on "local idiom" advertising in this second sense. That campaign promoted a bank whose founding intentions have been variously described as nationalist, localizing, and chauvinist. A small but aggressive agency, Phoenix, produced the advertising, and, in constructing Sampath Bank as "A Truly Sri Lankan Bank for Sons of the Soil," made its reputation for mastering "the local idiom." The heart of this chapter derives from my conversations with the man who oversaw Phoenix's advertising for Sampath, focusing on how Phoenix positioned Sampath as an altogether different kind of bank.

Appreciating the allure of "A Truly Sri Lankan Bank" requires knowing a few things about that larger scene, especially how foreign banking has been in Sri Lanka. There have been Afghans, Arabs, and Europeans involved in lending money to Sri Lankans in the colonial period, but over the last two centuries two ethnic categories stand out. Tamil Chettiars furnished capital to the more traditional parts of the economy, and the British dominated modern banking. The dominance of these people meant that banking has been alien twiceover. The institution itself has been alien because of its bureaucratic formality, and the majority community has regarded the kinds of people who controlled most banks and other lending enterprises as foreigners.

From the Dutch period onward, a variety of Chettiar groups worked in Sri Lanka. All were Tamil, and most were Hindu. Some worked as laborers, but the caste became identified with trade in general and finance in particular. In South India Nattukottai Chettiars had once been a localized salt-trading caste. By the end of the eighteenth century, however, they had gained control of the pearl fisheries in Sri Lanka, then moved into coastal trade between South India and Sri Lanka, and eventually controlled the importing of rice from Thanjavur and Bengal to the island.[1] By the late nineteenth century, they had become financial intermediaries in Burma and Malaysia, transforming themselves into merchant-bankers across the Bay of Bengal. Their reliability, cleverness, and long-distance connections soon made them rich.

At the beginning of the British period, Nattukottai Chettiars became an important part of the local banking system by advancing money to European merchants. When European exchange banks established themselves, Chettiars lost that trade, but they continued to provide credit to Sri Lankan farmers, shopkeepers, coconut millers, arrack renters, and estate owners.[2] They linked the village and plantation sectors of the economy, supplying planters with rice for their laborers, selling rice to villagers, and often owning paddy land themselves. A credit crisis brought down many Chettiar firms in 1925, forcing many merchants into pawnbroking. Colombo Chetties had earlier gravitated toward the profession of shroff, serving in British banks as a local expert as to which borrowers were reliable and which not. That meant that virtually every Sri Lankan seeking a loan from a British bank had to arrange things by first securing the support of a shroff.

Even after Independence, when the state established its own banks, banking retained its foreign character. Chettiars continued doing business in the Pettah, lending large amounts of money on a short-term or long-term basis. The children of men who had served as guarantee shroffs followed them into the banking business, taking on new roles as the system evolved. Tamils with no family connection to banking were attracted to the profession because it constituted a respectable, white-collar profession. Their educational accomplishments and competence in English gave them an advantage over other Sri Lankans. With the establishment of the Bank of Ceylon and later the People's Bank, more Sinhalas entered the banking business. But even these state banks remained "British" to the extent that their procedures were marked by a set of checks and balances, a high level of formality, and a subservient cadre of workers—minor employees and "peons," as the job was known in colonial English—who moved paper around and attended to the needs of other employees.

When J. R. Jayewardene came to office in 1977, he acted to renovate banking and finance as a step toward expanding the economy. First, get banking right, Jayewardene's administration thought, and the economy will follow. Making the transition from a business dominated by European and state-controlled banks to private banking represented a transition neither from local to foreign practice nor from foreign to local practice. It was a transition from one kind of foreign practice to another, from British ways of banking—which the state banks followed as much as the foreign banks—to American.[3] The state's goal was to encourage the private sector, not to drive Tamils from the banking business. But favoring private banks invited banks constructed in "the local idiom," and that change brought the growing estrangement of Sinhalas and Tamils into print advertising.

Enthusiasm for "modernizing" the state banks reached a high point in 1991 when the Premadasa government hired an American management firm—Booz, Allen, and Hamilton—to consider how the state banks could be operated more efficiently. Even if the firm had not been American, the association with free-wheeling enterprise and electronic technology marked it thus in local eyes. The firm enjoyed the sponsorship of the World Bank and International Monetary Fund, which is to say, it entered the local scene with government support and, in turn, enough leverage to seriously threaten local interests. In particular, the proposal threatened Bank of Ceylon employees, who numbered over twenty thousand. Their union's response makes clear what has been at issue in the establishment of new forms of banking.

> Under the recommendation, great stress is being laid on the need to cultivate a commercial culture against state-bank culture. Booz Allen say the state bank culture is (a) volume focussed (b) process driven (c) slow and inefficient (d) bureaucratic (e) unsupervised and (f) traditional, while commercial culture is (a) profit focussed (b) market customer driven (c) productive and efficient (d) streamlined (e) intensively managed and (f) operating with new/enhanced functions. These assessments are mere exaggerations and may not be a realistic evaluation of the current situation.[4]

The contrast between state-bank culture and commercial culture depends on both institutional differences and economic forces. Between 1977 and the mid-1980s, the number of private banks in Sri Lanka jumped from eleven to twenty-five.[5] But the state banks continued to control some 70 percent of the lending business despite being undercapitalized and weighed down with the burden, rumored to be as high as 30 percent, of nonperforming loans.[6] For consumers, the state banks had other problems. The Bank of Ceylon and People's Bank were notorious for being overstaffed—the two banks had security forces of some 2,500 men protecting their various offices—and inefficient. Customers complained of the banks' needing thirty minutes, after the customer had reached the front of the queue, to process a cash deposit. But most of all state banks were seen as indifferent to customers.[7] Its populist origins notwithstanding, the People's Bank managed to create the same air of indifference as the Bank of Ceylon. As a businessman put it to me, "How do I know it's the People's Bank? I know because they treat people so poorly."

What made banking such a profitable sector in an economy making the transition from state control to unrestrained capitalism is not far to seek—profit at relatively low risk. In the 1980s banks paid interest on savings accounts ranging from 12 to 18 percent; they lent money at rates of 17 to 21 percent, creating a spread that could amount to as much as 8 to 9 percent. That margin was often twice as great as margins in other Asian economies and sufficient to attract a steady flow of new banking enterprises. The state banks set the prevailing deposit and lending rates, and the private banks followed their lead. But the productive use of the new capital put into the economy by the growth of private banking was undone by still another factor related to the government's role in the economy. Banks could invest money in treasury bills paying up to 18 percent interest and avoid all risks. Treasury bills covered the government's budget deficits, but their high rate of return acted against the state's efforts to persuade banks to lend money to the underdeveloped parts of the economy—the shopkeepers, coconut millers, estate owners, and small businesses the state sought to support.

The state banks—the Bank of Ceylon, the People's Bank, and the National Savings Bank—were complemented by four large private banks—Hatton National Bank, whose origins reached back to the nineteenth century, Sampath Bank, Seylan Bank, and Commercial Bank.[8] These private banks have their head offices and most of their branches in and around Colombo, but banks regularly pop up in smaller places where once only the state banks ventured. Seylan Bank has over ninety branches nowadays (although a decade ago it had only twelve). Opening new branches makes little sense in a market that is "overbanked," but new banks keep appearing.[9] Something more than banking money and lending it out was going on here—the transition between banking as a state function and private enterprise, between colonial tradition and "modernity." Asked when Britain had entered the modern era, the historian J. G. A. Pocock once said, "1690, when the Bank of England began to give credit." In Sri Lanka the coming of aggressively managed private banks constitutes a similar transition, also linked to the proliferation of credit facilities.

The private bank that burst most spectacularly on the scene was Sampath Bank, which brought both new practices and striking advertising to the local market. I was interested in the bank because of its "local idiom" advertising campaigns of the early 1990s, but as I investigated that campaign I learned how inextricably advertising has been bound together with technology, everyday life, and economic change. What makes the Sampath case instructive is the way it refigured the relationship between culture and commerce, the more so because Sampath Bank went off in two directions at once. It developed itself as a local institution at the same time it cultivated modern technology and transnational connections. On the one hand, an advertising campaign with overtones of ethnic chauvinism, on the other, new kinds of technology and "American" forms of business organization—Sampath Bank exemplified not only the "local idiom" but also global modernity locally remade.

Sampath would be a Sri Lankan bank, standing alone in a market dominated by foreign banks, state institutions, and private banks with no claims to a local personality. It would invoke Sinhala tradition, linking itself to time and place. One striking set of print ads portrayed Sampath as the heir to a rebellion of 1848 when Kandyans tried to overthrow the British (see fig. 13). Just as their Kandyan ancestors struggled for economic independence, print advertisements argued, Sampath Bank was now carrying on that struggle. Independence from foreign banks? From state institutions? From underdevelopment? Another series of advertisements celebrated the opening of a branch in the countryside in an unprecedented way, saying that the bank had become one with the people of Matara (*api matara;* see fig. 8). What gave that claim its force was not simply the presence of a Sampath branch in Matara, but computer technology that would allow a customer from Matara to do business with a Sampath Bank branch in Colombo or Kandy. In this way technology raised the identitarian claim to a higher level. While the advertisement invoked a regional identity, technology allowed a merchant to operate his account in Matara without leaving Colombo. Sophisticated computer technology and dedicated telephone lines in fact made it possible for him to operate his account in either place.

The bank's founder, N. U. Jayawardena, was, as the Sri Lankan English expression puts it, a man from down South.[10] He was well known in banking circles, having run the Central Bank of Ceylon—which functions as a federal reserve bank. He was removed from office under suspicion of misconduct, eventually exonerated, and then went on to a private career, founding a finance company that became hugely successful.[11] As a British-educated Sri Lankan, Jayawardena had the social graces to mix confidently with foreign donors and middle-class Sri Lankans. As a former governor of the Central Bank, he had an insider's knowledge and social connections. As the founder of a successful finance company, he also had a reputation as an entrepreneur. An editorial writer called him "a living legend in the country's financial sector."[12] Against the background of the failure of finance companies during the 1980s, his position at Mercantile Credit and his adversarial relationship to the Central Bank gave him a roguish reputation in the bargain.

Jayawardena's plan was to establish a bank that would be both modern—driven by the same technologies that organize banking in developed countries—and consumer-oriented (or "American"). The support of USAID, the Asian Development Bank, and the World Bank made that prospect not only possible but inevitable.[13] USAID's support for Sampath developed in parallel with its efforts to support and broaden public participation in the Colombo Stock Exchange. Each of these institutions was to be inclusionary and egalitarian. On the one hand, the bank would treat customers as a resource; on the other, the bank would introduce new business practices.

In his first public statements, Jayawardena was less explicit about the future bank's technological plans than about his intention to reconfigure the way the bank worked as a human institution. Besides eliminating the battery of minor employees, he began hiring executives at salaries several times higher than their counterparts in other banks.[14] Computer technology would allow the bank to pay higher salaries because its employees would "work smarter" without having to work harder. An article that profiled one of the first executives to join the bank suggested that the bank brought change to a range of everyday behaviors: "I have never seen," the writer said—revealing in passing the prejudice against the generality of bank employees, "any of the employees at the Sampath Bank smoking cigarettes, chewing betel or having their lunch when dealing with customers."[15]

Jayawardena also wanted to make the bank a popular institution in a way that was democratizing but not populist. He organized a public issue of shares on the belief that a Sri Lankan bank should be owned by Sri Lankans. Where other banks with a Sri Lankan base had state support or foreign backing, Jayawardena guaranteed that the ownership of Sampath

Bank would be broadly based by a provision restricting the maximum share-holding of any statutory body to 10 percent. Eventually the number of Sampath Bank shareholders rose to eighteen thousand people, an enormous number of shareholders by local standards. Of the first eleven thousand, four-fifths of them held one-fifth of the capital in amounts of Rs. 10,000 or less.[16] The bank, in other words, would not only be owned by Sri Lankans, but their number would include Sri Lankans who had previously never imagined investing in a bank. They would be people who might have been intimidated by entering a bank. Now they would be owners of one.

USAID was committed to Jayawardena. "He's a scallywag," said one USAID bureaucrat, "but he's our scallywag." It fostered the bank's relationship with a local advertising agency, Phoenix, on the belief that an advertising campaign was essential to putting the bank and its share offering in public view. Sampath Bank grew to be a leading bank as Phoenix grew to be a leading advertising agency, tied together by an advertising campaign that made both players in the Sri Lankan economy. Previously the Colombo Stock Exchange limited advertising to a statutory newsprint advertisement announcing the issuing of shares and listing brokerage firms, guaranteeing that only a few Sri Lankans would invest in such shares. USAID and Sampath, by contrast, wanted a "shareholding democracy."[17] They got it almost immediately. The first offering of shares, worth Rs. 25 million was quickly oversubscribed. A second offering for Rs. 50 million was announced on 8 July 1987 and oversubscribed by 15 July. Eventually the Bank raised shares worth Rs. 125 million and had eighteen thousand shareholders.

"As a financial institution engaged in a highly competitive business," Jayawardena said in a press release, "the bank will offer its services to all irrespective of community or creed," an assertion notable for promising something that did not seem to be at issue. In retrospect, what he added was more portentous. "The bank has a special obligation to take care of the disadvantaged members of the community whom it will seek out deliberately and develop into creditable customers."[18] On its face, which "community" Jayawardena meant to serve was unclear, but it came to mean Sinhalas. The bank, he said, would value human capital, not just collateral in considering loans, and reach out to parts of the population underserved by banks, developing such people into banking customers at the same time it developed itself. Dealing with the press, Jayawardena spoke inclusively. But in other contexts, he spoke in narrower terms. He said that the thought of starting the bank came to him by accident when some members of the World Federation of Buddhists asked him to establish an International Buddhist Bank. "I asked them whether they could raise $200 million. They couldn't. So I told them I would start a bank of a different kind." [19]

The present-day Sampath Bank began its life as the Investment and Credit Bank, quickly moving on to its present name, Sampath. Under both nameplates the bank carried a tag line that insisted on its local identity: "A truly Sri Lankan bank for sons of the soil." It said the same in Sinhala ads—*upan bimē urumakkārayan haTa niyama sri lankika bankuvak.* And it did something less fulsome, but equally radical. It became the only Sri Lankan bank—and one of very few businesses of any kind—to employ its Sinhala name, written in Sinhala characters, on signboards, advertising, and printed material. In a world in which banking had been a British or cosmopolitan institution, a small gesture made Sampath Sinhala, thereby making the modern local.

The indigenizing expression "sons of the soil" has had a transnational career. In most contexts, it refers to indigenous people, and more narrowly to peasant farmers, but it has a troubled history in the region. The best-known usage is the *bumiputra* (Sanskrit, sons of the soil) legislation that Malaysia enacted after the anti-Chinese riots of 1969, giving Malays educational and economic preferences because they were the indigenous people of Malaysia. They were peasant farmers, "sons of the soil." Despite being the majority population, they were disadvantaged by Chinese control of the economy. To meet its responsibilities to the majority population, the Malay-majority political party that controlled the national government sought to gain 20 percent Malay control of corporate assets. By most accounts, affirmative action for the Malay majority has been successful, and Chinese advantages have been balanced by twenty-five years of prodigious economic growth.

In India the expression has had an equally fractious history. It arose amidst several anti-immigration movements in the late 1960s. The governments of Assam, Andhra, and Maharashtra responded to these movements by imposing restrictions on migrants through a system of preferences for local people, the "sons of the soil," in employment, education, and housing.[20] The effect of these policies has been to protect some middle-class people, defined as local, from others, defined as immigrants.[21] In the Malaysian case, the legislation distinguishes Malays as farmers and fishermen from Chinese as merchants and professionals; in the Indian case it distinguishes the long-time inhabitants of a region from newcomers, identified by their place of birth.[22]

The expression has an older Indian origin, and that usage follows the expression's even earlier transnational trajectory. The first appearance of the expression I can find dates to the 1940s and a Hindi film by K. A.

Abbas, *Dharti ke Lal* (Sons of the Soil). Abbas was a member of the Indian People's Theatre association, which had a loose connection to the Indian Communist Party. At this historical moment, the expression had a Hindi provenance and expressed a concern with social justice that still marks some parts of the Indian film industry. Abbas's connection to the Communist Party means that the expression had Western motivations, but more to the point, it expressed the movement's concern with the poor and oppressed, defined without regard for ethnic origins or place of birth. However much the expression has come to serve the interests of the middle classes or ethnic chauvinists, its original focus fell on the poor.

Sinhala politicians of the 1980s appropriated the expression to distinguish Sinhalas as the indigenous people of the island from communities that arrived later and especially those that had a close connection to trade. Some of those politicians were explicit about their being influenced by Malaysian policies giving preference to Malays. What *bumiputra* legislation had done for Malays they wanted done for Sinhalas. By invoking "sons of the soil," Jayawardena linked his bank to the Sinhala majority. The bank's Buddhist imagery also made the ethnic connection because to be Buddhist is to be Sinhala. But the expression had a more general referent. It was a local bank, not a foreign one, and, chauvinism aside, a good place for all local communities — Tamils, Muslims, and Christians alike — to do business.

Constructing a Local Idiom

Over the past ten years, I have had regular conversations with Guy Halpe about the advertising business. We have talked about matters ranging from advertising aesthetics and the organization of local agencies to music and popular culture. At the beginning of that interval, he had just begun his career at Phoenix, where he worked on Sampath Bank advertising. In the intervening years, he took jobs at a succession of other agencies, rising through the ranks at Minds Lanka, Masters, Zenith, and Holmes, Pollard, and Stott. Nowadays he works as a creative consultant, spending about half of his time at his old agency, now Phoenix, Ogilvy and Mather. As his reference to the "Brechtian concept of alienation" suggests, Guy is not a simple practitioner, but he remains a creative director with practical knowledge of banking, Sampath's advertising, and business in Colombo.

My role in what follows is less ethnographer than fellow student of advertising and culture. Showing the conversation preserves that equality, while allowing Guy to speak for himself.[23]

S: So suddenly in 1977 the local banks started to compete in new ways?

G: When private banks were given license to operate as retail banks, when the industry was deregulated, then they started to advertise.

S: And that would have been 1977 or after? Sampath was established in 1987. So the banking situation did not change until ten years had passed and Sampath came along and started to do business?

G: Sampath was not the forerunner, but they did business in a different way. Let's say that Grindlay's and Hatton National Bank were actually modern commercial banks at that time.

S: I had an account at Hatton National Bank in Kandy in 1985, and they were obviously dealing with individual, retail customers.

G: It's just that they didn't have the technology. Sampath came in with several innovations. First of all they actively publicized their share offering by way of advertisements.

S: So what? What did that mean?

G: It meant that they wanted ordinary people to participate. There was this idea—as I have been told by Irwin Weerackody [the chief executive at Phoenix and the executive most closely identified with local idiom advertising] — that N. U. Jayawardena wanted to make it a Sri Lankan bank for sons of the soil.

S: Yes. He had several partners. Albert Edirisinghe [a successful businessman and one-time president of the World Federation of Buddhists], for example.

G: Jayawardena was a very cosmopolitan, British-educated, public-school type. The other thing is that Sampath Bank brought in technology. People had heard of automatic teller machines before. The first ATM came in with Hong Kong and Shanghai Bank. Lots of young people, working in middle management, opened an account at Hong Kong Bank just for the sake of being able to flash the plastic card.

S: The appeal was status or the prospect of being able to get your hands on money night and day?

G: Both, but I suspect more status. In my case, I don't lead much of a public life. So it wasn't that I flashed the card. It was the convenience. Next to hospitals and hotels, the place I least want to go to is a bank. So all of my accounts [pulling an array of bank cards from wallet] I operate with plastic.

S: All of this rush to plastic did not begin with Visa or Master-Card. It began with ATM cards.

G: Yes, that was Hong Kong and Shanghai Bank. They were first. Sampath then came in with the SET [Sampath Electronic Transfer, the bank's acronym for its ATM product] card, and at the same time Sampath tied up with MasterCard and they very cleverly linked several services together. For example, I don't have a SET card. I have a MasterCard, but it can debit my Sampath savings account.

S: So you have a MasterCard that functions like a SET card?

G: Yes, if I use it at Sampath Bank.

S: You can deposit money late at night with Sampath?

G: Not only that, but I can also deposit checks. None of the other banks allows me to do that.

S: You get a check from a client and you put it in the ATM, and it is automatically credited to your account.

G: Well, the check is manually cleared.

S: So you don't get credit right away.

G: No, the next banking day. So that is what they did in account-ing. The third thing was what Irwin Weerackody brought to the question. He built a very cultural, Eastern thing for the bank.

S: That was N. U. Jayawardena's or Irwin Weerackody's con-ception?

G: Well, N. U. Jayawardena had this idea of a truly Sri Lankan bank for sons of the soil, but then if it is such a bank you would have expected it to develop heavily into the rural areas and to encourage microcredit, which he did not do.

S: So Irwin Weerackody actually guided the direction of the bank's services?

G: He stayed in the city centers and he invested in technology.

In this context, the "sons of the soil" that Phoenix's advertise-ments spoke of and to were a group of Colombo dwellers who would be attracted to the bank's ability to offer modern banking technology.[24] Guy described that clientele as including everyone from the CEO to the man who drives the CEO's car, but who also speaks English, as drivers often do in Colombo. Sampath hoped to create an unprecedented community of consumption, using the campaign to establish an indigenous form of banking—highly technological but culturally Sinhala—as a way to attract customers who, as a group, would scarcely have done their banking with any one bank under other circumstances.[25]

A central part of constructing advertising for the bank was to give the bank a "Buddhist" character without calling it the International Buddhist Bank.[26] But the medium of instruction for constructing this community of consumption was to be print and the language was to be English.

> S: At one point they wanted to be the Buddhist Bank. Their model of a religious bank was the Vatican Bank, which at that point in history had reached a low ebb because of massive fraud. [Actually it was] an Italian bank which did business with the Vatican. So that was a strange paradigm to choose.[27]
>
> G: They were not allowed to call the bank the Buddhist Bank. You know how easy it is to offend.
>
> S: Even in a Buddhist-majority society, that was too Buddhist?
>
> G: Well, it's got something to do with the popular conception of what can be used in advertising and what cannot.
>
> S: Right, but what I am saying is that you would think that a Buddhist-majority society might have trouble with someone trying to open another Vatican Bank here but might not have trouble with a Buddhist bank . . . it all depends on whose ox is being gored. But that is not what happened?
>
> G: All I'm saying is really that the idea of a Buddhist Bank brings together two words that don't seem to be matched.
>
> S: [Picking up an advertisement centered on the Lord Buddha and a Pali text]. Why isn't this ad too close to Buddhism (see fig. 7)? We talked of having to tread very softly, very gingerly when it comes to religion. But this isn't too much?
>
> G: The thing that immediately swings into my mind is the Brechtian concept of alienation, where there is a subject but there has to be a removal between the subject and the secondary subject, which is what you actually want to say. He's taken a quotation from the Buddha, and you will notice that the quotation is not directly linked to Sampath Bank. It's there on its own even in terms of the visual space. There is a picture of the Buddha and a Pali quotation, so this entire area has nothing to do with banking. It's purely Buddhist. Then Sampath

FIGURE 7.   The Buddha's wisdom remembered on *Vesak,* his birthday (*Daily News* [Colombo], 9 May 1990).

  Bank comes in at the end and says, "We realize the wisdom of these words." It's not really as if they've taken the words and said, "Okay, this is the way we do our banking."

S: That's right. They haven't made the Buddha a spokesman for the bank.

G: So I think he has achieved balance.

S: Yeah. That's clever.

G: The thing that connects with [the cultural reference] is the bank's symbol. It's pretty powerful, and maybe that did more to build the image of the bank than the name.

S: Sampath means "good fortune?"

G: It's a complex word that includes "good fortune" and "resource." The logo is the *pun kalāsa,* the urn of plenty.

S: The horn of plenty. The cornucopia.

G: In Western culture, it is the horn. Here it is the pot. *Pun kalāsa. Kalāsa* is the word for pot and *pun* . . .

S: Merit.

G: Yes.

S: Where would people have seen a *pun kalāsa* prior to its becoming a bank logo? [28]

G: Ancient architecture. It is a popular feature on entrances. I
think you have it on some of the architecture in Kandy. The
university? It is not at the entrance to the Arts faculty, which
has the two lions . . . Somewhere else I remember having seen
the pot. You know, the symbol of the New Year?

S: Yes, the overflowing pot.

G: The idea of the pot as a receptacle for rice or money. All of
these things are there.

S: It's more than storage, it's abundance. The pot must overflow.

G: Yes.

S: So people have a referent for it. It's something that works
without instruction?

G: Yes.

S: Well, tell me about those early Sampath ads. Sampath did
television advertising in those early days?

G: No, come to think of it, they didn't do television for a long
time. I think I did the first Sampath Bank commercial . . . and
that was not particularly Sri Lankan. It was not aimed at rural
people. It just publicized the Unibank system, the electronic
network.

S: So this attempt to create a Sri Lankan persona was limited to
print?

G: In retrospect, I think that may have been a mistake, Irwin's
mistake. It may have been Irwin's background as a print
journalist.

The emphasis on print had several motivations. Television did not
strike Weerackody as the right medium to announce a bank, much less a
share issue, which requires careful explanation when appealing to people
who have never held shares previously. Print advertising was relatively
cheap, making it an effective way to spend his client's money. But the
emphasis on newsprint and English-language advertisements also had a
social motivation. The bank also wanted to draw business from the people
who traditionally banked, not just newcomers. They wanted to do business
with Colombo's disparate population. They went where the money was—
the import-export business—and that is not part of the economy where
Sinhalas predominate. I once asked another advertising executive whether

he found this combination unlikely: Sampath Bank was the bank for "sons of the soil" but it tried to do business in the Pettah, that part of Colombo dominated by Muslims and Hindus in the import-export trade. Wouldn't they be put off by the ethnic pitch, I asked? His reply: "Money knows no race."

Guy and I looked over photocopies of the early print advertisements for Sampath, and he thought over my questions about what lay behind the photos and texts. What he said in response suggests the bank's attempt to create a local character for an institution that had been irremediably foreign. We spoke about the way Sampath advertised its opening of branches in provincial cities, despite doing most of its business in Colombo. I remembered having seen other banks that advertised the establishment of a branch office in a small town.

S: [looking at print ads] Certainly there is nothing unique about advertising the fact that you are opening a branch someplace in the island. Bank of Ceylon has always done that.

G: No, they didn't. Not until Sampath. That's what added to the corporate image of a bank—announcing where it was opening.

S: But what I was struck by is that once Irwin Weerackody got that going, other banks and finance companies did the same. I remember the series of ads that began with *Api Matara* [we are Matara] (see fig. 8).

G: That's the one. *Api Matara* was Sampath Bank. Somebody might have stolen the copy later because there is a tremendous lot of emotion invested in that statement, *api matara*. You know that Southerners often think of themselves as a great nation. Similar to affairs in Quebec.

S: Well, they are a separate nation. In terms of their ethnic origins, they came from India in relatively recent times. All of those Low Country caste groups—Karava, Salagama, Durava—are people who were Tamil four hundred years ago, eight hundred years ago. There's an article by Michael Roberts that collects what little evidence there remains.[29] They came between the thirteenth and seventeenth centuries from India. So they became Sinhala, but they were newcomers, and in a sense their difference is not just a caste difference. I think it is also ethnic, Kandyans must have seen them as newcomers, as Indians.

G: *Api matara* relates to this thing about Matara . . . being very separate, very individual, very proud. It is exactly what the text says. These people identify themselves with [the place] and they are proud of it. It's a tribute.

S: What I remember from seeing this advertisement the first time was thinking *api matara* meant we—Sampath Bank—are Matara. And it does mean that, but the primary reference is we—the people of Matara—identify ourselves as Matara. Right?

G: I think there is equal weightage on both concepts. It is part of the Irwin Weerackody style to have a double play. It's fifty/fifty Sampath Bank saying we are Matara and saying it in the same words as the people of Matara say it.

S: Next question. Can I say *api ratnapura* [we are Ratnapura] or *api nuvara* [we are Kandy]? It doesn't have the same force?

G: It doesn't have the same meaning.

S: There's not as much localism?

G: And also there is a dialect . . . a way of talking that's there in just these two words.

S: It's a way of projecting yourself.

FIGURE 8.   Celebrating a branch opening in Matara against the background of a business district in Colombo (*Times* [Colombo], 27 May 1990).

G: Yes, and if you try to translate the concept to another place, they would say *api inne ratnapura* [we are from Ratnapura] or a guy from the hills would say, *api nuvara kotiya* [we are the clan from Kandy, we are people from Kandy]. *Api matara* is a very good choice of phrase. It's not just saying we are Matara. It's saying we are Matara in the other way. Matara is us.

S: It's a metaphor that changes both sides. If that's the case, tell me if you don't see something strange about this advertisement [showing Guy a photocopy of the advertisement seen in fig. 8].

G: Meaning that there is no clear connection between Sampath Bank and the people of Matara?

S: No. Here, "You meet them everywhere . . ."

G: As it says at the top . . . "From Matara to all parts of the country." Okay, it is a fact that you find the people of Matara everywhere.

S: Right, Matara people are not just in Matara. But this is an advertisement that is celebrating the opening of a branch in Matara, and making a very strong claim, mimicking the voice of someone who actually lives there, but where are these buildings in the advertisement?

G: The buildings are in Matara.

S: No.

G: Oh . . . yes, the buildings are in Panchikawatte [a commercial area in Colombo and center of the auto parts trade].

S: Don't you find that strange? Isn't something going on here?

G: You see, Panchikawatte is the epitome of the self-made man—the small entrepreneur, the man who owns a shop. And there is a personality for Panchikawatte, aggressive, a little bit sneaky . . . not beyond doing things like getting you to park your car in front of their shop. There are these stories about Panchikawatte. You park your car and you want a couple of hubcaps and they sell you a couple of hubcaps. You go home and find that the hubcaps you have bought were taken off the other side of your car. Things like that, you know, streetwise?

S: Street-smart.

G: Yeah. But these guys are migratory. They've become famous, but not in Matara, outside Matara. I'll give you another example. There are about four or five drivers at one of the agencies I've worked at. One guy, just one guy, is basically the

kingpin there. He's a money lender. He has a little business
on the side. He comes to work in his own trishaw, so he probably has a trishaw business as well, running on the weekends
and nights. This guy has a certain attitude. He's respectful,
he's deferential, but he's very self-possessed. Calm, confident,
and not beyond a little brawling if the need arises. He's the
sort of guy whom we would take to the police station if one
of our people were in trouble.

S: He's the man.

G: He's the Man, capital m. He's the man who comes from
Matara.

S: What I was thinking with regards to the Panchikawatte part
of it: you're opening a branch located way down south, you're
showing a picture of Panchikawatte in Colombo. It's exactly
what we were talking about. This is a bank that was going after Colombo people. It's important to have the branch down
south, to be sure, but the real business is going to be done in
Panchikawatte and places like it. It's going to mean something
to people here [in Colombo] to see that reference to Matara,
that is, *api matara,* but the ad is not really focused on Matara.
It's focused on people who come from Matara who live all
over the island and might be charmed by the local reference.
That's my idea.

G: Yes.

The Sampath customer might have been a "son of the soil," but the advertising was aimed at urban-dwellers, sympathetic to an "ethnic imaginary"
that referred to themselves only indirectly by evoking a rural identity that
most had lost. A few of the early ads in Sinhala and English showed another paradigmatic Sri Lankan figure, not the paddy farmer but the *mudalali,* the small businessman, selling foodstuffs in a local market, and
making a living by trucking merchandise from a central place such as the
Pettah to that place.

S: Take a look at this second advertisement, the *mudalali* from
Matara (see fig. 9).

G: Now I worked on this advertisement.

S: Good, you know exactly what the author intended.

G: Well, I basically . . .

S: Did you do the Sinhala or the English.

G: I did the English.

එදා, කොළඹ යන කල අතේ සල්ලි හිතේ ගින්දර
අද, සම්පත් බැංකුවේ 'යුනිබැන්ක්' ක්‍රමය නිසා
හිතට සහනය වැඩට පහසුව

සේ මාතර ව්‍යාපාරිකයෙකි.

වෙත ද මෙත් කොළඹ යන කල සල්ලි පොදියක් අත තබා ගෙන මග යෑවීමට දැන් ඔහුට සිදු තො වේ. ඔහුට සම්පත් බැංකුවේ ජංගම ගිණුමක් තිබේ.

ඔහු දුන් කරන්නේ එදිනෙද ආදායම මාතර සම්පත් බැංකුවේ තැන්පත් කිරීම යි. එසේ කළ විට එක හරියටම කොළඹ හෝ කුරුණෑගල හෝ මහනුවර හෝ අනෙක් තැනෙක හෝ සම්පත් බැංකුවේ මුදල් තැන්පත් කළා වැනි ය.

ඒ පහසුකම ලැබී ඇත්තේ සම්පත් බැංකුවේ 'ශාඛා' තැති තිබා. ඒ තැන්වල තිබෙන්නේ සම්පත් බැංකුවේ කාර්යාල. 'යුනිබැන්ක්' ක්‍රමය නිසා සියල්ල එක ම පද්ධතියකි. ඒ නිසා කොතන මුදල් තැන්පත් කළත් ඔහුට ම තැනෙකින් ගනුදෙනු කළ හැකි යි. ශ්‍රී ලංකාවේ මේ පහසුකම ඇත්තේ සම්පත් බැංකුවේ ම පමණ යි.

ඔහු සතු ව SET කාඩ් පතක් ද තිබේ. ඒ මගින් ඕනෑ ම තැනෙකින් මුදල් ආපසු ගැනීම, ගිණුමකින් ගිණුමකට මුදල් හැරවීම, තැන්පත් කිරීම, චෙක් පොත් ඉල්ලා සිටීම, ගිණුම් පරීක්ෂණ සියල්ල කර ගත හැකි යි.

එන යන වේලාවල් කුමක් වුවත් කමක් තැ. රෑ දවල් වෙනසක් තැති ව දවසේ පැය 24 මුළුල්ලේ ම පාහේ බැංකු තිවාඩු දින වත් තො තකා සතියේ දින ගණතේ ම. ඒ නිසා ව්‍යාපාරිකයාට පමණක් තොව සියලු දෙතාට ම පහසුවක්.

සම්පත් බැංකුවේ ජංගම ගිණුමෙන් අත් තැනෙකින් තො ලැබිය හැකි පහසුකම් රැසක්.

සම්පත්බැංකුව
SampathBank

උපන් බිමේ නියම උරුමක්කාරයන් හට නියම ශ්‍රී ලාංකික බැංකුවක්.

FIGURE 9.   "Those days, carrying money to Colombo was painful. These days, Sampath's Unibank system makes it easy" (*Divaina* [Colombo], 28 July 1991).

S: And Irwin Weerackody did the Sinhala?

G: His way of working is to give the concept in the headline and to give the idea of the visual, and then we carry it out. Which is a little hard sometimes because it is quite hard to think like him, but that is something I've been able to learn over the years. Anyway, sorry, I interrupted.

S: No, no . . . What came first . . . the English or the Sinhala or do you remember?

G: The English. What we did was sit down . . . you see the reason for this campaign was that Sampath Bank realized that they should be talking about their unique data communication system [which linked all the branches together].

S: Which they had and others didn't?

G: Others did but not to the extent that Sampath did. At the point when we ran this campaign, nobody else was offering the same facilities, like night deposits. I mean . . . this little box [in the ad] with all those facilities. That's unique. It was a fairly strong campaign.

S: Yeah.

G: So?

S: The intended audience . . . Every stage play has an intended audience. Every ad has one. Is the intended audience here people who actually live in Matara or people who do business in different places and might be persuaded by the example of this *mudalali?*

G: I think it was not as directed as that. I think it was a campaign aimed at the general public, not even the customers . . . to say, you know, this is what Sampath is doing. Can your bank actually do the same? I don't think it was a hard sell.

S: Well, I didn't think it was a hard sell . . . I just wondered whether it had a sharp focus.

G: I would say this was a more diluted focus.

The data communication system itself made Sampath a more Sri Lankan institution despite the Sinhala focus of the advertising. It made the bank a national institution, one branch linked electronically to all the others.[30] The logic of the campaign, by contrast, was to put the bank into a variety of "zones of display," usually chosen on some metonymic basis. Panchikawatte stands for Matara which stands for Sinhala economic life; Sinhala economic life represents the economic life of the nation; and the Matara *mudalali* represents the customer who needs to move money from one place to another. He used to move money by carrying it in his jacket pocket; now he does so electronically.

Phoenix's early campaign for Sampath Bank also put the Pettah to the same metonymic end. But for a bank drawing on its Sinhala and Buddhist character, Pettah's role was even more problematic because of its strongly non-Sinhala character.

S: Let's look at the "Saga of Pettah" advertisement (see fig. 10). There is a series of these in different forms.

G: Yes, this was when Sampath Bank was launching.

S: But their first branch was not really in the Pettah.[31] Their first branch was on the other side of the Pettah railway station [so this advertisement is not referring to their first launch].

G: Yeah. I'm not saying that this was the very first advertisement. The target group was more specific in the ads that we've just gone through. Here they are actually soliciting business. They're trying to build an image for Sampath Bank in order to appeal to certain people.

S: People who work in Pettah?

G: No, not people who work in Pettah.

S: People who see themselves as heirs to the Chinese, Arabs, and Portuguese [the three ethnic types represented in the advertisement]?

G: Well, it is for a branch opening in Pettah, so it's not really an appeal to the heirs.[32] It is not an appeal to the businessmen in the area so much as it is saying, "We are going to be locating ourselves in a certain place, and we are doing this because we have the foresight to think of ourselves as being part of this community," and so on. I don't think there was a serious intention that they would actually be serving the needs of the Pettah traders.

S: Well, that's . . . why did they open a branch there? It's a strange place to open a branch if you don't want to [appeal to traders]. I mean it's off-putting for people who don't want to have any connection to Pettah. You're not going to open your business in Pettah if you are trying to be modern and upscale. If you open a branch in Pettah, saying something about the history of the place in the advertisement, it seems that you either want to capitalize on what might be a liability or else there's something else going on here that I don't understand.

G: Maybe it's not as clear as we both think it is. Ah, you see, a lot

FIGURE 10.   Tying Sampath Bank to Colombo's primary market area and the vanished ethnic groups who once dominated it (*Daily News* [Colombo], 20 July 1988).

of these things just . . . at the time when these campaigns actually took place, there wasn't really a strategy for advertising.

S: I see. It had to be done quickly . . .

G: It had to be done quickly. And also it all depended on an idea. That's why I told you about the way Irwin Weerackody works. The idea, the concept of the advertisement, pops into his head first, and he tells his writers to execute it.

S: Well, on to the Sinhala businessmen in Pettah. What's your reaction to this advertisement (see fig. 11)? We talked about the advertisement briefly before.

G: Again, it is a series. These campaigns ran at a time when press was still an affordable medium. So you could afford to have what is called a teaser ad, followed up by another teaser ad, and finally a big bang launch. He's done that for the Kandy advertisements [a similar series of advertisements announcing the opening of the branch at Kandy]. The first was "The Saga of Pettah" advertisement, and then he's trying to make it more specific by talking about businesspeople . . . who incidentally are mentioned in the previous advertisement, but not so prominently.

S: What do you mean they are mentioned?

G: Not the same people, but he does put in businesspeople.

S: Right. But these are businessmen of the past. The Chinese came and they disappeared. The Arabs came and were edged out by the Portuguese, who were followed by the British.

G: And then there are the local businessmen. The Sinhala headline reads, "*Sri lankika vyāpārikayan ge nijabima . . . pitako*

FIGURE 11.   Pettah, the cradle of Sri Lankan businessmen, all Sinhala (*Daily News* [Colombo], 22 July 1988).

Tuwa." That is, "The ground . . . from which these brilliant business people . . . have sprung . . . Pettah."

S: They are all Sinhala: H. Don Carolis, William Pedris, W. E. Bastian, Punchisingho, E. G. Hinniappuhami, M. D. Gunasena. No Lebbes. No Pillais [distinctive Muslim and Tamil names].

G: Let me see if he has mentioned anyone else in the text. No. He's calling [these six] the pioneers and saying, "This heritage and tradition we will join." I don't know. I think we did mention that there might have been an element of racism here.

S: It's the "sons of the soil" part of the campaign.

G: At this point, it may have been N. U. Jayawardena saying . . . By the way, I discovered since last time that Jayawardena was Durava [a caste whose traditional occupation was harvesting coconuts and tapping coconut palms].

S: Very interesting.

G: I didn't think . . . I'm a little curious about the caste system, so I mentioned this to my father-in-law, and he said, "Oh, it makes perfect sense . . . that N. U. Jayawardena should hook up with Irwin Weerackody because they are both Durava.

S: That's right, . . . *api matara* [A large concentration of Durava people live in and around Matara, and many people who do business in Colombo also see Matara as their native place].

G: Exactly. I didn't think that this advertisement had a clear focus. I think it is simply that Weerackody wanted to do something that would catch the interest of the reader.

S: The last Pettah advertisement is entitled "Living by Trade" (see fig. 12).

G: It's more of the same. Now instead of talking about personalities, he's now talking about the way business is actually done in the Pettah. He's talking about, you know, the high turnover. Here [reading from the ad]: "over half a million people conclude roughly three million transactions a day." It's basically saying that this is the sort of business that happens in Pettah.

S: It's as didactic as the previous advertisements. The former teaches you something of the Pettah's history; this is teaching you about how business is negotiated—the volume, the number of people involved directly and indirectly.

G: This is what I found interesting about this campaign. At every stage the advertisements said, "We are going to be a part of

this," when everyone knew that this wouldn't happen. It's
wishful thinking. Because the Pettah traders have their own
way of doing business. They prefer to work with cash.

S: Yeah, they get their money from Pillai [one of several famous
Pettah moneylenders] who has 75 million rupees on the street
every day at 1 percent interest per day.

G: So maybe there is something here. The Sri Lankan public is
now willing to tolerate a polite fiction . . . merely because
there is something that they can relate to in the fact that [the
ad] is taking the trouble to say that we are going to be a part
of this.

S: Exactly. Here's the contrast. It's the Hong Kong Bank on the
one hand. They're not going to identify with any part of the
island. They're going to give you wonderful service and lots
of efficiency . . . and that is no small virtue, but this is a bank
that is going to indulge in a polite fiction. It's going to use
Pettah as a trope. The place that stands for the entire island.
It's localism. Pettah stands for the island in general, especially

FIGURE 12.   Bazaar capitalism
as metaphor for Sam-
path's local aspirations
(*Daily News* [Colombo],
29 July 1988).

the Sinhala parts of it, even though it is the prototypically non-Sinhala place.

There are of course Sinhala businessmen who do business in the Pettah, and there are Pettah traders of other ethnic communities who opened an account at Sampath Bank. And the Matara *mudalali* could make direct use of the Pettah branch when he finally got his truck to pick up goods nearby, but the strategy is clear enough. Phoenix exploited the Pettah connection not because it spoke directly to prospective customers, but because it spoke indirectly of the bank's rootedness. It was going to do business in a distinctively commercial and consummately local place, the Pettah. As against all other Sri Lankan banks, Sampath was the one that dared to celebrate its being a local bank. It did so in a chauvinist way, assuming that Sinhala culture could plausibly represent the "local way of life" for Sinhalas and non-Sinhalas alike, hoping that such a jarring "zone of display" could overwhelm the contradictions.

What the agency thought would compensate for the incongruity was the notion of economic independence, of a local bank offering world-class service despite being local and congenial. I asked about another early campaign that exploited that theme.

S: Right. Tell me about "A Milestone" (see fig. 13).

G: Now this is a general advertisement.

S: Weerackody did three or four of these. I saw some on the wall of the reception area at Phoenix in 1990. The theme is economic independence.

G: No, this is celebrating our fortieth anniversary as a country. Political independence. Throwing off the colonial yoke.

S: Right, only it seems to me that there is an economic message here. [Reading] "With the establishment of Sampath Bank Limited in 1987, a new financial force moved into the forefront of this crucial struggle. The year marked a milestone in Sri Lanka's march to economic emancipation and prosperity for her people. We are confident of continuing to remain in the forefront of the struggle."

G: Well, the copy is a little bombastic

S: Of course. You think it's inadvertent that he turned the political struggle into an economic struggle?

G: Oh no. He's done it quite skillfully.[33]

S: Exactly. His purposes are to launch a bank which is an economic institution, so he rereads the past and sees economic

Reproduced from Illustrated London News of August ?? ??

The battle that ensued when British troops attacked this house
in Wariyapola where Gongalegoda Banda had taken refuge, was
one of the final episodes in the 1848 Matale rebellion – a
milestone in Sri Lanka's struggle for Independence.

This battle ground had earlier been immortalised by Ven.
Wariyapola Sumangala Thera, who pulled down the Union Jack
and hoisted the Sinhala flag for which act of defiance, he paid
with his life.

In 1948, exactly a century after the Matale rebellion, we won
Independence. And today we celebrate our 40th Independence
Commemoration Day. Independence brought with it full political
freedom. But the struggle for economic freedom still continues.

With the establishment of Sampath Bank Limited in 1987, a
new financial force moved into the forefront of this crucial
struggle. The year marked a milestone in Sri Lanka's march to
economic emancipation and prosperity for her people. We are
confident of continuing to remain in the forefront of the struggle.

A Milestone

සම්පත්බැංකුව
SampathBank

SAMPATH BANK LIMITED
WIJEWARDENE MAWATHA COLOMBO ??
TELEPHONE 541132, 11582, 26395, 54132
TELEX ?????? CBANK ????? NAMBE

A truly Sri Lankan Bank for sons of the soil

FIGURE 13.   Political struggle becomes economic struggle (*Daily News* [Colombo],
4 February 1988).

significance in 1848. And there was some economic significance behind the uprising, but there was also political
significance.

G: There was more political significance.

S: Yeah.

G: What he has done is very clever, making a connection to the
political rhetoric—"march, "forefront of struggle," "economic emancipation." [laughter]

S: The rights of man. *Liberté, égalité, fraternité.*

Guy talked about his boss, Irwin Weerackody, because he has been as much
of a phenomenon as Sampath Bank. Looking at the "A Milestone" ad, Guy
evaluated the advertising as advertising.

G: There's nothing much here in terms of copy, in terms of a
concept. I've got to say this. This is not what we would call
professional advertising, but this is advertising that is so different from the mainstream of all the other things that were done
at that stage.

S: I think I hear you saying that this text is not meant to be read
word for word and cashed out the way I'm doing.

G: Yeah.

S: It's meant to have an emotional impact. Some of the words
jump off the page, and the advertising agency will be happy
if you get a couple of these.

G: And also what I'm saying is that even though it is not professional in terms of advertising, I don't want to call it unprofes-
sional advertising . . . that's a strong word.

S: Yeah. Why isn't this advertisement fully professional? This is
what Weerackody does a lot of times. He doesn't want to
make readers of people. He doesn't want a close reading of
the text. He wants to . . .

G: Maybe then you're getting into the way I write, and I'm pretty
picky about grammar and syntax. For instance, I will never
write so much. I will try to cut down so people can actually
pick out the essence. So it's little things like that . . . technical
things. But I shouldn't be looking at it from a technical angle.

S: Sure, there is too much there.

G: But though it is less than technically perfect, it's very different.
And in being different, it creates a presence.

S: And this kind of advertising has had a long-term effect? What
    he did ten years ago has changed the ways advertisements are
    done now, no?

G: It's also changed the way Phoenix was perceived. Phoenix
    went from being, you know, a midrange, not-so-important
    agency to being a top agency.

S: The local-idiom agency?

G: Yeah, the local-idiom agency. The judges at the SLIM [Sri
    Lanka Institute of Marketing] awards ceremony that particu-
    lar year [1990 or 1991?] thought so. Phoenix carried away 13
    or 14 golds, basically for this campaign. With all the technical
    imperfections.

S: Sure, well, it may have its imperfections, but it is as profes-
    sional as the competition, no?

G: No.

S: Do you think Grant McCann-Erickson and JWT would have
    been more meticulous about their copywriting?

G: Not Grant's, but JWT would have . . . at this very time . . .
    they would have done advertisements for IBM. you know,
    corporate clients overseas.

S: Well you can't get away with anything less than clear English
    when you are dealing with a global client, I'm sure.

As Sampath Bank opened branches in the suburbs of Colombo, it
continued to stress that it was not only a local bank, but also a grassroots
one. When it launched its Nugegoda office, Phoenix put Sampath in a
"zone of display" so homely, so mundane as to be unthinkable for another
bank. In the "What has Delkanda Pola [market] got to do with the Sampath Bank?" advertisement, Phoenix celebrated the juxtaposition between
a ramshackle weekly market where business is carried out in cash and
weights measured on a scale and a bank with electronic transfers of funds
and a consumer orientation (see fig. 14).

The subtext is just as important as the text itself. Most Sri Lankans
have had suspicions at one time or another that they have been overcharged
for fruits, vegetables, rice, or any commodity that needs to be weighed—
in a place just like the Delkanda Pola—by a merchant who manipulated
his scales to make the scale read heavier than the actual purchase. Sampath
Bank will be just as much an institution in Nugegoda as Delkanda Pola.
But it will be different in one way: "And so, we shall tip the scales in your
favor." This is a bank, the advertisement says, that will be fully local but
consumer oriented, as modern as any bank, but as familiar as the village

bazaar. With this workaday scene—its ready-to-hand quality, naturalness, and presence in town and village—local-idiom advertising reaches its logical extreme. The exemplary alien, bureaucratized, intimidating institution

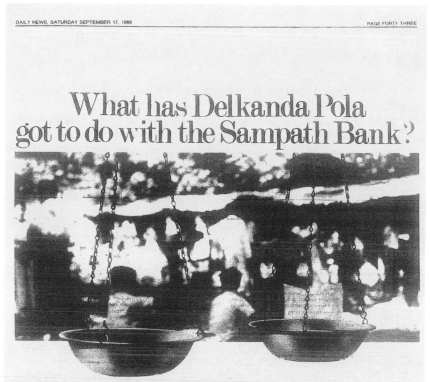

FIGURE 14.   A local bank brings consumer-oriented service to the hinterlands of Colombo (*Daily News* [Colombo], 17 September 1988).

appears in a "zone of display" very close to where most people live. The global becomes local; the British, Sri Lankan; the cold, warm and supportive. Sampath Bank would offer ATM machines, credit cards, and electronic transfers between branches in the bargain. Whether the generality of Sri Lankans would be engaged by all this is another matter.

NOTES

1. David Rudner, *Caste and Capitalism in Colonial India: The Nattukottai Chettiars* (Berkeley: University of California Press, 1994), 53–60.

2. See W. S. Weerasoria, *The Nattukottai Chettiar Merchant Bankers in Ceylon* (Dehiwela: Tisara Prakasakayo, 1973), 1–41.

3. I am speaking of the more modern parts of the banking business. Traditional sources of finance capital remained in place, although the rising threat of violence against Chettiars in Pettah has given them reason to maintain a low profile.

4. "Americanisation of the Bank of Ceylon," *Island* (Colombo), 1 December 1991.

5. Statistics Department, Central Bank of Sri Lanka, preface to *Report of the Survey on Customer Services of Commercial Banks in Sri Lanka,* December 1986.

6. "Who Reaps the Benefits of Economic Growth," *Financial Times Survey* (London), 27 October 1992.

7. The present Bank of Ceylon was founded as a private bank in 1939 and nationalized in 1962. The Peoples' Bank owes its existence to the support of Philip Gunawardana. a fiery Troskyite of the period that immediately preceded and followed independence in 1948. He wanted government to establish a bank that would serve not British agency houses or Tamil merchants but ordinary Sri Lankans, especially Sinhala farmers, petty traders, and other rural people.

8. There have also been a number of private and foreign banks doing business in Sri Lanka. Chief among them are Hong Kong Bank, Grindlay's, and Standard Chartered Bank. As of 1990, Bank of Ceylon had 243 branches; Peoples' Bank, 305; Hatton National Bank, 36; Sampath Bank, 13; Seylan Bank, 12; and Commercial Bank, 18 (H. N. S. Karunatilake, "Re-orienting Banking Policy and Practice to Meet the Needs of the People," *Central Bank of Sri Lanka, Occasional Papers,* no. 20, 1990.

9. Colombo may be overbanked, but villagers seeking to borrow money usually rely on sources of credit other than banks. Rauno Zander's study of two villages—one a semi-urban village near the Katunayake free-trade zone and the other in the remote northern part of Kurunegala district—found villagers borrowing from a variety of lenders. In the first setting, sources of credit included friends and relatives, 33.9 percent; NGOs, 17.9 percent; money lenders, 17.9 percent; traders, 14.2 percent; banks, 12.3 percent; and workplace 3.8 percent. In the more remote settings, banks did only slightly better: friends and relatives, 34.9 percent; NGOs 21.9 percent; traders 15.6 percent; banks, 14.1 percent; money lenders, 12.5 percent; and workplace, 1.6 percent ("Politics and Rural Financial Markets in Sri Lanka," [paper delivered at the Third Sri Lanka Conference, Amsterdam, April 1991], 9).

10. There are Sinhalas of other caste origins, including Goyigama, who come from or live in the southern part of the island, so it is useful to distinguish caste from region in many contexts. But to say of a person that he or she comes from "down South" in English, *dakuna palate* (southern province), or *Bentota gange eha* (on the far side of the Bentota River) is often to speak of caste identity. The three castes that dominate in either context are Karava, Durava, and Salagama (Michael Roberts, "From Southern India to Sri Lanka: The Traffic in Commodities, Bodies, and Myths from the Thirteenth Century Onwards," *South Asia*, n.s., no. 3 [June 1980]: 36–47).

11. Kotelawela suspected Jayawardena of misconduct as governor and dismissed him. His name was cleared by S. W. R. D. Bandaranaike when he became prime minister.

12. "Banking on Sampath," *Observer* (Colombo), 18 November 1991.

13. Speaking of the intervention of development experts in the cause of reducing hunger and malnutrition, Arturo Escobar argues that "only certain kinds of knowledge, those held by experts such as World Bank officials and developing country experts trained in the Western tradition, are considered suitable to the task of dealing with malnutrition and hunger, and all knowledge is geared toward making the client knowable to development institutions. The interaction of local field personnel . . . with their clients is conditioned by this need and automatically structured by the bureaucratic operations already in place. . . . This interaction is reflected in and organized by documentary practices— the elaboration of program descriptions, evaluation reports, research reports, meeting documents, scholarly papers, and so on—that ceaselessly take place as part of a process that is largely self-referential" (*Encountering Development: The Making and Unmaking of the Third World* [Princeton, N.J.: Princeton University Press, 1995], 111–12).

14. "New Bank Raises Rs. 125 m Equity," *Daily News* (Colombo), 15 May 1991.

15. Upali Dias, "Our Money Grows on Our Trees," quoted by Sugeeswara Senadhira, "Meet a Yuppie in Banking," *Observer* (Colombo), 16 June 1992. The word *yuppie* in the title of the second article suggests the bank's success in portraying itself as cosmopolitan.

16. "New Bank Starts Off with a Number of Firsts," *Daily News* (Colombo), 19 May 1991.

17. The report on the results of the survey that USAID commissioned to evaluate the success of Sampath's advertising for the share offering is entitled "Towards a Shareholding Democracy: Sampath Bank Share Marketing Experience" (1987). The author of the preface and, presumably, of the report itself is Anura Goonasekera.

18. "New Bank Starts Off." To judge from Sampath's career to this point, the bank sought to serve not the "disadvantaged" but the middle-class and urban people who depend on banking services.

19. "New Bank Raises Rs. 125 m.

20. Myron Weiner, *Sons of the Soil: Migration and Ethnic Conflict in India* (Princeton, N.J.: Princeton University Press, 1978), 12–14.

21. See Myron Weiner and Mary Fainsod Katzenstein, *India's Preferential Policies: Migrants, the Middle Classes, and Ethnic Equality* (Chicago: University of Chicago Press, 1981).

22. Weiner, *Sons of the Soil,* 272.

23. This dialogue is a transcription of tape-recorded conversations Guy and I had in July, 1997. I have preserved the temporal order of what was said but melded several conversations.

24. In the face of the general tendency to portray Sinhala tradition by adverting to temple

and tank images, the expression *upan bimē urumakkārayan* is doubly interesting. To an English speaker, "sons of the soil" has at least some reference to peasants and farming, but the Sinhala carries a less direct implication. *Upan bimē urumakkārayan* are people who have a claim on the land. They are natives—as opposed to immigrants—whether they work the land or not.

25. The questionnaire that produced the Sampath Bank's shareholders survey that I have mentioned previously in this chapter included the question, "Did these advertisements give you the impression that the Sampath Bank was a Sinhala Buddhist Bank?" The survey did not include responses to that question.

26. As late as the end of 1990, a director of the bank was still talking about opening branches in other Buddhist countries. In a statement that suggests interests more spiritual than financial, Stanley William "said that he had put forward the proposal for establishing overseas branches of the Bank at the seventeenth general conference of the World Federation of Buddhists held in South Korea this year. He said that [the] first overseas branch of the Bank is likely to be set up in Lumbini in Nepal" ("Sampath Banks on Buddhist Nations," *Week-end* (Colombo), 25 November 1990).

27. Calling the bank the Investment and Credit Bank had its ironies too because of the notorious career of the Pakistani-managed Bank of Investment, Credit, and Commerce.

28. The Sinhala *pun kalasa* and the ritual by which it is made to overflow on New Year's is related to the Tamil *pongal* pot, which is also made to overflow on New Year's. As in many other contexts, the affinity between Sinhala and Tamil culture disappears in a time of sharpening ethnic identities.

29. Roberts, "From Southern India to Sri Lanka."

30. The alternative is worth mentioning because it characterized the general shape of banking at the time. If a customer had an account in Colombo but found himself in Kegalle needing money, he could not go to the local branch of his bank and expect to cash a check, and if he deposited a check, gaining access to the new funds would require weeks.

31. That branch, which until recently served as the bank's headquarters, was located on D. R. Wijewardene mawatha.

32. None of those three social categories exist in contemporary Sri Lanka, although there are a few Chinese families still running restaurants in Colombo.

33. Sri Lankan opposition to new taxes imposed in 1848 underlay the "rebellion," but those grievances were as much political as economic. See K. M. de Silva, ed., *The "Rebellion" of 1848* (Kandy, Sri Lanka: K. V. G. de Silva, 1965).

CHAPTER SEVEN

No. 37, Sapugaswatte Road

Tilakasiri, his wife, Indrani, and their three children live on the ground floor of the house at No. 37, Sapugaswatte Road; Cedric, his wife, Anusha, and their baby live upstairs. Their lives provide a way to move from advertising to its audience, from consumption as a general phenomenon to middle-class consumers, and from the fashionable parts of Colombo where advertising agencies are located to outlying parts of the city where paddy fields and coconut gardens begin to replace urban sprawl. In what follows I get down to cases by scrutinizing what these two families own, what they want to purchase, and where and how they bank. Each family has a relationship to Sampath Bank and its local-idiom advertising, but my focus falls on their lives and the commodities that participate in them. I say "participate" in preference to "terminate" because the commodities that Sri Lankans purchase create the "regulated improvisations" of domestic life, organized by long calculative sequences of earning, saving, buying, and possessing, which lead on to other sets of calculations.[1]

Neither of the families at No. 37, Sapugaswatte Road started out as middle class. Tilakasiri's family leads a middle-class life almost inadvertently. The five of them are city-dwellers by accident too, and long to return to the Kandyan village where they spent most of their lives. Cedric and Anusha moved a few years ago to Sapugaswatte Road from villages some forty miles south of Colombo. They have a baby now, and they plan to stay, not forever at No. 37, but somewhere near Colombo. Downstairs Tilakasiri's family leads a modest life; upstairs Cedric and Anusha are acquiring the signs of prosperity. Each has plans for constructing the defining possession of Sri Lankan domestic life, a home of their own. These are people who exemplify the increasing reach of Sri Lankan advertising practice and people who should bear out the profession's characterization of Sri Lankan consumers as traditional, conservative, self-restrained and cautious. They are also the object of advertising done in the local idiom and the very people one would expect to be engaged by the advertising that Guy Halpe describes in the previous chapter. Points of contact notwithstanding, their calculations look very different from what advertising people imagine, and their lives bear as little connection to the national project as Robert Loo's feelings for the inchoate Malaysia.

Looking out from the house at No. 37, the neighborhood includes an accountant's family living in the adjacent house on the first floor, beneath a family headed by a man who works as a sales manager at Lakspray, the local powdered milk product. On the other side of No. 37 are two new houses owned by a man who is a middle-level manager at Coca-Cola and a marketing manager who works for Velona, a large garment manufacturer. These families are considerably better off financially than Tilakasiri, and because of their age, they have more assets than Cedric. On the opposite side of the road is another "American"-style house, belonging to a man who works for a local tile company.[2] Within one hundred yards of the house at No. 37, there are five or six other homes of the same age and style. As the road runs its course between the juncture with a larger road where it begins and another main artery where it ends, there are probably twenty or so more residences, ranging from wooden shanties *(mudukkuva)* located down in the floodplain to much more substantial houses.

These six or seven families constitute a small colony, clustered among more modest homes that long-time residents inherited from their parents. When Sampath Bank sought to strike a cultural connection, it had these people in mind, people with assets who might make banking decisions on the basis of ethnic identity, people living in Colombo with a strong sense of Sinhala identity. Tilakasiri's and Cedric's families have not only that identity but also active ties to the villages—from their fields and gardens to their kinship networks—from which they came. Everyone living along Sapugaswatte Road is Sinhala, but the area has developed by a thousand small events. Tilakasiri has frequent dealings with the families that live in the older houses, but Cedric and Anusha interact mainly with their first-floor neighbors and the people next door. These are *ganu-denu minissu* (people who give and take).

Middle-class life has its sources of independence but depends on considerable amounts of mutuality. When Tilakasiri sees the Coca-Cola manager on the road, he raises a gentle reminder about the job the man is scouting for Tilakasiri's oldest son. Before the people across the way went off to China, they left their washing machine with Tilakasiri to make life easier for Indrani. He is more outgoing than most people and likely to pop into anyone's house, but his neighbors are friendly and many exchange favors back and forth. All the same, the middle-class people have a distinctive position in the neighborhood, a pattern—people living on recently purchased land in newly built houses next door to people who inherited their houses from parents—that is repeated in Colombo's other outlying areas.[3] Most have live-in servants and are able to move about in their own cars.

It is convenient to speak of the newcomers as middle class, but doing so requires considering what it means to speak of a middle class in a society where an import-export economy has produced a small indigenous elite.[4] In common usage that elite was the middle class—"middle" by virtue of their mediating position between the colonial power and the generality of Sri Lankans. The prosperity that tea, rubber, and coconut exporting brought made it possible for such people to be chauffeured about in late-model cars, live in elegant homes, and travel to Europe and other parts of Asia. Whether that expression—even when naturalized in its Sinhala form—might be extended to a broader category of bureaucrats and professionals is open to argument. I know a university professor who takes the bus back to his village to collect paddy from his family's rice fields. Without it, he does not earn enough income to support his family. Even a paid sabbatical would not allow him to do research anywhere outside of the island. Is he middle class?

I raise the definitional issue not to offer a solution, but to make clear the particularity of the lives of these two families. Tilakasiri and Cedric are economic actors able to make substantial decisions about consumption—not whether to purchase a whole bar of soap or a half, but whether to invest in a television set or tuition classes (to which parents send their children to prepare them to take examinations for university admission). Tilakasiri's monthly salary comes to Rs. 13,000 (over US $200 in the late 1990s). By Sri Lankan standards, to have Rs. 13,000 a month is to be prosperous. Cedric's income is more erratic, depending on how much work he finishes in a month, but he schedules four or five major commissions in that interval, each worth on the order of Rs. 70,000 to 100,000. His monthly income ranges upward from Rs. 30,000 (US $500). By Sri Lankan standards, both families have advantages. But my being able to relate the entirety—and in what follows I will inventory just about everything each family owns—of two families' possessions in quick order says something about what being "middle class" entails in a poor country.

I started in the summer of 1997 to make an inventory of Tilakasiri's household. When I finished, I put similar questions to the couple who lived in the second-floor apartment. The questions I asked frequently embarrassed me with their impertinence and occasionally embarrassed them. But inquiring into everyday things—What do you keep in your bathroom? Why did you buy it? How much did it cost?—was the obvious way to track down exactly how the world system of culture and commerce enters the lives of ordinary consumers, enabling one style of life and closing off others.

I started with Tilakasiri, knowing that he would put up with my questions. He had taken leave from his job to nurse his wife at home, and that obligation meant that he had time on his hands. In the course of his adult years, Tilakasiri has done well enough as a driver and administrative assistant to own a house and a car; over the same period—roughly 1950 to the present—Sri Lanka entered the ranks of economies in which substantial numbers of people have resources sufficient to count as consumers in the global economy. By his own definition, Tilakasiri is middle class (*madhyama pantiya*). He once gave me an endearing definition of his condition in life: "Middle-class people are people who have enough to live on, but no more."

As it happens, Cedric, who rents the upstairs apartment, complements Tilakasiri's life story. He works in the lower reaches of the advertising business, having started a billboard and display business some ten years before I spoke with him. He grew up in a village—in this case to the south of Colombo—and he has made a considerable success of his life. Relative to the executives who run the major agencies in Colombo, his circumstances are modest, but the course of his life is extraordinary. Having finished his O levels, he moved to Colombo and found a job as a graphic artist at the same advertising agency that did the Sampath Bank campaign. He took that job without formal training, learning as he went. Within a decade he had started his own business, and in 1997 he employed twenty people in his workshop. Putting his life story in such abbreviated form races over the energy, skill, and self-sacrifice necessary to make all of this happen. Cedric and Anusha are as newly arrived as Tilakasiri and Indrani, but they are also some thirty years younger. They are consumers with obvious enthusiasm for things and the means to acquire them.

People such as Tilakasiri and Indrani, Cedric and Anusha are the beneficiaries of changes put into motion by the election of S. W. R. D. Bandaranaike in 1956. They are even more beneficiaries of very different changes that began during J. R. Jayewardene's administration. The four of them now live in a world that their parents could hardly imagine. A change in dress suggests the transition. Both Tilakasiri and Cedric are "trousered gentlemen," going off to work each day dressed in Western clothes.[5] They shift into sarongs when they return home, but in the public arena they wear trousers. Neither of their fathers ever did so, nor did Indrani's or Anusha's fathers. The everyday dress of the fathers has become casual wear for the sons. The village is something they put on as comfortable clothing.

All of their parents lived in village settings—Indrani grew up in Polonnaruwa district, Tilakasiri in the Kandyan highlands, and Cedric and Anusha in two villages inland from Kalutara. Tilakasiri's ability to make a living these days owes to both his having been raised in a village that happened to have a mission school and joining the army in the 1950s, where he mastered the English the missionaries had taught him. To that extent he owes his good fortune to a demographic accident, the moment and place of his birth. He has always been a Buddhist and has no feelings about his missionary teachers other than remembering their proselytizing. Cedric, by contrast, can read English, but really cannot speak it to any extent. He learned a little in school, but in the village he had no need for the language that nowadays dominates his life.

Since he left the army, Tilakasiri has worked for a series of nongovernmental organizations, themselves a product of a transnational practice that has replaced the missionary efforts of his youth. Cedric's livelihood depends on the upturn in both consumer capitalism in Sri Lanka over the last twenty years and the advertising business. These are people, in other words, who live in several places at once—village and town, the local context and the global one. They also live in a world increasingly "choisified," to put Aimé Césaire's expression to a new use, and some of those commodities come from afar. But the conversations that follow reveal how much their connection to the world economy is shaped by local people, practices, and purposes. To varying degrees, their homes reveal the effects of "cultivation," that process of interpretation that both reflects and creates the goals of a person's life.[6] The contrast between the people on the first floor and the second is equally much to the point. Both apartments are identical in size, but each family has followed a distinctive consumption regime. Tilakasiri lives his life almost in spite of the commodities that surround him; Cedric and Anusha are consumers in the full sense of the word.

Having a television may not be the defining mark of middle-class life, but televisions, radios, and newspapers are both possessions and channels of communication, the part of life that celebrates, contextualizes, and domesticates consumption. I think there are real-life forces substantially more important in determining what Sri Lankans buy than anything seen on television or read in print. There are Sri Lankans who surprise me with their capacity to spend money extravagantly. But neither Tilakasiri nor Cedric have anything in common with such people, and neither comes close to consuming conspicuously. Like the great majority of human beings—middle class and otherwise—they find themselves enmeshed in a net of relationships that both makes it possible to enjoy possessions without purchasing them and constrains how those possessions get used.

The Ground Floor

The two-story house where Tilakasiri and Indrani live sits close to an asphalt road linking their neighborhood to a stretch of shanties just down the hill. The low-lying land to the east is swampy, and when the monsoon comes, the people who live by the edge of the flood plain are washed out. As Sapugaswatte Road rises to the west, the quality of the housing follows suit. No. 37 is a substantial place, an "upstairs" house, surrounded by other houses built twenty to thirty years ago when people who worked in Colombo began to put up houses in increasingly more distant and less likely places. As the city has grown, new houses have appeared in paddy fields, coconut gardens, and marshes where no one would have built in earlier days. Although Colombo has avoided the runaway growth of Calcutta or Bombay, most areas close to the city have been heavily developed in the last two decades and the mosquitoes forced to look after themselves.

Approaching the house requires a bumpy ride from the High Level Road, which leads out of Colombo some six miles away. Sapugaswatte Road is asphalted, but the pavement is broken up by craters often filled with muddy water. Early on Sri Lankans learn the art of walking over unreliable ground, keeping themselves unmarked, while moving at a pace just slow enough to avoid breaking into a sweat in the one hundred-degree heat. I was neither dry nor clean when I rattled the driveway gate that serves as the entrance to No. 37. Tilakasiri hurried out of the house, and we walked through the garden that occupies what little remains of open space between the house proper and the masonry wall surrounding the property. This is a house built to occupy as much of the land as possible, and the garden exploits what little is left, producing bananas and the leaves *(karapincha)* essential for making a curry.

Tilakasiri pulled up a chair, I sat on the couch, and we started talking about how much he earns and how he spends it. Tilakasiri was sixty years old, having served in the army for twenty-five years, then working as a driver and administrative assistant for fifteen. When he enlisted in the Sri Lankan army, it was a ceremonial force. By the end of his career, he served in a unit that put down the Che Guevarist insurgency of 1971. But what he learned in the army had more to do with bureaucratic procedures than the arts of war. His commanding officer once regaled me with stories about Tilakasiri's ability to keep order and get things done. After he retired from the army, he exploited what he had learned—the driving and organizational skills as well as the ability to speak and write English—putting those skills to work as a driver and administrative assistant. Despite being hired as a driver, his competence, integrity, and high energy led to his being given more and more responsibility. He became the secretary who knows more than the boss, the irreplaceable man. Just out of the army, he found a job with a nongovernmental organization near Kandy, and when his first employer left the island, he recommended him to another expatriate. These days he earns Rs. 9,750 a month—two to three times more than a driver makes. His army pension pays him another Rs. 3,124 a month, giving him an income that compares with a bank manager or senior lecturer in a university.

The circumstances that brought him to No. 37, Sapugaswatte Road are equally anomalous. The village where he grew up sits in a spice-growing region some twenty miles north of Kandy. When he got married, he put up a small house adjoining a family plot of land that produces nutmeg, cloves, and coconut. Once retired from the army, he took the bus to Kandy to work, cared for his mother, who lived into her nineties, in the family house next door, and helped his wife raise their three children. One of his uncles had spent his life in the monkhood, giving Tilakasiri a familial relationship to the religious life of the village. As Buddhism has become transnationalized in Sri Lanka, more and more Japanese Buddhists have come to visit the village monastery, some becoming supporters of a monastery that could only have been built with large contributions from beyond the village. When Tilakasiri was a boy, English missionaries ran a school in his village. Today Japanese people patronize the monastery.

He always had hopes for educating his children, and as they reached school age, they began to commute to Kandy with him in order to attend schools with better facilities than their village school. In the late 1980s, his second son did well enough on his Grade Five examination to win a place at Royal College in Colombo. For a village boy, a place in the premier secondary school in the island was a singular opportunity. It came with a price, because he had to board in a hostel near the school. In 1988 Tilakasiri's wife came down with a pneumonia that developed into a chronic lung and heart condition. She lost fifty pounds, and her doctor suggested that living in a warmer, sunnier climate would help her condition, allowing her to cough up the congestion that made it impossible to care for children and do housework. They began to talk about moving the whole family to Colombo.

On the face of it, Tilakasiri would have little means to move his family to Colombo, which is an expensive place for a man to start up a new life even with his monthly income. But he had relatives, and in Sri Lanka relatives, neighbors, and friends make many things possible. Although Tilakasiri's wife came from a village near Polonnaruwa, her sister had also married a man from Tilakasiri's village. The two families lived side by side. As time went by, his niece married a man who had made a great leap out of the village. Chandrasena passed his exams to become a chartered accountant and took a job with a Japanese firm in Colombo. Over a period of years he acquired enough savings to buy a piece of land in order to put up his own house. Coming from a village, he hardly knew how to begin. But he asked his coworkers, and they led him to the nine perches (a colonial measure of land equal to 1/160 acre) of land where eventually he was able to put up the house at 37 Sapugaswatte Road.

In 1994 Chandrasena had even better luck. He had moved on to a job with a Korean firm doing business in Sri Lanka, and his employers asked him to take a position in their New Zealand office. Tilakasiri had organized his niece's wedding, standing in for her father who was bedridden at the time. One would not expect an offer of free housing from just any relative, but Chandrasena knew Tilakasiri's efforts had made his wedding ceremony possible, and he felt sympathy for Indrani because of her deteriorating condition.[7] He had been the beneficiary of the East Asian economic expansion into Sri Lanka—now it was taking him to another part of Asia where his firm was doing business. Tilakasiri got a place to live while his wife recovered her health and his son attended Royal College. They moved into the house in February 1995.

I looked around the living room. The walls were plaster and needed paint; the floor was tile. I assumed that Tilakasiri purchased the furniture or brought it from the village. But the couch with a carved wooden frame, two chairs, and a dining table with four chairs came from Chandrasena. So did the lithograph of a Burmese village scene—the leg-rowers of Inle Lake—and a faded reproduction of a milk-product advertising still of a fat and healthy baby. The telephone also came with the apartment. Nailed to the wall behind Tilakasiri was a calendar, an annual gift from the people next door. In the corner of the room rested a low table that supported a National television and a Sharp tape deck. The black-and-white television was 13 years old, a gift from one of the Europeans for whom Tilakasiri drove in the 1980s. The vertical hold was defective, causing the picture to flop over and over as we talked. The tape deck was even older and likewise a gift from another employer. The tape player was broken, but the radio worked, giving the children a way to listen to music. A pile of their tapes sprawled over the table, now without hope of being heard.

> S: "Isn't there anything in this room that you've purchased?"
> T: "Nothing."
> S: "Are you sure? What about the curtains?"

I was surprised, assuming that I could understand Tilakasiri's major capital purchases by discovering how he had set up his household in Colombo. He hadn't purchased much of anything. Everything seemed to come from friends and relatives, but I was right about the curtains. They had been bought—although not on the open market—from a lady who runs a weaving center for young women in Tilakasiri's village. Now bleached by the sun, the curtains were purchased because of their bright colors, but their being inexpensive was also a factor. So there was nothing in the public part of the house that had been purchased except for the curtains that came from a village acquaintance (at a price Tilakasiri cannot remember, and he is a man who remembers prices). If the room represented "cultivation," much of it had been achieved by default. These are people who live in Colombo because of circumstances—education and ill-health—and their home says as much.

Looking under the dining table, I saw two *Vesak* decorations *(pan kudu)*. Tilakasiri's younger son had made both from construction paper, which was purchased. There was also a Kandyan drum that belonged to his daughter, who had once wanted to try drumming and had borrowed this one from a village friend. Two wooden badminton rackets, leaning against the wall, were left behind by Chandrasena. Finally I spotted a large pile of Sinhala and English newspapers—surely a consumption decision, and a prolific one because almost every Sinhala and English-language newspaper was there. They turned out to be gifts too, purchased by Cedric, who buys every daily and weekend newspaper—in Sri Lanka that means five or six papers every day—and then passes them on. Tilakasiri's family goes through them, they get tied up, and when enough pile up, they are sold to the paper man for Rs. 10 to 12 per kilogram.[8] The world of middle-class consumption did not look very consumer-oriented. True, the house was someone else's, but the only purchase in the public part of the house was still the curtains.

I asked to see the bathroom, and Tilakasiri walked me into a completely dark room, the toilet, directly connected to what Tilakasiri called the bathroom, a separate room containing a sink and mirror. There was nothing in the toilet except for a Western-style commode and little more in the bathroom proper. Below the mirror was a bar of Sunlight soap for doing laundry and washing hands and a bar of Lux for washing faces and shampooing hair. Everyone in the family uses Lux for the latter. Only well-to-do Sri Lankans make a practice of using shampoo. There were no other toiletries but for some Bic disposable razors, which the three men in the family use. Toiletries for a family of five consisted of two bars of soap and three razors, although Tilakasiri's daughter sometimes buys a sachet of Sunsilk shampoo for her hair. The bathroom also serves as a laundry area. Because Indrani is incapacitated, everyone in the family does laundry. Their equipment included two plastic tubs and Rinso washing powder. Tilakasiri prefers Bic razors to Gillette because they last longer, and he buys Rinso because it also goes a long way.

In the rear of the house, the kitchen was fitted out with several consumer items. The most substantial appliances were a gas cooker (roughly equivalent to a camp stove) and a refrigerator. The cooker was a gift from another employer, who gave it to Tilakasiri in appreciation of his hard work. Many Sri Lankan families cook over a wood fire, including several who live down the road. But a gas cooker is a convenience, and Tilakasiri wanted to make cooking as little demanding as possible for his wife. When the family moved to Colombo, he brought the cooker down from Kandy for her. But now that Indrani is even less able to get about, the three children do most of the cooking and they manage the cooker. The LP gas canister that supplies fuel for the cooker is a major expense at Rs. 304 for 13.5 kg of gas. A tank lasts two months, and replacing it rocks the family budget.

The kitchen had the items that make Sinhala cooking possible—a stone grinder, an egg beater, knives, spoons, plates, a mixer for making coconut gravy for curries, and a coconut breaker *(pol bidiniya)*. All were left behind by Chandrasena. The item that would not be found in many middle-class homes was a washing machine, which was another convenience for Indrani. It was on loan from neighbors across the way, who went off to China on a study trip. The kitchen also housed a small collection of staples: tea leaves (unbranded and purchased in small quantities, usually 100 grams) and a variety of dried milk products—Nestomalt, Sustagen, and Ratri—for nursing Indrani and making milk tea.

Next to the kitchen, a pantry served as living space for a servant, storage, and a passageway between the two bedrooms and the living room. The Sisil refrigerator was the room's major item. It belonged to Chandrasena. It was only a quarter or so full, and several items were there to be stored as much as to be refrigerated—several limes, one onion, spinach, curry leaves, bitter gourd, two halves of a coconut, and green chilies. Lined up directly next to the refrigerator was a Singer sewing machine that Tilakasiri bought in Kandy some fifteen years ago. To this point, what economists would call consumer durables included just one item that Tilakasiri had purchased—a sewing machine. Singer advertises on television and in newsprint regularly and for almost a decade sponsored one of the most successful programs on Sri Lankan television, *Dynasty,* itself a celebration of high living and consumer behavior.[9] But Tilakasiri said he was never influenced by any of it, insisting that he purchased the sewing machine because of Singer's reputation for quality.

On the floor were two irons—the family iron was broken and the other was borrowed from the people upstairs. On the wall hung a flat rattan basket, the kind used to cover food on the table. Below it on the floor sat a blue plastic bag full of boiled rice brought from the village and a red basket full of unboiled rice. There was also an empty red plastic satchel, used for carrying vegetables and supplies from the Saturday market, where the family shops because fruits and vegetables there are slightly cheaper than in the shops along High Level Road. There were two other items in the room. One was a mosquito net, formerly used by the Tamil lady who took care of Indrani until last April, when she went home for New Year's and never returned. On the floor rested a rolled-up carpet that could be dragged into the living room to serve as a place for four people to sleep when relatives come to stay. The servant formerly slept on it.

There were several ritual items in the pantry. Indrani kept an image of the Lord Buddha on a makeshift altar high above the refrigerator. There was also a four-foot-high oil lamp, topped off by a rooster. The oil lamp is the artifact that creates a visual center at Buddhist occasions and public events. This one came from the neighbors who went off to China. At the same level as the image of the Buddha was a lithograph of Pattini, a goddess supplicated in times of sickness. Indrani brought it down from Kandy along with the Buddha image. She made a vow to Pattini in hopes of recovering her strength. Tilakasiri said that she did not know who Pattini was until she got sick. To that extent, these ritual items represent the only active example of "cultivation" in the house—fostering Indrani's health so they can all move back to their village.

Two bedrooms open off the pantry, one in the front of the house; the other on the rear side. Tilakasiri and Indrani started off living in the rear bedroom, but it receives dust and exhaust fumes when cars travel along Sapugaswatte road. The rear bedroom has the advantage of being adjacent to the bathroom, but for the sake of Indrani's health they moved to the front. During the time when Tilakasiri is away working in Kandy, his fourteen-year old daughter sleeps in the double bed with her mother. When Tilakasiri returns, she shifts to the boys' bedroom, and the younger son moves to the couch in the living room. All of the beds were equipped with mosquito nets. During those times of the year when the nighttime temperature goes down only to the 80s, it is difficult to sleep in the confined space under the nets. Those nights the family burns mosquito coils, which provide less relief from mosquitoes but more air.

Tilakasiri and Indrani share a bedroom without either a closet or much furniture. He hung his clothes on hangers suspended from a nail driven into the wall. She stored her frocks in the same way but kept her sarees in an *almāriya* (comparable to a French armoire; it too belongs to Chandrasena) that sat in the other bedroom. All told, Indrani had ten sarees. She had not bought one since she became ill in the late 1980s. The newer ones were hand-me-downs from Anusha, just as Indrani used to give her older sarees to her Tamil servant. There was a dressing table in the room and a small table where Tilakasiri's daughter did schoolwork. Next to those pieces of furniture sat a small cupboard where the daughter kept her textbooks. Curtains, in this case purchased from a textile shop in Kandy, hung over the windows. A small fan sat on the reading table. Chandrasena left it behind, and it served to allow Indrani to get a few hours of sleep before she awoke with a coughing attack and needed to go to the toilet.

The other bedroom was fitted out with two twin beds and two mosquito nets, which Tilakasiri had purchased in Colombo. Mosquito nets, in fact, had been a major investment since his family moved into this house. Chandrasena left behind the *almāriya* that dominated this bedroom, housing his family's porcelain dishes, ceramicware, and glasses. The boys kept their shirts on hangers as their parents did. They draped their pants on a wooden towel rack that sat on the floor and was used at other times for drying clothes. Each boy had two or three shirts and two pairs of trousers. Because Tilakasiri's daughter was still in school, she had a set of school uniforms, as well as tee shirts and skirts. Most of the tee shirts that the children wore displayed English expressions and Western brand names—from Reebok to American colleges to European NGOs. A small reading table sat in the room, and it was covered with the boys' purchases—plastic racing cars, felt-tip markers, and combs.

A tally of all the items in the house would not come to much. Subtract the consumer durables and furniture that belong to Chandrasena, and there was quite a lot less. Almost all of the consumer items that Tilakasiri himself owned were gifts—the television, tape deck, and gas cooker.

This was a household with middle-class possessions, but few of them were Tilakasiri's purchases. Before the tape deck broke, the boys had acquired a collection of tapes of Sinhala popular music, but they had gotten the money from their father (himself not a fan of pop music whatever its national origins). There were the toiletries I listed—two bars of soap and three razors—but the list of personal products was so small as to call to mind the things stored in the refrigerator—an onion, two half coconuts, two limes, a bunch of spinach. Relative to Western expectations, both larders were bare.

Tilakasiri was exhausted from answering questions about household items, but I asked him one more: Why aren't there more things in the house? He said that older people don't like having things. As people get older, they want less. Men in particular, he said, stop wanting things after they reach fifty-five or sixty. Tilakasiri is a Buddhist, but he did not attribute any of his self-restraint to religious values. He traced it to his being sixty years old.

> S: "So where does all of your income go?"
> T: "Medicine for my wife and education for my kids. I spend it all on those two things."

The big expense was the medicine Indrani had been taking since she fell ill nine years ago, and it was an expense for which the family was not prepared. Although the Sri Lankan state provides free medical care, in most cases it is minimal care. If a family has a loved one with a serious problem, it will often seek out a physician in private practice. The move to Colombo came at the suggestion of Indrani's doctor in Kandy. Once in Colombo, Tilakasiri had her treated at Colombo General Hospital, but when she continued to founder, he began to talk to others about her treatment.

A neighbor from across the road suggested a doctor at Nawaloka Hospital in Slave Island. It has become the preeminent private hospital on the island, and the doctor she sees has a graduate degree from the United Kingdom. She sees him perhaps once every three to six months, but each visit costs Rs. 325. The bigger expense is medicine. Her prescriptions cost Rs. 580 a week; and to clear her chest she goes for physical therapy once a week at Rs. 250 a visit. Her doctor suggested that eating fruit would help to break up her congestion, so Tilakasiri spends some Rs. 150 a week on bananas, sugar cane, and mangoes. Everything related to medical expenses comes to Rs. 3,320 a month. Coupled with the family's monthly food bill of some Rs. 4,000, well over 50 percent of Tilakasiri's salary is gone.

Having three children in school has also exerted a serious effect on family resources, even though education is another state service. Tilakasiri's older son attended a private school in Kandy but did not pass his A-level examinations in 1994, and he began private tutoring to improve his chances the next time. His second son graduated from Royal College and also failed his A levels the first time around. Tilakasiri arranged to have him tutored by a teacher who came to the house, preparing him to sit for the examination a second time. On this attempt, he passed, making the tuition of Rs. 1,000 a smart investment. Although he passed three of four subjects at the A-level examinations, his results were not strong enough to secure a place in the university system, and he joined his brother in looking for a job. Meantime he was taking a computer course that cost Rs. 6,000 and an English language course at Rs. 2,000. Neither son had found a job, at least in part because Tilakasiri is a villager living in the big city. The people most likely to help the boys are back in the village.

Tilakasiri's daughter was attending the local high school, and he was paying Rs. 300 a month for a van to take her there and back. She was also attending a science class after school that cost Rs. 200 a month. The government provides books for students and the cloth for one uniform set. In a tropical country where students travel by bus or van under conditions that are both humid and dirty, everyone needs two or three uniform sets to get through the week. These are petty expenses, but clothing three children, feeding and tutoring them, and then providing the occasional Rs. 50 so that they can go out with their friends requires several thousand rupees a month. Together, expenses for education, food, and medicine took almost 80 percent of Tilakasiri's monthly income.

Amidst his concern for his wife and children, there was an apparent luxury: the 1975 Nissan that sat in his driveway. He spent Rs. 100,000 for it back in Kandy, and then invested another Rs. 10,000 to have it repainted iridescent green. As a result, the exterior looked fresh, but the interior revealed twenty-five years of hard traveling on cratered roads. It never had air-conditioning, and the fan had quit. Looking down at the floorboards, the driver had a direct view of the pavement below. Tilakasiri used the car for only one purpose—to drive his wife to medical appointments and visits with the physical therapist. No one else drove it, and the few times he took it out each month did not roll up many miles. But it burns gasoline, not diesel (which is three times cheaper in Sri Lanka because of government subsidy), and it cost him Rs. 2,600 to fill the tank, one-fifth of his monthly income. That meant that he simply did not fill his tank. He would buy two liters at a time and do a lot of coasting, sometimes with the ignition off.

Include the expense of insurance, registration, and maintenance, and the car becomes a major investment. Many middle-class people in Sri Lanka—let's say people drawing Rs. 13,000 as Tilakasiri does—do not own cars, but he bought the car to take care of his wife when she got sick, and he regarded it as an investment. While the car was dilapidated, it was not likely to depreciate any more, because what Tilakasiri paid for it represented the cheapest price one was likely to find for an automobile of any kind. With inflation, the car was likely to be worth more in the future. If he had to sell it to meet his wife's future medical expenses, he would come out all right. The car sat idle most of the time in the garden, making it as much a savings account as a vehicle.

I asked Tilakasiri what he would be hoping for if his wife had not gotten sick. He said he would have put his money into enlarging his house back in the village. If he could have remained in the village, he said, his family would have had money in the bank and a second story completed on the house he started some fifteen years before. As the house stands now, the concrete floor of the second floor serves as a roof for the first floor. The second story floor is ready to anchor the masonry walls of an addition that would provide bedrooms for his children. Even though his sons were in their twenties, they would not move out until they get married, and that could be a decade off. His daughter would remain at home for probably as long. It would be even nicer to have a separate bedroom for her. That was where Tilakasiri would have spent his money. He owned a house, and lived rent free in another, but he still had housing needs.

Having more discretionary income would have meant that he could also have purchased a new television, because that seductive window on the larger world had become an important family possession—less practical than the car but more used and appreciated. He had his eyes on a Sony or National 14-inch set. His children do most of the viewing, but the family watches at night, especially prime-time teledramas. I would say that television represents the family's one indulgence. Everyone prefers Sinhala programs. I asked Tilakasiri whether there were Western programs he liked. He watched only one and could not at first remember the name. It was a British program about a man who never speaks but acts like a malicious child, he said. The man walks in a funny way and has big ears. One of his sons yelled out from the back room, "Mr. Bean."

Upstairs

The people who live upstairs were in their early thirties, and they married only in 1994. Both grew up in villages south of Colombo—Cedric comes from Agalawatte and Anusha from Neboda. After he finished his O levels,

Cedric came to Colombo and managed to find a job as a graphic artist. He had no connections whatsoever. He had the ability to draw, however, and the advertising business has been hungry for artists for the last twenty years. A teacher at his high school had given him some instruction, but he mostly learned how to draw after he was hired. First, he convinced the creative director that he could do the job—by the usual method, he drew something on the spot—and then he made himself into a graphic artist. At Phoenix he also discovered the demand for outdoor advertising—billboards, dealer signboards, and the other forms of signage. By the late 1980s he had quit Phoenix and gone into the outdoor advertising business.

There were no other artists in Cedric's family. His skill, in his words, is not *āriya* (from his ancestors), it is *sahaja* (from his own inclinations and efforts). He was intimidated the day he tried for the job at Phoenix, but he got the position. Then he saved his earnings, living at home in the village, commuting forty miles to work each morning. Once he had the job, he began nursing the idea that someday he would work for himself. His chance came when a friend asked him to paint a banner for a school exhibition. Having managed a small job, another friend came and asked him to produce a billboard, a large, metal sign painted with a scene, faces, and a brand name. Putting up a billboard is a larger task. Besides the artwork, it requires finding space to be rented, negotiating a contract with the owner, moving the billboard by truck from the workshop to the site, and erecting it. It also requires start-up capital. Because he had saved faithfully, Cedric pulled off this task without a bank loan or family support. As his business grew, however, he became a regular borrower.

During the Jayewardene administration, there suddenly were more things to buy, which created growing demand for outdoor displays. It also created competition, especially from older companies with established reputations. Cedric pursued his business by reading the newspapers each morning, looking for advertisements placed by, or news items referring to, new businesses in Colombo, then trudging off to solicit their accounts. He spent most of his time managing the workshop located behind his office on the High Level Road. Now he employs twenty men as artists and welders, and to ensure that they stay on task, he needs to be on the spot. The work comes in bursts, but his workshop almost always works late. He seldom gets home before his baby daughter goes to bed at 8:00 or 9:00, and he sometimes works seven days a week.

Seizing another opportunity, he recognized the market for promotional gift items and started a second business. Operating out of the same building, he sells plaques and trophies, the kind that companies use to motivate their employees. That work has several transnational connections—American motivational psychology and Chinese suppliers—and Cedric pursues the wholesale side of his business in a transnational way. Once a year he flies to Singapore and buys new stock from Chinese vendors in the trophy and plaque business. When he first went to Singapore, he was astonished by all the things that make the place distinctive—its discipline, its tall buildings, its cleanliness. These days, he thinks about what a long way it is to Singapore from the village where he grew up.

He also makes an annual trip to Bombay or Madras to see what is new in the Indian world of billboards.[10] What he sees there is considerably more familiar than Singapore, but Indian billboards—technically and rhetorically—are much more sophisticated than graphic work in Sri Lanka. The Singapore trip is educational in its way, but the India trip is entirely so. When he flies to Singapore to get trophies and plaques or to India to look at billboards, he becomes an international businessman. Just as advertising agencies in Colombo look to India for technical sophistication and innovation, a single entrepreneur at the lower end of the advertising business looks to India for those same qualities. I never asked Cedric how he first learned about Indian billboards or how he got the idea of flying to India to see the latest innovations, but it is hard to overlook his initiative and self-confidence in doing so.

Cedric's business was almost a decade old when I spoke with him, and he had moved his office four times since he began. Constructing billboards requires a large workshop, which he must rent. Purchasing a place outright is too expensive in areas close to the city, and he needs a location convenient to other businesses in order to display his work for his customers. When he and Anusha were first married, he found the second-floor apartment on Sapugaswatte Road, choosing it because it was affordable and close to his business. Even when he has shifted his workshop from one location to the next, he has always stuck close to his rented home. Because he is not as outgoing as Tilakasiri and works late into the night, he has fewer social connections to the neighborhood. Still, Sapugaswatte Road is home. For the present, he rents both his place of business and the apartment, but he would like to own both.

Unlike the first-floor apartment, the upstairs apartment came unfurnished. Cedric and Anusha received a few of their possessions from their wedding and brought some from their parents' houses, but they have purchased most of the furniture and consumer items in the apartment over the last four or five years. They acquired these possessions for their present setting, and these acquisitions make it home. Cedric and Anusha had a "love marriage," which is to say that it was not arranged by their families. Also, Cedric refused a dowry, making him a self-made man in a second, quite unusual way. He told Anusha that he would provide everything for their home. Where Tilakasiri has been gifted most of the consumer durables in his house or has them on loan from Chandrasena or his neighbors, Cedric and Anusha have furnished their place.

When I spoke with Cedric and Anusha, the paint on the walls was fresh and all the appliances in the house worked. The floor is waxed a deep red every few weeks, the furniture was new and recently dusted, and the living room had the look of a public space. Cedric sometimes brings friends and business acquaintances home, and the living room has been organized for entertaining. The number of chairs itself suggested as much. Most of the chairs were the Rubbermaid plastic variety seen on patios in North America, two were caned wooden chairs of Low Country design, and the rest of the seating came by way of the living room set—a small couch and two chairs—that Cedric bought just after their wedding. On several occasions, Anusha said, laughing, all thirteen seats have been occupied, and Cedric has entertained by playing the guitar that rests against the corner of the room. The home as a place for entertaining and even for encountering nonfamily members is something new for people who grew up in villages.

The focus of the room was a 14-inch Sony color television that Cedric purchased before he got the furniture. He paid Rs. 18,000 for it, and he chose the brand. If price is no object, Sony is the brand name that people prefer because of its reputation for quality. Cedric makes all the major consumer decisions. When he has time, he and Anusha go shopping together; but when they buy something, she defers to him. He manages the household finances, giving Anusha whatever money she needs to purchase food, pay the servant, and make weekly purchases. The decoration of the living room was entirely Anusha's doing, and to that extent they have "cultivated" their home together, just as a successful business has allowed them to become consumers together.

An outsized bunch of green plastic grapes hung on the wall one faces on entering the living room. Just below it stood an étagère fitted into the corner of the room. It contained an extravagant plastic knick-knack that resembled a royal carriage—the cab was spherical and plastic but gold in color. It was topped with a spray of white plastic streamers that opened up like a fountain as it rose from the cab. On the middle shelf was a ceramic figure of a seated woman with a pot on her head, and on the lowest shelf, more artificial flowers. In the opposite corner stood a matching étagère decorated with a brass vase with a ruffled mouth, as well as ceramic figurines and more artificial flowers. The bulk of Anusha's knick-knacks were kept in the contemporary style *almāriya* with glass doors at the far end of the room, but that space also served as a place to keep her daughter's toys, family albums, and a lacquerware tray set. The wicker bookcase that sat next to the *almāriya* was filled with wedding photographs. On the wall above hung a plaque of Saraswati, whose presence was more aesthetic than spiritual, and in the corner, almost at the level of the ceiling, a ceramic figure of the Lord Buddha honored by a small oil lamp.

Anusha guided me through the curtain of wooden beads that separated the more public parts of the house from the kitchen, living room, bedrooms, and bathroom in the back of the house. The kitchen had a new Rashmi oven for making cakes and *wattalapam,* a palm sugar and coconut milk dessert that Cedric loves. She does most of her cooking on a Sanyo gas cooker that Cedric purchased. Many of the kitchen items would be found in most Sinhala homes—a coconut breaker and a scraper, knives, ladles, strainers, and pots. The electric kettle would be considerably harder to find, and the profusion of specialized tools—from melon ballers to tools for handling cake dough—would appear in an even smaller number of homes. Anusha cooks, and she has the tools for doing so. On the adjoining wall rested a shelf with an impressive array of spices, some thirty containers strong.

The kitchen is linked to the bedrooms and bath by a room that runs the width of the house and was separated from the living area by the hanging beadwork. Ten feet wide and twenty-five feet long, the space served as a dining area at one end and a baby's room—crib, changing stand, toys cascading out of a cupboard—at the other. A Sisil refrigerator marked the divide. Except for an enormous papaya that occupied most of the top shelf, the refrigerator was no more full than Tilakasiri's. There were a few other items on the lower shelves and door rack—limes, curry leaves, and coconuts. The rear portion of the kitchen was full of consumer items, including a Singer washing machine. The room onto which it opens was empty except for cleaning supplies. A Sanyo tape deck sat on the dining room table, and an ironing board stood next to it. Anusha's baby was three and still slept in the crib just outside the door to the master bedroom. At that moment, the toy that held the baby's attention was a battery-powered Ferrari, a gift from her father on returning from Singapore.

One of the reasons Anusha likes shopping is to see things, just to see—the buildings, the people, and the products. She wants to taste new kinds of food, and she knows that going to Singapore would be a chance to eat in the night markets around the city. What she understands less clearly are the possibilities for "shopping" in a newly industrialized economy such as Singapore's. All the sarees she desires, Anusha can buy locally. Usually she buys one in preparation for a wedding, the occasion above all others when people put on their best. Anusha wears lipstick and nail polish on that occasion and only then. I asked her whether there are not any other times when she might put on lipstick. She gave me a look that I interpreted to mean: wearing lipstick to a wedding is suitable; wearing it on other occasions is excessive. Clear nail polish, she said, is passable, but even that she does not wear often.

Her dressing table and bathroom gave the cosmetics business little reason for optimism. Although she had seen the talc commercial that says, "It's for you. It's for me. It's for all of us," she does not use powder or talc. Those entry-level cosmetics are inoffensive, while also modern and sophisticated. Anusha simply does not like them. She uses Lifebuoy soap for showering, fully aware that the soap is marketed for men. She uses Pear's Baby Soap for washing her hair, taking a product made for her daughter and using it as American adults sometimes use baby shampoo because of its mildness.[11] Once a week, Anusha shampoos with Sunlight shampoo, but she believes that shampoo is too strong for regular use, so she sticks to Pear's ordinarily. Cedric uses Lux when he showers, but Anusha prefers Lifebuoy because of its reputation for keeping skin healthy. The only other item in the bathroom is the Black Knight cologne that Cedric splashes on before he heads off to work.

Cedric runs a business that keeps him away from home until dark and often until the baby has gone to sleep. Although he brings friends home sometimes, he is not a man who has much leisure time, and he spends most of his life away from his home. Even making purchases is shaped by time constraints. When he is especially busy, he has a friend or business associate purchase an item for him and bring it home. Or he simply calls a shop and asks for a purchase to be delivered to his house—the gas cooker is an example. The major pieces of furniture that make the living room livable came from shops in Kalutara and Moratuwa, where Cedric has known people since the days when he was living at home. Most of it has been purchased when Cedric and Anusha were visiting their parents, and stopped in Kalutara on their way back to Colombo.

Instead of flying to Singapore or Madras with Anusha, Cedric travels with his assistant, Dinesh, who speaks English. Dinesh serves the same purpose locally, allowing Cedric to do business with executives in Colombo. One of the extraordinary parts of Cedric's career is that he has managed to enter the world of corporate business without having English at his command. He did not have it when he started out as a graphic artist, and he still has not mastered it. Like many non-English speakers, he reads English-language newspapers because job announcements and advertisements are often found only there, and Cedric needs to know about new businesses and corporate changes. He can read English well enough; speaking it is a problem.

Lacking the *kaduwa* (sword) that English provides its speakers, Cedric needs someone else to clear the way for him. For the last two years, Dinesh has provided that service. Dinesh sits in the air-conditioned office with two secretaries, handling phone calls and interacting with clients. To the outside world, Dinesh is Cedric. The creative director of a Colombo advertising agency corrected me when I said Cedric was an unusual example of a man who had entered the advertising business without English. She said that she had spoken to him on the phone several times and did so in English. She had spoken to Dinesh. Cedric usually works outside in the workshop, keeping his employees on task. Besides the psychological cost involved in running a business from the workshop, there is a domestic cost. He needs Dinesh to negotiate with Chinese businesspeople in Singapore and to book hotels, order food, and give directions to taxi drivers in Madras. Anusha cannot do that, so Dinesh travels and Anusha stays at home.

Instead, Anusha has the companionship that a television set, a small child, and a servant provide. It would not be right for her to flit about the neighborhood as Tilakasiri does, but she visits downstairs with his family. She runs the house and spends most of her time carrying the baby about and entertaining her. An elderly lady helps her with the housework and spells her with the baby. She also helps with the washing and cooking. Even with a servant in the house, however, Anusha is housebound the same way that Cedric is businessbound. Cedric has the car, and Anusha cannot drive in any case. Her chance to get out comes on the weekend, when Cedric takes her someplace by car. Going places—to shopping malls, to theaters, and to visit parents—sounded to me to be a central part of the time they spend together, so I asked Anusha how they met. After she stopped giggling, she said that she met Cedric after she had finished school, but she became quiet about the details of their romance. A love marriage is not scandalous, but the romance that led to it is embarrassing to recount to a stranger. She was drawn together with her husband in a modern relationship, despite the traditional form that relationship now takes.

Take all the commodities that create domestic order in Cedric and Anusha's apartment, and the total would probably come to several hundred things. The most substantial are consumer durables from Japan, Korea, India, and Sri Lanka. Their clothing, toiletries, and household utensils have more local origins, in either India or Sri Lanka. The only Western-manufactured items are the Rubbermaid chairs that provide seating in the living room, and Cedric and Anusha have no taste for Western luxury items—watches, cosmetics, liquor, and clothing. They spend less time watching the television than Tilakasiri's family, and, like his family, they prefer Sinhala programs. Anusha regularly watches only one program, a show for women called *Kantha Lokaya* (Women's World). Neither of them has much interest in the Western programs, often sponsored by multinational corporations doing business in Sri Lanka. Television links them to the outside world, just as newspapers and periodicals do in a less animated way. But their community of consumption and their neighbors' has nothing in common with Asian consumers who smoke Marlboros, wear French perfume, and idolize Western and Japanese celebrities.

SAVING, CONSUMING, AND HOPING

In many ways Tilakasiri and his family and Cedric and his have reached a consumption cul-de-sac. Although Tilakasiri has a substantial number of consumer goods in his house, almost all are gifts or items given on loan. Other than his hopes for replacing his television set, he has no particular desire to acquire anything else. What he wants is to return to his village and add a second story to his house. Circumstances make doing so unrealistic, and other things are on his mind. Indrani's condition gets worse in the village climate, and Tilakasiri's two sons are less likely to find a job without a base in Colombo. Chandrasena's return will force them to find another place, but for the moment they are staying put. A woman who cannot move more than ten steps, two boys waiting for their first job, a daughter preparing for her O-level examinations, and a man who says he wants nothing—this is not a family of engaged consumers.

Cedric and Anusha have their share of consumer items, and they will acquire more things. But there is no natural next step on the consumption ladder, and what they dream of most is beyond their reach for the moment. Anusha has a well-decorated household and a full complement of appliances—fans, color television set, tape deck, refrigerator, gas cooker, oven, iron, and washing machine. Cedric drives a late-model Mitsubishi Mirage, the fourth car he has owned. He bought it from a friend for Rs. 300,000. Anusha regularly walks around Colombo's two shopping malls. The *almāriya* in her bedroom holds twenty-five sarees. She has ten Western outfits as well. Her baby has a large number of dresses and toys. I asked Anusha what her dreams were, and she hesitated. When she replied, it was clear she was not uncertain, just reluctant to say that she wants to own a house.

She discusses building a house frequently with Cedric. They agree, she said, that they will have to hire the masons, carpenters, electricians,

and plumbing contractors. Nowadays there are some fifteen general contractors who build houses on contract in and around Colombo, but it is a
new commercial role and unknown to Anusha. Cedric is not deterred by
the prospect of organizing the construction process himself and dealing
directly with subcontractors. The problem is finding open space and ar-
ranging the financing for the construction. The apartment is comfortable
enough, the location is perfect, and at Rs. 3,000 a month the rent is a
bargain. But having a house is everyone's dream in Sri Lanka, no less for
people in Colombo than for those in the countryside. What is harder to
explain is why the owner of a thriving business has not been able to finance
a house.

Cedric confronts two problems—the inflated cost of land in Colombo and the areas that surround it and the underdeveloped condition of
the credit market. When Chandrasena purchased the land at No. 37 in
1976, he paid Rs. 9,000 per perch. The nine perches cost some US
$6,000. A perch of vacant land in the neighborhood is now hard to find,
but what remains sells for Rs. 100,000 a perch, making the same plot
(allowing for the declining value of the rupee) worth US $15,000 nowa-
days. The underlying problem is that there are few such plots available,
and although they are advertised in the newspapers, locating a place to
build a house by way of the classified advertisements is a time-consuming
process. Putting up a house makes buying the land look easy. Duplicating
the house at No. 37 would cost several million rupees.

The major agency houses in Colombo have begun to construct
housing estates on village land outside Colombo. Houses are advertised in
the newspapers, sold by way of inspection tours, with financing arranged
through the agency house. Putting up a subdivision of houses creates
economies of scale, and financing puts them within reach of at least some
middle-class Sri Lankans. Seeing the cost of a new house in inflated rupees
evokes a shock in people first considering building. But the more fundamental problem is this particular form of development—the houses are
small and identical to their neighbors—which flies in the face of most Sri
Lankans' thinking about what makes a house a home. More Sri Lankan
housing will be mass-produced in the future, but for the present people
with resources want to build their own houses.

Cedric and Anusha do not want to live in any of the housing
developments that are being built around Colombo. The insurance companies, finance institutions, and agency houses that advertise developments
in Malabe, Boralanda, Punchiwatte, and beyond stress how easily financing can be arranged. Television advertisements show the handsome display
homes already constructed, the asphalted roads, and vacant plots in the

development, not to say the friendly way prospective customers are treated in the firm's Colombo offices. The newsprint advertisements make the rooms look well-built and spacious. Sometimes they show floor plans. Cedric and Anusha are not comfortable living in a development where every house looks like every other. They want to put up their own house. One either inherits a house or puts up a new one. That is the way their parents lived and the way they want to raise their family. That is what a house means.

Tilakasiri and Cedric are resolute savers, and they share that practice with a huge majority of Sri Lankans who are increasingly savvy consumers of the full range of bank products. The national savings rate has reached over 15 percent, although nowadays car buyers borrow as never before from a bank or finance company.[12] In this environment, a borrower should be able to find a lender, and local idiom advertising might reduce anxiety about the process. But Cedric and Anusha are anxious about the mortgage loan business, and Tilakasiri keeps telling them that getting a mortgage is a big headache. To make an application requires collateral, which is reasonable enough, but gathering together the documentation to support one's assets is an endless process. He told them that banks never make clear what kinds of information they require, and after a prospective homeowner has applied for a mortgage, the bank asks for additional information. He slapped his forehead as he described the frustrations of getting a mortgage.

Once the application process begins, reaching a decision takes a huge amount of time because of the slow pace at which banks move. If one makes an application at a branch bank, the application has to be evaluated by a loan officer or committee at the head office. The paperwork travels slowly within each office and between each. For their part borrowers may have to return to the bank a dozen times with more documents as the business proceeds. Having a job is essential to getting a mortgage, but if a customer has a job, there is no time to keep returning to the bank to nurse the process along. By some accounts, the application can take up to a year.[13] And when the mortgage is finally approved, the borrower needs someone to serve as guarantor. Who can Cedric find who would be acceptable to the bank? Someone from his village would not make a credible guarantor, and neither would Tilakasiri.

Absent a mortgage market that is friendly to consumers and efficient, even people with considerable assets hesitate to begin a house. The difficulties of the mortgage loan business do not deter most people from using other banking services, but for Tilakasiri and Cedric, banking is shaped by personal ties and long-term calculations. However liberating the effect of advertising, electronic media, and the global flow of commodities and culture, however deterritorialized the imagination under the regime of consumer capitalism, when the focus is tightened down to the lives of people living at No. 37, Sapugaswatte Road, human relationships play a countervailing role in determining what one saves, where one saves, and what one buys. The next time I went to Sapugaswatte Road, I pursued the first two of those issues by asking Tilakasiri where he kept his money. "You mean in the house," he replied, following the logic of my earlier questions about the location, value, and origin of everything else. "No, I'm sorry, where do you bank your money?"

He has no choice about his monthly pension check from the army. The government automatically deposits the Rs. 3,124 in a state bank, in this case, the People's Bank in Katugastota, just north of Kandy. Each month Tilakasiri travels the hundred miles to the bank and withdraws Rs. 3,000 from his checking account. When he stays in Colombo, it would make sense for him to write a check on his Kandy account and cash it at a People's Bank branch in Colombo or Nugegoda. He cannot do that because one branch will not honor a check drawn on another. Tilakasiri does not mind having to carry out the transaction in person, but getting to his bank is a long trek. First, he has to take a local bus to Pettah, then the intercity to Kandy, and finally a local bus to Katugastota. He is less happy with the time it takes to get his money withdrawn once he gets in line at the bank. "It is a state bank, no?" he said, assuming no further explanation was necessary. I pressed him. "At the end of the month, they are getting paid"—the second explanation as elliptical as the first. What he said reiterated the popular critique of government banks. Employees are not well-paid, but they have job security and no motivation to make life easy for their customers.

Tilakasiri also acts out of loyalty to People's Bank. The woman who runs the textile center back in his village got her start by virtue of a loan from People's Bank. It was her sewing center—now four sewing machines and four employees—that produced the curtains that hang in his living room. Because of that loan, she has a business—mostly she sells frocks, but she has also begun to sell plastic products—and he has curtains at a reasonable price. But that is only part of the bank's activity in the village. It has financed several carpentry shops, a spice-collection cooperative, a provision shop, a cool-drink shop, dairy and poultry farms, as well as the small operation of the villager who sells lottery tickets. Tilakasiri likes the way employees of the bank come out to the village. Operating from a van, they allow people to do their banking, pay their water and electricity bills, and make payments on their loans. Other times the bank sends loan officers to the village, and they hold a meeting in the temple, explaining how to apply for a loan. Private banks do not do any of those things.

"Even though you have to wait for two hours to clear a check, you still feel loyalty to People's Bank?" I asked. Tilakasiri said yes. Besides, he has a way of avoiding the queue altogether. If he goes directly to his village from Colombo, he can get up the next morning and meet a relative who works at the People's branch in Katugastota as he walks to the bus stop. All Tilakasiri needs to do then is hand him a filled-out withdrawal ticket, and his relative will get the job done during the course of his workday at the bank. Tilakasiri meets him after he returns from work and picks up his Rs. 3,000. It sounds like a lot of effort to make a withdrawal, but it is also a lot of work to take the bus to Katugastota, wait two hours in the queue, and then take another bus back to the village. Bureaucratic involution constrains the transaction, to be sure, but personal relationships give Tilakasiri a way to make it relatively efficient.

Tilakasiri keeps his savings in the Hatton National Bank in Nugegoda. Despite the bank's colonial origins and commitment to serving the estate sector of the economy, Hatton National Bank has become a retail bank over the last twenty years and now aggressively pursues individual clients. In some circumstances Tilakasiri would not have been a likely candidate for an account at the Hatton Bank. It is a friendly, convenient bank, but all of his previous experience was banking with government institutions. He started his account in Nugegoda so that he could have a source of funds in Colombo to draw on for his wife's medical expenses. When he opened his account in 1995, he put Rs. 98,000 on deposit. Indrani's medical bills have left the family with Rs. 22,000. Was he worried? "What to do? That is what a savings account is for."

I asked him whether he had been influenced by any bank advertising. He said that twenty years ago the only banks that he used were People's Bank and the National Savings Bank, and that was no problem. By way of doing errands for his employer, he got to know the Hatton National Bank, and he liked the way they treated people, so he opened his savings account there. Now he relies on the monthly statement the bank sends him. Thinking about the local-idiom advertising that Phoenix did for Sampath Bank, I asked him whether he was an *upan bimē niyama urumakkarayek* (a real son of the soil). He smiled and said he was influenced by people, not slogans. In another context he had admitted to being influenced by advertising for Signal toothpaste and Bic razors. Banking is more embedded in a network of relationships, but even with the advertisements that persuaded him, he said that he preferred Bic to Gillette razor blades because Gillette blades last only three or four shaves. Signal, he has heard, is good for teeth. In these cases, consumption decisions are influenced by forces that operate outside of the advertisements proper.

Unlike the People's Bank in Katugastota, the Hatton Bank in Nugegoda is close to his house. Tilakasiri can withdraw money 24 hours a day with his ATM card. He opened the account in his and his oldest son's names, ensuring that there would be someone living with Indrani who could withdraw money when he is away on his job. One son has an ATM card in his own name; and the younger son, daughter, and Tilakasiri himself have cards by way of that same account. It is a family account, and that is a very unusual practice. I kidded him that his children might withdraw his life savings while he was away. "I trust my children. They wouldn't take even a chocolate." Tilakasiri can expect all manner of help from neighbors and family. They lend him things, they give him other things. But he would not borrow money from any of them. Mutuality has its limits.

Cedric and Anusha follow a more complicated consumption regime, and they follow a more complicated savings regime, holding a lot of accounts. Some are essential to Cedric's business, but Anusha shows the same attention to organizing her savings accounts as to organizing her household. Cedric has three current accounts. When he was starting his business, he opened an account with the People's Bank in Nugegoda. The government helps small businesspeople, he knew, and People's was the logical place to go. As soon as Sampath Bank opened in Nugegoda, he started a second account, drawn there by the bank's reputation for technological innovation such as ATM machines and by the good name all private banks enjoy for handling customers efficiently and kindly. He later opened another account at Seylan Bank in Boralesgamuva, favoring it because until recently the bank did not charge customers the Business Turnover Tax on interest earned on accounts. Sampath Bank collected the tax from customers; Seylan, Cedric thought, paid it out of its own pocket.

As his business grew, Cedric took loans regularly from Sampath Bank. He borrowed to buy the truck that makes it possible for him to deliver and erect his own billboards and to put up the sheet metal structure that serves as his workshop. Each time he applied for a loan, he was impressed that Sampath Bank gave him a decision quickly. The Nugegoda branch manager was free to act without the application having to go downtown to be evaluated by a loan committee (as is the case with People's Bank). Then Seylan Bank came along, making it possible for Cedric to close out his two other accounts and transact all of his business with one nearby bank. But he would not do that. He feels a sense of obligation toward the bank that helped his business in the past. He knows the manager. The mutual dependence, the reciprocity that characterizes everyday relationships in Colombo and beyond extends into the commercial relationship he has with his bank.

Cedric has his savings account; Anusha has hers. He started his account at Sampath Bank because the bank was offering high rates of interest on fixed-rate accounts. Anusha's savings program is more interesting. She has three savings accounts. The Sampath account she started for reasons identical to Cedric's. Both accounts draw 14 percent. The other two accounts, at Hatton National Bank and People's Bank, have different motivations. Neither pays a high rate of return, but both offer regular drawings. At the end of the year, there is a giant drawing. The monthly drawings offer savers keeping a minimum balance in their accounts—usually Rs. 10,000—a chance to win. The winners of those monthly lotteries, and savers who keep more substantial accounts, namely, more than Rs. 60,000, compete in an annual drawing that pays substantial prizes. In 1997 Hatton Bank's drawing offered a house worth 37 lakhs (Rs. 3.7 million).

Banks introduced the practice of holding drawings—I will not call these drawings lotteries, in order to distinguish government "lotteries" from bank "drawings"—some five years ago.[14] The first bank to do so was Standard Chartered Bank, which was having trouble attracting accounts despite the expansion of the banking business over the last decade. It was not the advertising agency that represented Standard Chartered Bank those days that suggested the drawing. It was the chairman of the bank's board, who saw it as a way to increase the number of private accounts. The bank had been seen as British and unfriendly. The drawings would counteract that perception. Here was a bank offering hope as well as service.

The only problem was that a number of other banks quickly got into the drawing business, not the other business-oriented banks, but banks that already had a reputation for being friendly and customer oriented. These were simply banks that recognized a good thing when they saw it, adding these drawings to other promotional strategies. The National Savings Bank established a savings scheme called *Ridi Rekha* (Silver Leaves), aimed directly at small savers and people living in the countryside. The bank's advertising agency produced a television commercial featuring a group of dancing women, mimicking a love scene from a Hindi film without benefit of a leading man.[15] With the ubiquitous presence of Hindi film shorts now seen on television—there are three channels that screen Hindi films—there are few television viewers who would not recognize the referent, the Hindi film world of fantasy and forbidden pleasures.

This surely is the low end of the drawing market—a government bank originally intended to encourage savings from schoolchildren, offering no interest on some accounts but now advertising chances in a drawing on a par with a Rs. 10 lottery ticket. The National Savings Bank has always fixed its attention on small savers, it has spread its branches into villages and beyond by way of Post Office Savings Banks, and now it entices people to save with prospects of winning their drawing. And the circle remains unbroken because those savings are used to finance the government's deficits.[16]

Lotteries and savings schemes alike have turned increasingly to women.[17] The *Mahajana Sampatha* (People's Resource) lottery recently ran a print advertisement showing a smartly dressed woman speaking into a cordless phone as she stands next to another, far less well-dressed woman seated behind a sewing machine in a newly built garment factory. Entitled "Sew Lucky," the advertisement explains: "Sewing was our profession. We had to report to work before the sun rose and we returned to our cubicles after dark. But the 'Mahajana Sampatha' ticket made us not only so lucky, but so successful. Now under my roof we carry on our business, sewing to our hearts' content" (*Daily News,* Advertising Supplement, 28 February 1997).

Wealth, upward mobility, and "sewing to our hearts' content" aside, neither Cedric nor Anusha plays the lotteries. In that regard, the advertising profession's perceptions are right on target about these two Sri Lankans. They are conservative and cautious. Both deny being influenced by advertisements, either in print or on television, with the exception of a Signal toothpaste commercial that persuaded Anusha. Cedric replied to my question about his being an *upan bimē niyamu urumakkurayek* by saying that he did business with Sampath because the bank had an ATM machine, and he kept his account there because the manager had treated him well. To judge from their example, men make decisions about banking based on technology, interest rates, and how the bank treats them. Women do not often see the interior of a bank, and it would be improper for a woman to have a relationship with a bank manager as familiar as Cedric's. But women also make decisions based on forces that transcend the semiotic boundaries of the advertisement itself. Whether they play the lotteries or not, they make banking decisions on the hope for a vacation with their husbands or the dream of a house of their own.

Cedric had made it clear that finding a mortgage was too improbable at the moment. Besides, he was too busy to even start the process. I asked Anusha how saving and consuming, calculation and hope fit together.

S: "Is it more important to get a high rate of interest or a chance
    to win the drawing?"

A: "A chance to win the drawing, because I still get interest."

S: "So you are not interested in consolidating your savings ac-
    counts to get a higher return?"

A: "I want to win a house. We cannot afford one now. The
    drawing is my good luck."

When the advertising business characterizes Sri Lankans as self-restrained
and cautious, it has her pegged. For Anusha, risk-taking is as cautious as
keeping a savings account that animates her life with a monthly drawing.
By saving, she gambles.

Anusha's servant brings distinctly different views to long-term calculation. She buys lottery tickets every time she gets paid, keeping her
sights on the enormous jackpot the state lotteries offer. She has won small
prizes occasionally, but she has put in a lot of money and recovered only a
fraction of it. Now she wants Anusha or Cedric to purchase lottery tickets
for her. She will give them the money, they will buy the tickets, and the
money having passed through the hands of prosperous people such as Anusha or Cedric will improve the servant's chances of winning. Anusha tells
her she is crazy—she would be much better off banking her wages or
sending the money to her family. The odds against winning the lottery
are enormous, and the buyer's prosperity has no bearing on her chances
of winning. But for the servant, even gambling is embedded in a nexus of
social relationships. Good luck will rub off people who have already had
good luck. She can use their advantages to create her own. For their part,
Anusha and Cedric are middle-class to the extent that they put their faith
in long-term planning, saving, and self-reliance. And wherever foreign
commodities enter their lives, those same acts of agency keep the interactive center of the global system of culture and commerce closer to Sapugaswatte Road than faraway centers of material and symbolic production.

NOTES

1. The opening paragraph of Arjun Appadurai's "Consumption, Duration, and History"
    is to the point: "Consumption as a topic has always come equipped with an optical
    illusion. That illusion, especially fostered by the neoclassical economics of the past cen-
    tury or so, is that consumption is the end of the road for goods and service, a terminus
    for their social life, a conclusion to some sort of material cycle, . . . this view is indeed an
    illusion" (in Arjun Appadurai, *Modernity at Large* [Minneapolis: University of Minne-

sota Press, 1996], 66. I have taken the expression "regulated improvisations" from Pierre Bourdieu, *Outline of a Theory of Practice,* [Cambridge: Cambridge University Press, 1977], 78.

2. What Sri Lankans call "American"-style houses are typically characterized by roofs that are either flat or sloping from one side to the other, a minimum of exterior decoration, two or more stories, no verandah (as older houses usually have), and the exploitation of land for the house itself, reducing the yard to a walkway and car park.

3. There is virtually no ethnographic work on such places. Sociological work on Colombo and its suburbs is also limited, but includes a comparative study of poor families in urban settings (Kalinga Tudor Silva and Karunatissa Athukorala, *The Watta-Dwellers: A Sociological Study of Selected Urban Low-Income Communities in Sri Lanka* [Lanham, Md.: University Press of America, 1991]) and a study of Dematagoda (Neville S. Arachchige-Don, *Patterns of Community Structure in Colombo, Sri Lanka* [Lanham, Md.: University Press of America, 1994]).

4. The evolution of the expression is treated in Michael Roberts, "Problems of Social Stratification and the Demarcation of National and Local Elites in British Ceylon," *Journal of Asian Studies* 33, no. 4 (August 1974): 554–55.

5. When I last purchased cloth for a sarong, I overheard two other customers say in Sinhala—"A white gentleman doesn't wear a sarong outside. He must be buying cloth for pajamas."

6. Mihaly Csikszentmihalyi and Eugene Rochberg-Halton, *The Meaning of Things: Domestic Symbols and the Self* (Cambridge: Cambridge University Press, 1981), 173–76.

7. Moving a relative into one's place has another motivation in a society where renters who decide to resist a landlord's attempt to reclaim his own house often succeed. Relatives are more likely to move out when the owner returns.

8. T. J. Jackson Lears concludes his treatment of American advertising with a brilliant chapter entitled "The Things Themselves." In the works of Henry James, Marcel Proust, and Joseph Conrad, Lears finds signs of the way an emergent consumer culture looked to things for their signifying force, "against the disenchanting power of productivist rationality" (*Fables of Abundance* [New York: Basic Books, 1994], 380). He says less about other signs of consumer culture—willingness to throw things away and indifference to the consequences of high levels of waste.

9. Singer and its advertising agency had just that connection in mind. According to Felicia Dean, the Managing Director of Zenith Advertising, "The wealth, stealth, passion, fashion, power, greed, aggression, obsession, treachery, lechery, deceit, conceit, humour and rumour that surrounded Blake Carrington and his super-rich set seemed to enthrall audiences from such unlikely places as Galagedera, Kamburupitiya, and Pilessa" [all out-of-the-way village settings]. "People from these places wrote in saying that they enjoyed the goings-on" ("Dynasty Was Good for Singer Says Company Boss," *Daily News* (Colombo), 23 July 1991).

10. R. Srivatsan, "Looking at Film Hoardings: Labour, Gender, Subjectivity and Everyday Life in India," *Public Culture* 4, no. 1 (Fall 1991): 1–23.

11. I once asked an executive at J. Walter Thompson whether Unilever was aware that many Sri Lankan women prefer baby soap for their hair. She said the company knew well enough, but saw no way to exploit that unintended use without undermining the larger market.

12. This percentage figure derives from the national account statistics that the United Nations publishes. To produce the percentage figure, I have looked at the table, "Cur-

rent Incomes and Outlay of Households and Non-Profit Institutions," starting with the current receipt figure for each year, subtracting the direct taxes figure, then dividing the balance into the net savings for that year. On those calculations, Sri Lankans are saving more all the time. For the following years, I have these percentage figures for household savings: 1980, 6.5 percent; 1983, 7.59 percent; 1984, 9.58 percent; 1985, 10.65 percent; 1986, 10.63 percent; 1987, 12.68 percent; 1988, 12.2 percent; 1989, 14.24 percent; 1990, 16.09 percent; 1991, 13.99 percent; 1992, 18.78 percent; 1993, 20.98 percent (United Nations, Department for Economic and Social Information and Policy Analysis, Statistics Division, *National Accounts Statistics: Main Aggregates and Detailed Tables, 1993*, part 2 [New York: United Nations, 1996], 1222).

13. H. N. S. Karunatilake, "Re-orienting Banking Policy and Practice to Meet the Needs of the People," *Central Bank of Sri Lanka, Occasional Papers*, no. 20, 1990, 9.

14. See Steven Kemper, "The Nation Consumed: Buying and Believing in Sri Lanka," *Public Culture* 5, no. 3 (Spring 1993): 377–93.

15. On television the dancing maidens do not bump and grind, they swoop and swirl, prominently holding the National Savings Bank's Silver Shares. In less active form they appear in print advertisements, where the text explains that buying a savings certificate worth Rs. 100 entitles the saver to ten chances to win the drawing. Banking has nowadays not only embraced the lottery principle, the National Savings Bank has found price parity. It would proliferate chances, each no more costly than a Rs. 10 lottery ticket.

16. Bernhard Fischer, "Rural Financial Savings Mobilization in Sri Lanka: Bottlenecks and Reform Proposals," *Savings and Development* 12, no. 1 (1988); quoted in Rauno Zander, "Politics and Rural Financial Markets in Sri Lanka" (paper presented at the Third Sri Lanka Conference, Amsterdam, April 1991).

17. The Bank of Ceylon has initiated a savings program for women, *Kantha Ran Ginum* (Women's Gold Account). Meant to appeal to working women with cash to save—the full-page advertisement run on the occasion of the fourth annual drawing in April 1997 shows women working in a garment factory, a school teacher, two potters, a woman standing behind a shopping cart in a supermarket, and a shoe salesperson—*Kantha Ran Ginum* pays a low-rate of interest, but it also offers a drawing. A minimum of Rs. 5,000 entitles savers to enter the monthly drawing. Just below the caption, the reader finds fifteen winners in each of ten provinces; above, the three big winners of two return air tickets to North India with cash, Rs. 25,000, Rs. 15,000, and Rs. 10,000. No Hindi film sequence here, but fantasy of a different kind—a woman wins a vacation with spending money, a chance to take a trip with her husband. As the tag line has it, "Kantha Ran Ginum, the innovative savings scheme from Lanka's premier bank—The Bank of Ceylon—encouraging thrift, helping national development."

CHAPTER EIGHT

The Home and the World

Theodore Levitt's *Harvard Business Review* article makes a breathless announcement. Now—the year was 1983—is the time to approach the world as one market, "ignoring superficial regional and national differences."[1] Levitt's conviction that the world had entered a new age made his article a seminal contribution to the study of global advertising, not to say its practice. What business confronts "is a new commercial reality—the emergence of global markets for standardized consumer products on a previously unimagined scale of magnitude." The future is equally clear: "If a company forces costs and prices down and pushes quality and reliability up—while maintaining reasonable concern for suitability—customers will prefer its world-standardized products. The theory holds, at this stage in the evolution of globalization, no matter what conventional market research and even common sense may suggest about different national and regional tastes, preferences, needs, and institutions" (94). Like other millennial visions, Levitt's assessment—"everywhere everything gets more and more like everything else as the world's preference structure is relentlessly homogenized. . . . No one is exempt and nothing can stop the process"—has a generality and absoluteness that is bound to be wrong.[2] His vocabulary itself reveals what is necessary to motivate an argument that begins by defying research and common sense alike—a "preference structure" that can be attributed to the world itself (thereby bypassing the extremely various human beings who entertain those preferences).

By the early twentieth century, the world had gotten small enough for the son of a Nottinghamshire coal miner to sojourn in places as far

away as Kandy and Taos. But the problem with D. H. Lawrence's concluding that the world was getting smaller is that the world is always getting
smaller, and it is never clear what is being said. Getting smaller—as with
Lawrence's happening into South Asia—is one thing; everything being
everywhere, quite another. Consider the "everywhereness" of three exemplary commodities—Coca-Cola, McDonald's, and Levis—in a place such
as Sri Lanka. Coca-Cola is certainly part of local life. It has been sold for
over three decades and is still offered to guests because it remains special.
But as recently as the 1990s it has also prompted protests for threatening
the indigenous way of life. McDonald's has recently put up its first two
restaurants in Colombo. Eating in such places will provide the locally in-
flected experience that it has become in other parts of Asia.[3] And as for
Levis, lesser-known brands are sold in Sri Lanka, but Levis are too expensive for the market. The appropriation of these commodities does not
suggest a world of sameness. The first exemplifies routinization and spo-
radic resistance; the second, an institution that will be fitted to local circumstances; and the third, absence and mimicry.

THE HISTORICAL GEOGRAPHY OF CAPITALISM

David Harvey's *The Condition of Postmodernity* brings considerably more
sophistication to the claim that the world is getting smaller, and it understands "getting smaller" in yet another way.[4] People the world over are not
being reduced to sameness, but their experience is increasingly marked by
time-space compression—by which Harvey means the speeding up of the
pace of life and overcoming of spatial barriers in ways that "revolutionize
the objective qualities of space and time . . . [forcing us] to alter, sometimes
in quite radical ways, how we represent the world to ourselves" (240).
Harvey marks the beginning of this compression to a world capitalism that
was taking shape by 1600. But the revolutionary moment came more recently, around 1973, when political-economic power acquired a Fordist-
Keynesian configuration (124).

   Where postmodernists have settled for exploring the aesthetic sensibility produced by this period of rapid change, flux, and uncertainty—
otherness, difference, fragmentation, and depthlessness (113–15)—Harvey sees a retreat from any metatheory (he is thinking of Marxism in particular) that might unpack the political and economic forces just now
reshaping the world. In the space where theory should be uncovering the
economic forces that drive the world order, he finds postmodernists "actually celebrating the activity of masking and covering up, all the fetishisms
of locality, place, and social grouping" (117). The argument is Marxist and

deductive. There are *a priori* grounds for believing that there is some kind of necessary relation between the rise of postmodernist cultural forms, the emergence of more flexible modes of capital accumulation, and a new round of time-space compression.[5]

To meet the postmodernists on their own turf, Harvey needs to address how time-space compression shapes postmodern consciousness. He follows Marshall Berman, Daniel Bell, and Fredric Jameson in asserting that both modernity and postmodernity entail a characteristic way of experiencing time and space (201) and uses Wim Wenders's *Wings of Desire* and Ridley Scott's *Blade Runner* for examples of movies that cut back and forth across time and space (308–23). What he does not do is explicate what viewers of those films themselves experienced or what time-space compression means for the generality of people who never saw either film. "As space appears to shrink to a 'global village' of telecommunications and a 'spaceship earth' of economic and ecological interdependencies," he writes, "as time horizons shorten to the point where the present is all there is (the world of the schizophrenic) so we have to learn how to cope with an overwhelming sense of compression of our spatial and temporal worlds."[6] Who constitutes the "we" in this assertion?

An anthropologist is obliged to like Harvey's attempt to bring postmodernity to ground and to think about it as a geographical phenomenon. But fidelity to any metatheory keeps him from reaching his own goals. Toward the end of his argument, Harvey praises Edward Soja for his willingness to address the problem of spatiality (284). Soja argues that social theory has privileged time and history over space and geography, leading to understanding modernity as destroying and replacing traditions. Instead, he says, it brings with it a reorganization of temporal and spatial relations.[7] That foundation seems to have been laid to describe the topography of late consumer capitalism, but both Harvey and Soja face a common problem. All force derives from capitalism, most of it emanates outward from Western centers of material and cultural production, and ordinary people are scarce to be found. For Harvey, the people shown to suffer most from time-space compression are postmodern theorists. They are the ones whose heads are ringing; they are the people overwhelmed by hallucination and schizophrenia. I want Harvey to complete the job by discussing the non-West and descending from postmodern cinema, architecture, and painting to the lives of ordinary people—somewhere, in either the non-West or the West. Instead we are left with assertions— "Wherever capitalism goes, its illusory apparatus, its fetishisms, and its system of mirrors come not far behind"[8]—just as apocalyptic as Levitt's.

The one that strikes me as particularly overstated is the notion that because capitalism is increasingly a global phenomenon, the compression of time and space is every human being's burden. When I read Harvey's argument that "the home becomes a private museum to guard against the ravages of time-space compression" (292), I know he is not talking about the South Asian homes I know. It is easy to forgive him for not appreciating just how the Internet would bring time-space compression directly into American homes. But I am less generous about the truth of his assertion when applied generally (which is how it is framed). Along Sapugaswatte Road, and most of the world's residential streets, the home does not guard anyone against the ravages of time-space compression. It guards people against the neighbors, thieves, stray animals, and the weather.

Because Harvey says so little of how most of the world's people live, he avoids one problem. He characterizes globalization in a way that avoids the "self-confirming allegory" of growing sameness, corruption, and lost authenticity.[9] Nor does he accuse advertising and commercialization of fetishizing commodities. By his account, fetishism "arises automatically in the course of market relations."[10] To that point I travel comfortably with Harvey. But he also assumes that human action is either clear-eyed—life in Marx's long-gone precapitalist society would qualify because when such societies interacted with the world, they encountered the thing in itself—or fetishized to varying degrees. And all fetishizing effects derive from capitalism, including the pathologies of place, locality, and social grouping.[11] For anyone who does not buy in on the metatheory, restricting to capitalist societies alone the effect that social action—exchange behavior, sumptuary practices, even material activities—exerts on consciousness seems unwarranted, as does the reduction of place, locality, and social identity to fetishes.

Harvey's use of the notion of fetishization would be beside the point were it not for the way he brings the idea to bear on advertising:

> advertising and media have come to play a very much more integrative role in cultural practices and now assume a greater importance in the growth dynamics of capitalism. Advertising is no longer built around the idea of informing or promoting in the ordinary sense, but is increasingly geared to promoting desire. . . . If we stripped modern advertising of direct reference to the three themes of money, sex, and power, there would be very little left.[12]

I am not carrying a brief for advertising, which is never innocent and often worthy of critique, but Harvey's characterization settles for popular imagery instead of scrutinizing the phenomenon. As a purely empirical matter, if one excluded advertisements emphasizing money, sex, and power, most advertising would remain untouched.[13] Like it or not, a large fraction of advertising is informational, and another large fraction puts the commodity—let's say, a wristwatch or a pair of shoes—in a "zone of display" that provides some informational content but makes no reference to money, sex, or power. Such advertisements have no role in fetishizing the commodities they promote and need to be ignored to make the metatheory plausible. As for fetishization, consider how many advertisements rely on images of family and home, or young people and friendship. If we are to understand how advertising has its way with us, we need to begin with a realistic conception of advertising as an imaginative literature that includes both sex and what Lucien Goldmann called "Frigidaire mystique."[14] Appreciating the full range of advertising's effects is even more important in non-Western places where there is a lot more family and friendship and a lot less sex.

Advertising between World and Home

I approach the historical geography of the advertising business as a descriptive problem, believing that Goethe was right about description—"there is a delicate form of the empirical which identifies itself so intimately with its object that it thereby becomes theory."[15] Independent of whether I have approached that ideal, it is clear that the power that attends theory is produced not when it emerges immaculately from the case at hand or enters the scene already locked away in the observer's heart but when thinking "identifies itself with its object" and evolves according to that encounter. Bourdieu's work has a sophisticated way of including the researcher's own self-awareness as part of the research project. It also has the virtue of giving no privilege to material causes or ideal ones. Sometimes both operate in tandem, each depending on the other; sometimes one is relatively more important in explaining some effect, and other times, the other comes to the fore. A materialist approach to the global system of commerce and culture—just as much as an interpretive one—needs to recognize the endless conversion, interdigitation, and equiprimordiality of the economic and the symbolic. As Bourdieu puts it (quoting Mauss): "society pays itself in the false coin of its dream."[16]

Although it is sometimes useful to distinguish material and symbolic production, commodities are never simply things. Like everything else, they are what they are because of the semiotic effects that attend them. When advertising agencies remake the relationship between a commodity and those effects, they draw on the full range of rhetorical devices to reimagine—sometimes by sensualizing a commodity and other times by do-mesticating it—the meanings that make the commodity what it is. Cre-ative directors do so each time they relaunch its advertising; copywriters, when they narrate a commodity's virtues; art directors and graphic artists, when they insert a product into a new "zone of display." The success of all of these symbol analysts in converting things into "libidinal images of themselves" is well documented, but the opposite side of the process is just as fundamental—taking highly charged things and moralizing them or bleaching them of the meanings they once carried.[17] Much of this transla-tion process occurs in the far reaches of the global system of advertising—in places such as Kuala Lumpur and Colombo—where commodities are domesticated for local consumption.

Advertising practice invites treatment in Bourdieu's terms, as re-lational, recursive, and reflexive. When people across the world confront print and electronic advertisements, they see those advertisements against a background—constituted of tacit knowledge, intersubjective meanings, a form of life—that includes structure, domination, and long calculative sequences as much as meanings. Advertisements take their force from their interaction with this background. To approach advertising as either "sex, power, and money" or the communication of information is to ignore the interaction of advertising content with the local form of life, because that interaction gives advertising whatever force it generates. Both Certeau and Bourdieu have illuminated the procedures of everyday creativity by which material objects enter human lives.[18] Rather than reducing advertising to its fetishistic exploitations, I would concentrate on the way individuals ap-propriate advertising, including its fetishes, as part of a form of life.

Savings, planning for the future, spending, and using commodi-ties to cultivate a particular kind of life—all are part of a process in which the actor's role is constructive without being sovereign.[19] Where Lévi-Strauss insisted that gift exchange was organized by deep principles un-known to the actor, Bourdieu argues that it is driven by a hundred small calculations, idiomatic to actors who reevaluate and change their strategies as the situation unfolds in time. To this extent, the actor's agency is recur-sive. But to imagine that the actor's agency allows the actor to stand apart from other people, social groups, and their pressures is to imagine that Cedric is likely to move his accounts to another bank offering more gen-erous terms for credit or savings. He is not, because where he banks is constrained by human relationships (in this case, with the bank manager).

Bourdieu's argument that practices carry their own interpretation recalls Geertz's saying that "societies, like lives, contain their own inter-pretations. One has only to learn how to gain access to them."[20] But Bourdieu's project owes more to Heidegger than simply the insistence that the background is essential for the possibility of social action. He shares with Heidegger an understanding of behavior that blurs the line between the individual and society. "The *habitus*—embodied history, internalized as a second nature and so forgotten as history—is the active presence of the whole past of which it is a product. As such, it is what gives practices their relative autonomy with respect to external determinations of the immediate presence. This autonomy is that of the past, enacted and acting, which . . . makes the individual agent a world within a world."[21] It is by reworking the *habitus*—"the durably installed generative principle of regulated improvisations"—that advertisements produce culture, insinuating themselves into ways people think of themselves as men, women, citizens, and consumers, there to interact once again with the background.[22]

Bourdieu's work gives little guidance toward sorting out the competing claims of citizenship and consumption. Nor does the nation-state ever enter Levitt's pipedream, and it hardly affects Harvey's. Levitt's thesis depends on the idea that markets operate independently of political forces; Harvey's, on the idea that the state functions merely to protect capitalist interests. Harvey treats the state as a form of otherness and regional resistance, to be sure, suitable for celebration by postmodernists, but incapable of resisting the forces that really count. The nation-state would be surprised to hear that, for it takes at least part of its legitimacy from protecting local society from global institutions—the World Bank, the United Nations, the multinational corporations, the West, and in some circumstances, the market itself. Or it legitimates itself by negotiating with those institutions and striking the best bargain possible. One does not have to swallow those self-justifications. But a moment's reflection suggests that the nation-state is as much a source of rupture and constraint as continuity and homogenization.

Thinking about the global system of commodities and culture needs to move beyond the idea that global capitalism provides a kind of physics, and local societies, locked into the reproduction of a way of life, provide a teleology.[23] Sometimes the global sweeps in and creates unprecedented flights of the imagination, in turn producing solidarities that transcend the nation-state.[24] At other times, global modernity sweeps in and is recapitulated as local diversity. Because of its large middle class, diasporic connections, and lusty entanglement with consumer capitalism in recent years, South Asia has become an especially fertile area for spawning local diversity. By joining religious chauvinism to a public culture increasingly enamored of media and markets, the Hindu Right, for instance, has produced a specifically Hindu kind of modernity.[25] And as the forces of globalization gather strength, internal divisions in South Asian society, as well as the differences that separate India and neighboring states, become all the greater.[26]

By deterritorializing the imagination, advertising transcends the nation; by domesticating the imagination, it inscribes it in new form. The interpretive function that advertising plays is more thoroughgoing than simply reinterpreting incoming commodities manufactured elsewhere. If one tallies all commodities sold in Sri Lanka, perhaps half are manufactured outside of the island, mainly in India or East Asia—foodstuffs, hygiene products, automobiles and motorcycles, and electrical products. The other half—from home furnishings to other foodstuffs—are commodities that are produced locally, and they especially provoke advertising that stresses the commodity's appropriateness for the Sri Lankan public. The local idiom, in other words, gets applied as much to commodities that are local as to ones that are foreign. Because political and economic forces motivate the distinction between the global and the local, the boundary work of culture bears on advertising practice and ethnic interactions alike.[27]

These operations confound the idea that global flows enter far-away markets without challenge or are uniformly resisted at their point of entry. That boundary draws fire from several directions. What flows into Sri Lanka from the outside world are advertisements for cigarettes, camera film, and medicines, and they have been constructed on a regional basis. The faces and practices may not be Sri Lankan but neither are they Western or East Asian. These advertisements represent a liminal moment in the production of worldly identities—organized by faces that are simultaneously us and not us. Where Burgher models appear as handsome and well-to-do Sinhalas, pan-Asian models in Southeast Asia and Sri Lanka represent a trope not seen in the bipolar operations of colonial and postcolonial economies, faces and practices that derive from nearby parts of Asia. But the general point is more interesting: advertising serves to produce two foreign forms of locality—the global and the regional. Sometimes the region exerts a claim on the popular imagination; other times it does not. In the Southeast Asia case, that sense of region is strong enough to constitute what Manthia Diawara calls a "regional imaginary" unlike anything seen in South Asia.[28]

TOWARD HOME

Linking the world to the home requires making a space for a final venue where coins are exchanged for dreams. When consumers enter the equation, however, the exchange metaphor distorts things by oversimplifying the relationship. Consumers respond to the semiotic effects of global flows of commodities in a way that lacks the balanced reciprocity by which one thing is given and payment passes in the opposite direction, concluding the relationship. Advertising, understood as a cultural phenomenon, produces a world, a system of generalized reciprocity in which commodities are constantly under semiotic reconstruction, some fraction of which end up in consumers' hands, but in which the productivity of the advertising system engenders effects on the imagination that far outstrip the total array of things one buys.[29]

Appadurai suggests that "where hedonistic and antinomian consumption practices have taken deep hold, there remains a tendency for those practices of consumption that are closest to the body to acquire uniformity through habituation."[30] The residents of No. 37, Sapugaswatte Road are largely untouched by what Appadurai calls "practices of reproduction," which periodically reinscribe signs of identity on the human body. While repetition is central to a bodily consumption regime, it has little effect in places where savings rates approach 20 percent and few consumers live hedonistic and antinomian lives. Instead of the valorization of the ephemeral—the extravagant dinner, the fashionable suit of clothes, the hairdo—one finds a consumption regime in which savings is central and buying a house is the decision that overwhelms all others.

The point is not that the people who live along Sapugaswatte Road are never swayed by advertising. They are persuaded, and sometimes directly so. Tilakasiri and Anusha admit being persuaded by the advertisements for Signal toothpaste that say the product is better for preventing cavities. But if that is the effect of advertising on their buying patterns, it hardly warrants the expense. Tilakasiri and Indrani, Cedric and Anusha make even small purchases against a background of long-term calculative schemes and dispositions very different from the simplistic model of advertising providing the stimulus and consumers responding. Amidst a world of global firms, multinational and local advertising agencies, and the onslaught of commodities, they make choices that range from direct influence to indifference and resistance. Anusha loves movies and watches television, but she has no interest in taking the next step on the ladder of consumption by buying a VCR. Sri Lanka's involvement in the global system of culture and commerce has destroyed the Sinhala film industry. She was interested only in Sinhala films when there were still theaters in every provincial town. Why purchase a new technology when there are no Sinhala films on videocassette?

When I asked Tilakasiri whether he was an *upan bimē niyama urumakkarayek* (a son of the soil, Sampath's tagline), his response was short but to the point. All of his other actions said "no" too—he makes his banking decisions not on the basis of identitarian blandishments of an advertising campaign but in terms of careful calculations of what is convenient and what is possible, which banks have treated him well, where his fellow villagers work, and whether he can find a bank accessible to a job that often has him on the move. If the Phoenix agency had a vision of just what kind of person—Sinhala, male, middle class—might be drawn to the claims of Sampath advertising, it looked beyond Tilakasiri in several ways. He is not persuaded by chauvinist appeals, life has taught him to accommodate himself to a banking system that is often frustrating, and he appreciates the way the state banks have provided services to villages such as his own.

As for advertising, the monthly bank drawing has considerably more appeal than advertising's more quotidian exercises of the imagination. As with Robert Loo's indifference to the prospect of a Malaysian nation, Tilakasiri's and Indrani's, Cedric's and Anusha's thoughts are not much fixed on either the faraway or the national. Although he admits liking *Mr. Bean,* Tilakasiri watches the program for its slapstick humor, not its exoticism or Englishness, and none of the residents of Sapugaswatte Road is prone to postmodern bouts of hallucination or to living in the moment. Nor do they suffer from time-space compression in any way I can detect. In this regard the world system comes right up to their doorstep, swirls around them, entertains them, furnishes them with all manner of tropes and figures, without much influencing their buying behavior. Announcements about bank drawings, by contrast, they follow with the intensity of a bettor at a race track. All in all, advertising's impact on these families is more a matter of the long-term reshaping of images—of self and other, male and female, home and work—than influencing what they buy these days.

To the extent that they have unmet desires, their minds are fixed on one of life's least commodified, least advertised commodities, the private home. Buying a home is an economic calculation, to be sure, but the home once bought becomes a domain where emotion and collective well-being reign. Even the calculations preliminary to acquiring a home—building it, buying it, finding mortgage money to pay for it—are consumption decisions where individual desires have their faintest effect, the place where individuality is most often subsumed by feelings and forces associated with family life. Whatever the efforts of the advertising industry in domesticating advertisements to fit the local imagination, domesticity speaks to Tilakasiri and Indrani, Cedric and Anusha in the strict sense of the word. And in this sense it speaks quite a lot more strongly. They want to live in their own houses. Having a house is the first step toward making it a home, and when that transformation occurs, coins are traded for dreams that are practical and familiar.

NOTES

1. Theodore Levitt, "The Globalization of Markets," *Harvard Business Review* 3 (May–June 1983): 92.

2. 93; I have reversed the order of the two sentences.

3. See James Watson, ed., *Golden Arches East: McDonald's in East Asia* (Stanford: Stanford University Press, 1997).

4. David Harvey, *The Condition of Postmodernity* (Cambridge, Mass.: Blackwell, 1990).

5. This compression effect is a product of the changing nature of decision making—"the time horizons of both private and public decision-making have shrunk, while satellite communication and declining transport costs have made it increasingly possible to spread those decisions immediately over an ever wider and variegated space" (Harvey, *Condition of Postmodernity*, 147). And shrinking time horizons reflect capitalism's innate tendencies: Capitalism seeks to speed everything up—production time and turnover time (the time taken for the value of a given capital to be realized through production and exchange) alike (David Harvey, *The Limits to Capital* [Chicago: University of Chicago Press, 1982], 62–64). The conquest of space also derives from the nature of capitalism: "the necessary geographical expansion of capitalism is . . . to be interpreted as capital in search for surplus value." (Harvey, *Limits to Capital*, 96). The shark either moves ahead or it dies.

6. Harvey, *Condition of Postmodernity*, 240. Harvey says little about how real-life interactions link people living in far-flung parts of this compressed world. The split-second decision an American pilot made to fire his rockets, shooting down an Iranian passenger jet, gives Harvey a poignant example but one that cannot speak to the experience of anyone but fighter pilots (306). Another example—the stock market collapse of 1987—better illustrates how time-space compression influences different kinds of people. Harvey quotes the *Wall Street Journal*: "'The crash aftermath is the tale of two cultures—processing different information, operating on different time horizons, dreaming different dreams. . . . The financial community—living by the minute and trading by the computer—operates on one set of values,' while 'the rest of America—living by the decade, buying and holding—has a different code,' which might be called the 'ethic of those who have their hands on shovels'" (356–57).

7. Edward Soja, *Postmodern Geographies: The Reassertion of Space in Critical Social Theory* (London: Verso, 1989).

8. Harvey, *Condition of Postmodernity*, 344.

9. James Clifford and George Marcus, eds., *Writing Culture* (Berkeley: University of California Press, 1986), 22.

10. Harvey, *Condition of Postmodernity*, 102.

11. The Marxist inclination to reserve the process of fetishization for capitalist society is itself a product of seeing the social world in a way shaped by economic forces. "Economism," Pierre Bourdieu argues, "knows no other interest than that which capitalism has

produced" (*Outline of a Theory of Practice* [Cambridge: Cambridge University Press, 1977], 177).

12. Harvey, *Condition of Postmodernity*, 287.

13. Michael Schudson draws a balanced picture of what characterizes the content of American advertising, not just the advertisements that catch the eye or offend one's sensibilities. See *Advertising, the Uneasy Persuasion: Its Dubious Impact on American Society* (New York: Basic Books, 1984).

14. See Michel de Certeau, *Culture in the Plural* (Minneapolis: University of Minnesota Press, 1997), 20.

15. The quotation comes from Goethe, but I know it by way of John Berger, who refers to Walter Benjamin as his source of Goethe's characterization. See "The Suit and the Photograph," in John Berger, *About Looking* (New York: Pantheon Books, 1980), 28.

16. Bourdieu, *Outline of a Theory of Practice*, 195.

17. Fredric Jameson, "Notes on Globalization as a Philosophical Issue," in *The Cultures of Globalization*, ed. Fredric Jameson and Masao Miyoshi (Durham, N.C.: Duke University Press, 1998), 70.

18. Michel de Certeau, *The Practice of Everyday Life*, trans. Steven F. Rendall (Berkeley: University of California Press, 1984).

19. Bourdieu, *Outline of a Theory of Practice*, 96–97.

20. Clifford Geertz, "Deep Play: Notes on the Balinese Cockfight," in *The Interpretation of Cultures* (New York: Basic Books, 1973), 453.

21. Pierre Bourdieu, *The Logic of Practice* (Stanford: Stanford University Press, 1990), 56.

22. Bourdieu, *Outline of a Theory of Practice*, 78.

23. Marshall Sahlins, "Cosmologies of Capitalism: The Trans-Pacific Sector of 'The World System,'" *Proceedings of the British Academy* 74 (1988): 4.

24. Arjun Appadurai, "Patriotism and Its Futures," in *Modernity at Large* (Minneapolis: University of Minnesota Press, 1997), 172.

25. Arvind Rajagopal, "Thinking through Emerging Markets: Brand Logics and the Cultural Forms of Political Society in India," *Social Text* 17, no. 3 (Fall 1999): 131–49.

26. Partha Chatterjee, "Beyond the Nation? Or Within?" *Social Text*, 16, no. 3 (Fall 1998): 57–68.

27. Marshall Sahlins, "Two or Three Things I Know about Culture," *Journal of the Royal Anthropological Institute*, n.s., 5 (1999): 414–15.

28. "Toward a Regional Imaginary in Africa," in *The Cultures of Globalization*, ed. Fredric Jameson and Masao Miyoshi (Durham, N.C.: Duke University Press, 1998), 103–24. Southeast Asian intellectuals, such as Sutan Takdir Alisjahbana, rector of Indonesia's national university, have envisioned a Malay-speaking transnational community. See Rehman Rashid, *A Malaysian Journey* (Petaling Jaya, Malaysia: Rehman Rashid, 1993), 68.

29. The distinction comes from Marshall Sahlins, "The Sociology of Primitive Exchange," *Stone Age Economics* (Chicago: Aldine, 1972), 191–96.

30. Arjun Appadurai, "Consumption, Duration, and History," in *Modernity at Large*, 67.

BIBLIOGRAPHY

Books, Journal Articles, and Conference Papers

Abu-Lughod, Lila. 1991. "Writing against Culture." In *Recapturing Anthropology*, edited by Richard Fox, 137–62. School of American Research Seminar Series. Seattle: University of Washington Press.

Amarasekera, Gunadasa. 1990. "Jathika Chinthanaya: What Does It Mean?" *Dana* 15 (5, 6): 6–8.

Anderson, Benedict. 1983. *Imagined Communities.* London: Verso.

Appadurai, Arjun. 1990. "Disjuncture and Difference in the Global Cultural Economy." *Public Culture* 2 (2): 1–24.

———. 1996. *Modernity at Large.* Minneapolis: University of Minnesota Press.

Appadurai, Arjun, and Carol A. Breckenridge. n.d. "Buying the Nation: Advertising and Heritage in Contemporary India." Typescript.

Arachchige-Don, Neville S. 1994. *Patterns of Community Structure in Colombo, Sri Lanka.* Lanham, Md.: University Press of America.

Aserappa, Antony F. 1930. *A Short History of the Ceylon Chetty Community.* Colombo: Catholic Press.

Baker, Chris. 1991. "Who Are the Space Invaders Now?" Paper presented at the Social Science Research Council Conference, "Advertising, Consumption, and the New Middle Class in India," Monterey, California, April 17–20.

Balibar, Etienne. 1990. "The Nation Form." *Review* 13 (3): 329–61.

Ballhatchet, Kenneth. 1980. *Race, Sex, and Class under the Raj: Imperial Attitudes and Policies and Their Critics, 1793–1905.* New York: St. Martin's.

Bandarage, Asoka. 1983. *Colonialism in Sri Lanka: The Political Economy of the Kandyan Highlands, 1833–1886.* Berlin: Mouton.

Barber, Benjamin. 1995. *Jihad vs. McWorld.* New York: Times Books.

Barth, Fredrik. 1974. Introduction to *Ethnic Groups and Boundaries,* edited by Fredrik Barth, 9–38. Boston: Little, Brown.

Basso, Keith. 1979. *Portraits of "the Whiteman."* Cambridge: Cambridge University Press.

Batuta, Ibn. 1983. *Ibn Battuta: Travels in Asia and Africa.* Translated by H. A. R. Gibb. London: Darf Publishers.

Bayly, Susan. 1999. "Race in Britain and India." In *Nation and Religion: Perspectives on Europe and Asia,* edited by Peter Van Der Veer and Hartmut Lehmann, 71–95. Princeton, N.J.: Princeton University Press.

Benjamin, Walter. 1968. "The Work of Art in the Age of Mechanical Reproduction." In *Illuminations,* 219–53. New York: Harcourt, Brace and World.

Berger, John. 1980. *About Looking.* New York: Pantheon Books.

Brohier, R. L. 1984. *Changing Face of Colombo.* Colombo: Lake House.

Brown, Judith M. 1989. *Gandhi: Prisoner of Hope.* New Haven, Conn.: Yale University Press.

Burchell, Graham, Colin Gordon, and Peter Miller, eds. 1991. *The Foucault Effect.* Chicago: University of Chicago Press.

Burgess, Anthony. 1992. *The Long Day Wanes: A Malayan Trilogy.* New York: Norton.

Burke, Timothy. 1996. *Lifebuoy Men, Lux Women: Commodification, Consumption, and Culture in Modern Zimbabwe.* Durham, N.C.: Duke University Press.

Camroux, David. 1996. "State Responses to Islamic Resurgence in Malaysia." *Asian Survey* 36 (9): 852–68.

Caplan, Lionel. 1995. "Creole World, Purist Rhetoric: Anglo-Indian Cultural Debates in Colonial and Contemporary Madras." *Journal of the Royal Anthropological Institute,* n.s., 1 (4): 743–62.

Certeau, Michel de. 1984. *The Practices of Everyday Life.* Translated by Steven Rendall. Berkeley: University of California Press.

———. 1997. *Culture in the Plural.* Translated by Tom Conley. Minneapolis: University of Minnesota Press.

Chatterjee, Partha. 1998. "Beyond the Nation? Or Within?" *Social Text* 56: 57–68.

Clifford, James, and George E. Marcus. 1986. *Writing Culture.* Berkeley: University of California Press.

Colley, Linda. 1992. *Britons: Forging the Nation, 1707–1837.* New Haven, Conn.: Yale University Press.

Crapanzano, Vincent. 1985. *Waiting: The Whites of South Africa.* New York: Random House.

Creighton, Millie. 1991. "Maintaining Cultural Boundaries in Retailing: How Japanese Department Stores Domesticate 'Things Foreign,'" *Modern Asian Studies* 25 (4): 675–709.

Csikszentmihalyi, Mihaly, and Eugene Rochberg-Halton. 1981. *The Meaning of Things: Domestic Symbols and the Self.* Cambridge: Cambridge University Press.

Daniel, E. Valentine. 1996. *Charred Lullabies: Chapters in an Anthropography of Violence.* Princeton, N.J.: Princeton University Press.

Dening, Greg. 1980. *Islands and Beaches: Discourse on a Silent Land, Marquesas 1774–1880.* Honolulu: University of Hawaii Press.

de Silva, C. R. 1978. "The Politics of University Admissions: A Review of Some Aspects of the Admissions Policy in Sri Lanka, 1971–1978." *Sri Lanka Journal of Social Sciences* 1 (2): 85–123.

de Silva, K. M. 1976. "Discrimination in Sri Lanka." In *Case Studies on Human Rights and Fundamental Freedoms: A World Survey.* Vol. 3. Edited by W. A. Veenhoven, 73–119. The Hague: Martinus Nijhoff.

———, ed. 1965. *The "Rebellion" of 1848.* Kandy, Sri Lanka: K. V. G. de Silva and Sons.

de Silva, Nalin. 1991. *Jathika Sanskitiya Saha Chintanaya.* Colombo: Chintana Parshadaya.

———. 1992. *Mage Lokaya.* Dehiwela, Sri Lanka: Mudanya.

de Silva, S. B. D. 1982. *The Political Economy of Underdevelopment.* London: Routledge and Kegan Paul.

Diawara, Manthia. 1998. "Toward a Regional Imaginary in Africa." In *The Cultures of Globalization,* edited by Fredric Jameson and Masao Miyoshi, 103–24. Durham, N.C.: Duke University Press.

Dwyer, Kevin. 1982. *Moroccan Dialogues: Anthropology in Question.* Baltimore: Johns Hopkins University Press.

Dyer, Gillian. 1982. *Advertising as Communication.* London: Methuen.

Escobar, Arturo. 1995. *Encountering Development: The Making and Unmaking of the Third World.* Princeton, N.J.: Princeton University Press.

Fabian, Johannes. 1983. *Time and the Other: How Anthropology Makes Its Object.* New York: Columbia University Press.

Foster, Robert J. 1995. "Print Advertisements and Nation Making in Metropolitan Papua, New Guinea." In *Nation Making: Emergent Identities in Postcolonial Melanesia,* edited by Robert J. Foster, 151–81. Ann Arbor: University of Michigan Press.

Foucault, Michel. 1984. "What Is an Author?" In *The Foucault Reader,* edited by Paul Rabinow, 101–20. New York: Pantheon Books.

Frank, Thomas. 1997. *The Conquest of Cool: Business Culture, Counterculture, and the Rise of Hip Consumerism.* Chicago: University of Chicago Press.

Geertz, Clifford. 1973. "After the Revolution: The Fate of Nationalism in the

New States." In *The Interpretation of Cultures,* 234–54. New York: Basic Books.

———. 1973. "Deep Play: Notes on the Balinese Cockfight." In *The Interpretation of Cultures,* 412–53. New York: Basic Books.

———. 1980. *Negara.* Princeton, N.J.: Princeton University Press.

———. 1988. *Works and Lives: The Anthropologist as Author.* Stanford: Stanford University Press.

Gell, Alfred. 1986. "Newcomers to the World of Goods: Consumption among the Muria Gonds." In *The Social Life of Things,* edited by Arjun Appadurai, 110–38. Cambridge, Mass.: Cambridge University Press.

Gombrich, Richard, and Gananath Obeyesekere. 1988. *Buddhism Transformed: Religious Change in Sri Lanka.* Princeton, N.J.: Princeton University Press.

Gooneratne, Yasmin. 1992. "The English-Educated in Sri Lanka: An Assessment of Their Cultural Role." *South Asia Bulletin* 12 (1): 2–31.

Goonetilleke, William. 1988–1989. "Dubash and Tuppahi." *Orientalist* 3: 212–13.

Grant, Wyn. 1997. "Perspectives on Globalization and Economic Coordination." In *Contemporary Capitalism: The Embeddedness of Institutions,* edited by J. Rogers Hollingsworth and Robert Boyer, 319–36. Cambridge: Cambridge University Press.

Greenblatt, Stephen. 1987. "Capitalist Culture and the Circulatory System." In *The Aims of Representation,* edited by Murray Krieger, 257–73. New York: Columbia University Press.

———. 1990. *Learning to Curse.* New York: Routledge.

Habermas, Jürgen. 1989. *The Structural Transformation of the Public Sphere.* Translated by Thomas Burger. Cambridge, Mass.: MIT Press.

Handler, Richard. 1988. *Nationalism and the Politics of Culture in Quebec.* Madison: University of Wisconsin Press.

Handler, Richard, and Joyce Linnekin. 1984. "Tradition, Genuine or Spurious." *Journal of American Folklore* 97: 273–90.

Hannerz, Ulf. 1993. "The Cultural Role of World Cities." In *Humanising the City?* edited by Anthony P. Cohen and Katsuyoshi Fukui, 67–84. Edinburgh: Edinburgh University Press.

Harvey, David. 1982. *The Limits to Capital.* Chicago: University of Chicago Press.

———. 1985. *Consciousness and the Urban Experience: Studies in the Theory of Capitalist Urbanization.* Baltimore: Johns Hopkins University Press.

———. 1989. *The Condition of Postmodernity: An Enquiry into the Origins of Cultural Change.* Oxford: Blackwell.

Hashim, Adnan. 1994. *Advertising in Malaysia.* Petaling Jaya, Malaysia: Pelanduk Publications.

Hobsbawm, Eric, and Terrence Ranger. 1983. *The Invention of Tradition.* Cambridge: Cambridge University Press.

Hong, Jinhao. 1994. "The Resurrection of Advertising in China." *Asian Survey* 34 (4): 326–42.

Horowitz, Donald. 1989. "Incentives and Behavior in the Ethnic Politics of Sri Lanka and Malaysia." Working Papers in Asian/Pacific Studies. Durham, N.C.: Duke University.

Hulugalle, H. A. J. 1960. *The Life and Times of D. R. Wijewardene.* Colombo: Lake House.

Ivy, Marilyn. 1988. "Critical Texts, Mass Artifacts: The Consumption of Knowledge in Postmodern Japan." *South Atlantic Quarterly* 87 (3): 419–44.

Iyer, Pico. 1988. *Video Night in Kathmandu.* New York: Knopf.

Jameson, Fredric. 1998. "Notes on Globalization as a Philosophical Issue." In *The Cultures of Globalization,* edited by Fredric Jameson and Masao Miyoshi, 54–77. Durham, N.C.: Duke University Press.

Jayawardena, Kumari. 1984. "Some Aspects of Class and Ethnic Consciousness in the Late 19th and Early 20th Centuries." In *Ethnicity and Social Change in Sri Lanka,* no editor, 74–92. Colombo: Karunaratne and Sons.

Johnston, Alexander. 1827. "A Cufic Inscription Found in Ceylon; with a Translation by Rev. Samuel Lee." *Transactions of the Royal Asiatic Society (Great Britain and Ireland)* 1:545–48.

Jones, Geoffrey. 2000. *Merchants to Multinationals: British Trading Companies in the Nineteenth and Twentieth Centuries.* Oxford: Oxford University Press.

Karthigesu, Ranggasamy. 1988. "Television as a Tool for Nation-Building in the Third World: A Post-Colonial Pattern, Using Malaysia as a Case-Study." In *Television and Its Audiences,* edited by Phillip Drummond and Richard Paterson, 306–26. London: British Film Institute Publishing.

Karunanayake, Nandana. 1990. *Radio Broadcasting in Sri Lanka: Significant Dates and Events, 1921–1990.* Moratuwa, Sri Lanka: Center for Media and Policy Studies.

———. 1990. *Radio Broadcasting in Sri Lanka: Potential and Performance.* Moratuwa, Sri Lanka: Center for Media and Policy Studies.

Karunatilake, H. N. S. 1971. *Economic Development in Ceylon.* New York: Praeger.

———. 1990. "Re-orienting Banking Policy and Practice to Meet the Needs of the People." Occasional Papers, no. 20. Central Bank of Sri Lanka.

Kemper, Steven. 1979. "Sinhalese Astrology, South Asian Caste Systems, and the Notion of Individuality." *Journal of Asian Studies* 38:477–97.

———. 1991. "Culture and Consumption in the Sri Lankan Advertising Business." Paper presented at the Social Science Research Council Conference, "Advertising, Consumption, and the New Middle Class in India," Monterey, Calif., April 17–20.

———. 1991. *The Presence of the Past.* Ithaca, N.Y.: Cornell University Press.

———. 1993. "The Nation Consumed: Buying and Believing in Sri Lanka." *Public Culture* 5 (3): 377–93.

Khoo, Boo Teik. 1995. *Paradoxes of Mahathirism: An Intellectual Biography of Mahathir Mohamad.* Kuala Lumpur: Oxford University Press.

King, Anthony D. 1976. *Colonial Urban Development: Culture, Social Power, and Environment.* London: Routledge and Kegan Paul.

Kleinman, Arthur. 1995. *Writing at the Margin: Discourse between Anthropology and Medicine.* Berkeley: University of California Press.

Lavie, Smadar. 1990. *The Poetics of Military Occupation: Mzeina Allegories of Bedouin Identity under Israeli and Egyptian Rule.* Berkeley: University of California Press.

Lears, T. J. Jackson. 1994. *Fables of Abundance.* New York: Basic Books.

Levitt, Theodore. 1983. "The Globalization of Markets." *Harvard Business Review* 3 (May–June): 92–102.

Lynch, Caitrin. 1999. "The 'Good Girls' of Sri Lankan Modernity: Moral Orders of Nationalism and Capitalism," *Identities* 6 (1): 55–89.

McDaniel, Drew O. 1994. *Broadcasting in the Malay World: Radio, Television, and Video in Brunei, Indonesia, Malaysia, and Singapore.* Norwood, N.J.: Ablex Publishing.

McGilvray, Dennis. 1982. "Dutch Burghers and Portuguese Mechanics: Eurasian Ethnicity in Sri Lanka." *Comparative Studies in Society and History* 24 (2): 235–63.

McLaughlin, Thomas. 1996. *Street Smarts and Critical Theory: Listening to the Vernacular.* Madison: University of Wisconsin Press.

Mahathir, Mohamad. 1986. *The Challenge.* Petaling Jaya, Malaysia: Pelanduk Publications.

Mahathir, Mohamad, and Shintaro Ishihara. 1995. *The Voice of Asia: Two Leaders Discuss the Coming Century.* Tokyo: Kodansha International.

Marcus, George. 1998. "Ethnography in/of the World System: The Emergence of Multi-Site Ethnography." In *Ethnography through Thick and Thin,* edited by George Marcus. Princeton, N.J.: Princeton University Press.

Mintz, Sidney. 1985. *Sweetness and Power: The Place of Sugar in Modern History.* New York: Viking Books.

Moeran, Brian. 1996. *A Japanese Advertising Agency: An Anthropology of Media and Markets.* Honolulu: University of Hawaii Press.

Moore, Mick. 1985. *The State and Peasant Politics in Sri Lanka.* Cambridge: Cambridge University Press.

———. 1989. "The Ideological History of the Sri Lankan 'Peasantry.'" *Modern Asian Studies* 23 (1): 179–207.

Muller, Carl. 1993. *The Jam Fruit Tree.* New Delhi: Penguin.

———. 1994. *Yakada Yaka.* New Delhi: Penguin.

———. 1995. *Once upon a Tender Time.* New Delhi: Penguin.

Needham, Rodney. 1981. "Inner States as Universals: Skeptical Reflections on Human Nature." In *Indigenous Psychologies: The Anthropology of the Self,* edited by Paul Heelas and Andrew Lock, 65–78. London: Academic Press.

Newman, Gerald. 1987. *The Rise of English Nationalism: A Cultural History, 1740–1830.* New York: St. Martin's.

Noyelle, Thierry J., and Anna B. Dutka. 1988. *International Trade in Business Services.* Cambridge, Mass.: Ballinger Publishing Company.

O'Barr, William, and Mauricio Moreira. 1989. "The Airbrushing of Culture: An Insider Looks at Global Advertising." *Public Culture* 2 (1): 1–19.

Obeyesekere, Gananath. 1972. "Religious Symbolism and Political Change in Ceylon." In *The Two Wheels of Dhamma: Essays on the Theravada Tradition in India and Ceylon,* edited by Gananath Obeyesekere, Frank Reynolds, and Bardwell L. Smith. Chambersburg, Pa.: American Academy of Religion.

———. 1977. "Social Change and the Deities: The Rise of the Kataragama Cult in Modern Sri Lanka." *Man* 12 (December): 377–96.

———. 1984. *The Cult of the Goddess Pattini.* Chicago: University of Chicago Press.

———. 1995. "On Buddhist Identity in Sri Lanka." In *Ethnic Identity: Creation, Conflict, and Accommodation,* edited by Lola Romanucci-Ross and George A. DeVos, 222–47. Walnut Creek, Calif.: AltaMira Press.

Ondaatje, Michael. 1982. *Running in the Family.* New York: Norton.

Ong, Aihwa. 1987. *Spirits of Resistance and Capitalist Discipline: Factory Women in Malaysia.* Albany: SUNY Press.

Orlove, Benjamin, ed. 1997. *The Allure of the Foreign: Imported Goods in Postcolonial Latin America.* Ann Arbor: University of Michigan Press.

Ortner, Sherry. 1999. *Fate of "Culture": Geertz and Beyond.* Berkeley: University of California Press.

Perera, S. J. 1962. *Historical Sketches: Ceylon Church History.* Colombo: Catholic Book Depot.

Pujitha-Gunawardana, C. L. 1990. *This Is Colombo Calling.* Nugegoda, Sri Lanka: Perali Publishers.

Rajagopal, Arvind. 1999. "Thinking through Emerging Markets: Brand Logics and the Cultural Forms of Political Society in India." *Social Text* 17 (3): 131–49.

Rashid, Rehman. 1993. *A Malaysian Journey.* Petaling Jaya, Malaysia: Rehman Rashid.

Ratnakara, Tilak, ed. n.d. *Collected Speeches of Dr. Anandatissa de Alwis.* Colombo: Government Press.

———. n.d. *Some Ideas on Communication: Speeches by the Hon. Dr. Anandatissa de Alwis.* Colombo: Department of Information.

Redfield, Robert, and Milton Singer. 1954. "The Cultural Role of Cities." *Economic Development and Cultural Change* 3:53–73.

Reich, Robert B. 1991. *The Work of Nations: Preparing Ourselves for 21st-Century Capitalism.* New York: Basic Books.

Report of the Survey on Customer Services of Commercial Banks in Sri Lanka. 1986. Statistics Department, Central Bank of Sri Lanka.

Roberts, Michael. 1974. "Problems of Social Stratification and the Demarcation of National and Local Elites in British Ceylon." *Journal of Asian Studies* 33 (4): 549–77.

———. 1980. "From Southern India to Sri Lanka: The Traffic in Commodities, Bodies, and Myths from the Thirteenth Century Onwards." *South Asia* 3:36–47.

Roberts, Michael, Ismeth Raheem, and Percy Colin-Thome. 1989. *People Inbetween: The Burghers and the Middle Class in the Transformations within Sri Lanka, 1790s–1960s.* Ratmalana, Sri Lanka: Sarvodaya Book Publishing.

Rudner, David. 1994. *Caste and Capitalism in Colonial India: The Nattukottai Chettiars.* Berkeley: University of California Press.

Sahlins, Marshall. 1972. "On the Sociology of Primitive Exchange." *Stone Age Economics,* 185–275. Chicago: Aldine.

———. 1988. "Cosmologies of Capitalism: The Trans-Pacific Sector of 'The World System.'" *Proceedings of the British Academy* 74:1–51.

———. 1993. "Goodbye to Tristes Tropes: Ethnography in the Context of Modern World History." *Journal of Modern History* 65:1–25.

———. 1999. "Two or Three Things That I Know about Culture." *Journal of the Royal Anthropological Institute* 5 (3): 399–421.

Schudson, Michael. 1984. *Advertising, the Uneasy Persuasion: Its Dubious Impact on American Society.* New York: Basic Books.

Schumacher, E. F. 1973. *Small Is Beautiful: Economics as if People Mattered.* New York: Harper and Row.

Seligmann, C. G., and Brenda Seligmann. 1911. *The Veddas.* Cambridge: Cambridge University Press.

Selkirk, James. 1844. *Recollections of Ceylon.* London: J. Hatchard and Son.

Seneviratne, H. L. 1999. *The Work of Kings: The New Buddhism in Sri Lanka.* Chicago: University of Chicago Press.

Senaveratne, John. 1939. "The Past Might and Glory of the Sinhalese Nation." Colombo: Lorenz Press. Pamphlet.

Silva, Kalinga Tudor, and Karunatissa Athukorala. 1991. *The Watta-Dwellers: A Sociological Study of Selected Urban Low-Income Communities in Sri Lanka.* Lanham, Md.: University Press of America.

Siriwardena, Reggie. 1990. "Jathika Chintanaya or Multi-Culturalism." *Dana* 15 (5, 6): 6–8.

Snodgrass, Donald. 1966. *Ceylon: An Export Economy in Transition.* Homewood, Ill.: Richard D. Irwin.

Soja, Edward. 1989. *Postmodern Geographies: The Representation of Space in Critical Social Theory.* London: Verso.

Souchou, Yao. 1994. *Muhathir's Rage: Mass Media and the West as Transcendental Evil.* Canberra: National Library of Australia.

Spencer, Jonathan. 1990. *A Sinhala Village in a Time of Trouble.* Delhi: Oxford University Press.

Squiers, Carol. 1988. "Big Brother Goes Bicoastal: An Interview with Jay Chiat." In *Global Television,* edited by Cynthia Schneider and Brian Wallis, 171–81. New York: Wedge Press; Cambridge, Mass.: MIT Press.

Srivatsan, R. 1991. "Looking at Film Hoardings: Labour, Gender, Subjectivity and Everyday Life in India." *Public Culture* 4 (1): 1–23.

Stirrat, R. L. 1988. *On the Beach: Fishermen, Fishwives, and Fishtraders in Post-Colonial Sri Lanka.* Delhi: Hindustan Publishing.

Stoler, Ann Laura. 1989. "Rethinking Colonial Categories: European Communities and the Boundaries of Rule." *Comparative Studies in Society and History* 31 (1): 134–61.

———. 1989. "Making Empire Respectable: The Politics of Race and Sexual Morality in 20th-Century Colonial Cultures." *American Ethnologist* 16 (4): 634–60.

Tambiah, S. J. 1976. *World Conqueror and World Renouncer.* Cambridge: Cambridge University Press.

Tandon, Prakash. 1971. *Beyond Punjab.* New Delhi: Thompson Press.

Taussig, Michael. 1987. *Shamanism, Colonialism, and the Wild Man: A Study in Terror and Healing.* Chicago: University of Chicago Press.

Tedlow, Richard S. 1990. *New and Improved: The Story of Mass Marketing in America.* New York: Basic Books.

Temple, R. C. 1920. "Topaz-Topass." *Ceylon Antiquary and Literary Register* 7 (4): 210–17.

Thurston, Edgar. 1987. *Castes and Tribes of Southern India.* 7 vols. New Delhi: Asian Educational Services.

Tobin, Joseph. 1992. *Remade in Japan: Everyday Life and Consumer Taste in a Changing Society.* New Haven, Conn.: Yale University Press.

Tsing, Anna. 1993. *In the Realm of the Diamond Queen: Marginality in an Out-of-the Way Place.* Princeton, N.J.: Princeton University Press.

Tucker, Mary Ellen, and Duncan Ryuken Williams, eds. 1997. *Buddhism and Ecology.* Cambridge, Mass.: Harvard University Press.

Tyler, Stephen A. 1986. "Post-Modern Ethnography: From Document of the Occult to Occult Document." In *Writing Culture: The Poetics and Politics of Ethnography,* edited by James Clifford and George Marcus, 122–40. Berkeley: University of California Press.

United Nations. 1996. *National Accounts Statistics: Main Aggregates and Detailed Tables, 1993.* Part 2. New York, United Nations.

United Nations Development Programme. 1994. *Human Development Report, 1994.* Oxford: Oxford University Press.

United Nations, Economic and Social Commission for Asia and the Pacific. 1980. *Migration, Urbanization, and Development in Sri Lanka.* New York: United Nations.

———. 1993. *Urbanization and Socio-Economic Development in Asia and the Pacific.* Asian Population Studies Series, no. 122. New York: United Nations.

Watson, James. 1997. *Golden Arches East: McDonald's in East Asia.* Stanford: Stanford University Press.

Weerasoria, W. S. 1973. *The Nattukottai Chettiar Merchant Bankers in Ceylon.* Dehiwala, Sri Lanka: Tisara Prakasakayo.

Weiner, Myron. 1978. *Sons of the Soil: Migration and Ethnic Conflict in India.* Princeton, N.J.: Princeton University Press.

Weiner, Myron, and Mary Fainsod Katzenstein. 1981. *India's Preferential Policies: Migrants, the Middle Classes, and Ethnic Equality.* Chicago: University of Chicago Press.

Williams, Raymond. 1974. *Television: Technology and Cultural Form.* Hanover, N.H.: University Press of New England.

———. 1980. *Problems in Materialism and Culture.* London: Verso.

Wills, John E., Jr. 1993. "European Consumption and Asian Production in the Seventeenth and Eighteenth Centuries." In *Consumption and the World of Goods,* edited by John Brewer and Roy Porter, 133–47. London: Routledge.

Wolf, Eric. 1982. *Europe and the People Without History.* Berkeley: University of California Press.

———. 1996. *World Advertising Trends 1996.* Oxfordshire: NTC Publications.

Woolf, Leonard. 1961. *Growing.* New York: Harcourt Brace Jovanovich.

Yule, Henry, and A. C. Burnell, eds. 1968. *Hobson-Jobson: A Glossary of Colloquial Anglo-Indian Words and Phrases and of Kindred Terms, Typological, Historical, Geographical and Discursive.* New edition edited by William Crooke. New Delhi: Munshiram Manoharlal.

Zander, Rauno. 1991. "Politics and Rural Financial Markets in Sri Lanka." Paper presented at the Third Sri Lanka Conference, Amsterdam, April.

Magazines, Trade Publications, and Other Materials

"'AAI' Picks Next Major Marketers." 1995. *Advertising Age,* supplement. 18 September, I33–I43.

"Ads: Truth Should Be Stressed." 1989. *Business Times* (Kuala Lumpur), 22 March.

"Agents for Whom?" 1975. *Logos* 14, no. 3 (August).

"Apple Wants Unified Worldwide Image." 1993. *Advertising Age.* 12 April, 3.

"A Review of Advertising in Singapore and Malaysia during Early Times." 1971. Kuala Lumpur: Federal Publishers. Pamphlet.

"Asian Media Guide." 1993. *Advertising Age.* 8 November.

"BSB Sharpens Its Global Focus." 1993. *Advertising Age.* 7 June, 12.

Buddhadeva, Asoka. 1970. "Ceylonese in Danger of Losing Their Values." *Tribune* (Colombo). 24 May, 7–10.

Ceylon Chamber of Commerce. *The Story of Economic Development in Ceylon.* Colombo: Colombo Apothecaries Co., 1964.

Fairnington, Alain. 1980. "Kuala Lumpur—The Imminent Ad Capital of Asia." *Malaysian Advertising Association Bulletin* 8 (1): 12.

"53rd Annual Agency Report." 1997. *Advertising Age,* special section. 21 April, S1–S42.

"Global Campaigns Don't Work; Multinationals Do." 1994. *Advertising Age.* 18 April, 23.

Healey, Tim, and Law Siu Lan. 1995. "New Bird in an Overcast Sky." *Asiaweek.* 8 December, 55.

Heilemann, John. 1997. "Annals of Advertising: All Europeans Are Not Alike." *New Yorker.* 28 April and 5 May, 174–81.

"Heritage in Communication." 1984. Colombo: Tele-Cine Limited. Video.

Johnson, Bradley. 1996. "IBM Hammers out Worldwide Media Deals." *Advertising Age.* 8 January, 4.

Kementerian Penerangan Malaysia. 1989. "Advertising Code for Television and Radio." Typescript.

"Media Scene, Peninsular Malaysia, 1996." 1996. Malaysia: Batey Advertising. In-house publication.

"Medium and Message." 1993. *Far Eastern Economic Review.* 25 February, 52.

"Revlon Eyes Global Image, Picks Young and Rubicam." 1993. *Advertising Age.* 11 January, 1.

"Sampath Banks on Buddhist Nations." 1990. *Week-end* (Colombo). 25 November.

"Seeking the Right Look." 1989. *Asiaweek.* 21 April, 39.

"Selling of Asia." 1989. *Far Eastern Economic Review.* 29 June, 61.

Seno, Alexandra A. 1998. "Manufactured for Export." *Asiaweek.* 8 May.

Sri Lanka Rupavahini Corporation. 1985. *Sri Lanka Rupavahini Corporation Code of Advertising Standards and Practice.* Colombo: Government Press. Pamphlet.

"Targeting Asians." 1993. *Far Eastern Economic Review.* 21 January, 40–41.

Tefft, Sheila. 1994. "Ad Boom Unsettles China." *Advertising Age International,* supplement. 19 September, I3–I4.

Teinowitz, Ira. 1994. "Why A-B Bounced Bud." *Advertising Age.* 21 November, 1–2.

USAID. 1987. "Towards a Shareholding Democracy: Sampath Bank Share Marketing Experience." Typescript.

Wentz, Laurel. 1994. "Upstart Brands Steal Spotlight from Perennials." *Advertising Age International,* supplement. 19 September, I13–I14.

Wijewardena, Gehan. 1991. Book review. *Lanka Guardian* (Colombo) 14, no. 2 (15 May): 27.

Voice. 1988. Voice of America. 28 (August–September): 24.

INDEX

Abbas, K. A., 167–68
account managers, 121. *See also* advertising profession
advertising: Asian attitudes toward, 36–38; awards for, 114, 119, 188; code for, 52–53, 54–55, 71 nn.21, 23; colonial attitude toward, 103–4; defining and characterizing, 19–23, 39 nn.2, 3; expenditures for, 35, 118; interactive force of, 229–32; local adaptation of, 14–15, 31; multinational, 31, 41 n.36; origins of, 19, 39 n.2; persuasion by, 218–19, 221, 232–35; pervasiveness of, 13, 226; product-oriented, 32; roles of, viii, 2–3, 4; tutelary, 124, 150–57. *See also* global advertising; "local-idiom" advertising; print advertising; regional advertising; television advertising
advertising agencies. *See* American advertising agencies; Japanese advertising agencies; local advertising agencies; transnational advertising agencies; *specific agencies*
advertising code. *See* code of ethics in advertising; "local content" regulations
advertising executives: client services provided by, 119; cultural generalizations by, 131–32, 135–36, 141–42, 151; cultural views of, 75; as ethnographers, 3–8, 16 n.1; salaries of, 121; self-reflection by, 23; skills of, 14; social background of, 24, 25, 119–20, 122. *See also* advertising profession
advertising profession: annual ceremony of, 119; bi-directional focus of, 16; code of ethics for, 112, 113–14; cultural

perceptions of, 221, 222; cultural production by, 123–27; defining, 20; English language in, 24, 25, 212–13; ethnic groups in, 6, 122; growth of, 110–12; organizational structure of, 24–25, 119–23; origins of, 104–10; practices and vocabulary of, 7–8, professional promotion in, 112–16, 128 n.17; role of, 2–3; scandals in, 116; self-reflection in, 22–23; as symbol analysts, 2, 22–23, 229–30; transnational affiliations of, 116–19. *See also* advertising executives; creative directors; graphic artists
Afghans, 83
agency houses, 101–4, 108, 215–16
agricultural commodities, 101–2
alienation, "Brechtian concept of," 168, 171–72
Almeida, Peter, 62
Amarasekera, Gunadasa, 90, 91, 99 n.54
American advertising agencies: expansion of, 26–27; revenues of, 19; style of, 22. *See also* United States
Americans, advertisements portraying, 146
Anchor milk, 7, 155
Anderson, Benedict, 48, 77, 94–95
Anheuser-Busch, 27
anthropology: cultural representations in, 75; focus of, 3; "follow the thing" approach to, 15–16. *See also* ethnography; folk ethnography
Anuradhapura, 138
api Matara (we are Matara) campaign, 164, 174–77, 183
Appadurai, Arjun, 13–14, 77–78, 96 n.8, 222 n.1, 233